THE 100 MOST INFLUENTIAL ENTERTAINERS OF STAGE AND SCREEN

The Britannica Guide to the World's Most Influential People

The 100 Most Influential
ENTERTAINERS
Of Stage and Screen

Edited by Virginia Forte

Britannica®
Educational Publishing
IN ASSOCIATION WITH

ROSEN
EDUCATIONAL SERVICES

Published in 2017 by Britannica Educational Publishing (a trademark of Encyclopædia Britannica, Inc.) in association with The Rosen Publishing Group, Inc.
29 East 21st Street, New York, NY 10010

Distributed exclusively by Rosen Publishing.

To see additional Britannica Educational Publishing titles, go to rosenpublishing.com.

First Edition

Britannica Educational Publishing
J.E. Luebering: Director, Core Reference Group
Anthony L. Green: Editor, Compton's by Britannica

Rosen Publishing
Virginia Forte: Editor
Nelson Sá: Art Director
Michael Moy: Designer
Cindy Reiman: Photography Manager
Sherri Jackson: Photo Research
Introduction by Danielle Weiner.

Library of Congress Cataloging-in-Publication Data

The 100 most influential entertainers of all time / edited by Virginia Forte.
       pages cm. — (The Britannica guide to the world's most influential people)
Includes bibliographical references and index.
ISBN 978-1-68048-278-2 (library bound : alk. paper)
    1. Entertainers—Biography—Juvenile literature. 2. Actresses—Biography—Juvenile literature. 3. Actors—Biography—Juvenile literature. I. Forte, Virginia, editor. II. Title: One hundred most influential entertainers of all time.

PN1583.A15 2015
791.092'2—dc23

2015034549

Manufactured in China

CONTENTS

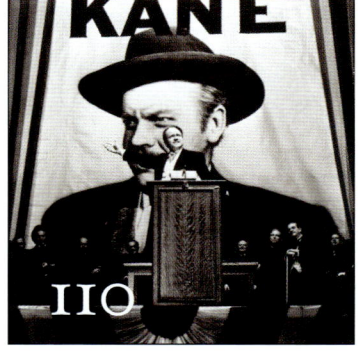

189

281

294

350

358

The media and entertainment industry is one of the most pervasive and profitable markets in the world. The U.S. entertainment industry alone accounts for one-third of the total global entertainment enterprise. In the 20th and 21st centuries, it evolved as it grew, changing our standards of entertainment and the definition of an entertainer. Broadly speaking, the title of "entertainer" has been given to performers, actors, comedians, musicians, and other creative figures in the music, television, theatre, and motion picture industries. Their work amuses and brings people together. In times of economic or political stress, the entertainment industry persists and not only brightens mundane life, but also builds upon it, using art as a lens through which to view universal human experience. Through this, the entertainment industry produces role models and defining icons of our culture. As the world becomes increasingly smaller through more rapid and widespread dissemination of media, the entertainment industry has acted as an increasingly prominent agent in producing critical thought about serious issues.

Key figures in the entertainment industry advance the progress of their craft, ask questions about society, and attempt to unite people in mutual enjoyment. Yet what makes some entertainers more influential than others remains a nebulous concept. As influence cannot be measured quantitatively, a definitive list of the one hundred most influential entertainers of stage and screen is not without debate. What definition of influence would allow us to compare that of different actors, directors, and other key figures in the entertainment industry? The best one can do is argue that the individuals in this volume possess certain qualities (however ambiguous the definitions of those qualities may be) that distinguish them from the rest in their field. Fame can be achieved with talent, hard work, and luck, but influence requires innovation of craft and impactful engagement with an audience—and society at large.

The effects of influence are more easily impressed and perceived than measured. However, market indicators such as monetary gain, public consumption, and institutional recognition serve as markers by which a quantitative assessment of influence can be attempted. During the 20th and 21st centuries, developments in motion-picture technology and studio production quality—including increasingly advanced cameras, media for recording and transferring video, special effects, and projection technology—paved the way for film and television to become influential fields of entertainment. Perhaps most notably, the capabilities that entertainers of all stock are afforded by the Internet for unmediated contact with the public have allowed performers to more directly craft their artistry and the trajectory of their career by choosing when and how to release new media, as well as how much (if anything) to charge for it.

Madonna (1958-), who moved from pop star to noted actress to fashion icon, was at the vanguard of a new generation of multi-talented performers who would venture beyond their initial niche to influence and even dominate numerous corners of the entertainment industry. In what is often considered the golden age of stage and screen entertainment, there were legendary "song-and-dance" men and women and so-called "triple threats" who were trained on the vaudeville stage—entertainers like Bing Crosby (1903–1977), Judy Garland (1922–1969), and Sammy Davis Jr. (1925–1990)—who were as adept at acting and dancing as they were at singing, adapted to changing entertainment tastes, mediums, and technology, and became powerful creative forces on stage, in film, and on radio and television. Led and influenced by Madonna and Michael Jackson (1958–2009), a new crop of post-modern triple threats have emerged in the late 20th and early 21st centuries—including Beyoncé and Justin Timberlake (1981–). For these performers, music is only one of the arrows in their quiver. Music is a jumping-off point, from which they move into innovative video projects, major feature films, television specials, and multimillion-dollar tours, not to mention product endorsement deals and 24/7 social media presences.

Like music, film provides entertainment that can be both light-hearted and serious; it can serve as entertainment for its own sake or as a medium for social change. One notable person who took advantage of film's ability

Popular entertainers in the music industry gathered in New York City on March 30, 2015, for the launch of the music streaming service Tidal.

to address social issues is filmmaker Spike Lee (1957–). Lee is known for his uncompromising, provocative approach to controversial subject matter. His debut film, *She's Gotta Have It* (1986), is a prismatic character study about the love life of a contemporary black woman. It grossed over 40 times its low production budget of $175,000 and made Lee a name to follow in film circles. However, it was his 1989 film, *Do the Right Thing*, that truly established Lee as one of the major provocateurs in the history of film. *Do the Right Thing* centres on a single summer day in a diverse New York City neighborhood and pulls no punches in its depiction of the racial turbulence that underlays the so-called "post-racial" modern society. His signature is present in all of his films, as he has taken on the role of writer, producer, director, and editor throughout his career and often appears in his own films in supporting character roles. Lee largely addresses issues of race and gender in his movies—despite mixed reviews throughout his career, three of his films received Academy Award nominations. Lee worked with actor Denzel Washington in his monumental biographical film, *Malcom X* (1992). Washington (1954–), an American actor praised for his engaging and powerful performances, is best known for taking on roles that confront issues of identity. Washington earned an Academy Award nomination for Best Actor for his portrayal of Malcolm X, and won an Oscar for Best Actor for his role as a violent police detective in *Training Day* (2001). Washington was only the second African American actor to win an Oscar for Best Actor.

Not all of film so directly addresses complex social issues. Much of the film industry has pure entertainment as its goal; the measure of this kind of success is reflected in box-office earnings and the creation of genre standards. American motion-picture director and producer Steven Spielberg (1946–) has created such popular and high-grossing films as *Jaws* (1975) and *Close Encounters of the Third Kind* (1977), each of which scored over $100 million in grosses. Spielberg also directed such classics as *E.T.: The Extra-Terrestrial* (1982) and *Jurassic Park* (1993). Throughout his career, Spielberg continued to direct and produce films both in the realms of sci-fi as well as more serious and controversial pieces.

Of course, comedy should not be forgotten as an indispensable segment of the entertainment industry. In the early days of silent cinema, comedy was one of the first genres to gain global appreciation. While comedians often work in film and television, unscripted stand-up comedy has become one of culture's primary means of processing and commenting on political leaders, current events, and popular culture; comedy is an influential genre in and of itself. Comedy's enduring nature, however, does not imply a stagnant one. The genre remains relevant and contemporary as influential comedians revise the realm and boundaries of comedy.

Well-known comedian Johnny Carson (1925–2005) was among the first to establish the now-standard format for comedic television chat shows. Host of *The Tonight Show* for nearly three decades, he came to be considered the king of late-night television. He held an unprecedented influence on a generation of viewers as well as the television industry; Carson's decision to move *The Tonight Show* from New York to Los Angeles was instrumental in shifting the geographic centre of the comedy industry. Carson has won numerous awards, the range of which signify the scope of his influence; in addition to four Emmy Awards, Carson was given the Presidential Medal of Freedom and a Kennedy Center Honor.

Carson's show was also a gateway for other entertainers to come into their own. Joan Rivers (1933–2014) rose to prominence through her appearances on the show in the mid-1960s. A housewife when she first started her stand-up career, Rivers drew comedic inspiration from the everyday world. She was always quick to entertain by mocking both herself and other celebrities. Rivers' bold personality was novel in the world of male-dominated comedy at the start of her career. Her audacious and sometimes blunt comedic style nevertheless allowed her to be a pioneer in comedy and celebrity culture, as she became a fixture on the E! Entertainment cable network, and later became the host of the E! show *Fashion Police*, on which she commented on celebrities' red-carpet ensembles. Rivers' influence as a woman in comedy persists to this day. Her brazen nature, willingness to speak her mind, and ability to spin truth into comedy allowed her to connect to a wide audience.

Larry David (1947–), too, is best known for his own bitingly sarcastic personality, on which he bases much of the content of his skits and sitcoms. David is known for, among other things, his role as the star of his own HBO sitcom, *Curb Your Enthusiasm*. While his type of humor could be alienating to some in mainstream audience, it was always influential in the field of comedy itself. David's bold honesty rendered his characters unforgivable, yet still likeable. He earlier teamed with friend and fellow comedian Jerry Seinfeld (1954–) to create *Seinfeld*, a landmark of American popular culture in the late 20th century. The sitcom's iconic style (it was deemed "a show about nothing") would inspire similarly formatted sitcoms to appear later in American entertainment. Jerry Seinfeld's comedic voice is comparable to that of Larry David's, making their collaboration an overwhelming success. Seinfeld resumed a thriving stand-up career in the late 1990s after stepping away from the still-popular TV series. He became a model for American stand-up comedy success.

Entertainers in all genres are among the most influential people on the planet. They have the power to touch individuals on a global scale. They enter homes and lives through film, television, radio, audio, and print media. Their art makes people laugh, contemplate, cry, and question. It is impossible to arrive at a complete, objective, and definitive description of the nature of influence. The necessary perspective to discern its effects and merits only become visible with time. Furthermore, the sheer massiveness of the entertainment industry and proliferation of localized movements makes it nearly impossible to achieve a global perspective; our scope remains largely limited to the Anglo-American entertainment industry. However, it is safe to say that the entertainers included herein have influenced society in ways that will be remembered for years to come.

LILLIE LANGTRY

(b. Oct. 13, 1853, Isle of Jersey, Channel Islands–d. Feb. 12, 1929, Monte-Carlo, Monaco)

Lillie Langtry, the byname of Emilie Charlotte, Lady de Bathe, née Le Breton (also called Emilie Charlotte Langtry from 1874 to 1897), was a British beauty and actress, known as the Jersey Lily.

She was the daughter of the dean of Jersey. In 1874 she married Edward Langtry, who died in 1897, and in 1899 she married Hugo de Bathe, who became a baronet in 1907. In 1881 Langtry caused a sensation by being the first society woman to go on the stage, making her first notable appearance at the Haymarket Theatre, London, as Kate Hardcastle in *She Stoops to Conquer*. For some time the critics did not take her seriously, but she became a competent actress, her most successful part being Rosalind in *As You Like It*. She also toured the provinces and the United States. She turned the old Aquarium Theatre in London into the Imperial Theatre, modeled on a Greek temple, and opened it under her own management in 1901. Her last appearance on the stage was in 1917. Lillie Langtry also maintained a successful racing stable at Newmarket. One of the most beautiful women of her time, she had many distinguished admirers, including the prince of Wales, subsequently King Edward VII.

ALBERT CHEVALIER

(b. March 21, 1861, Notting Hill, London–d. July 10, 1923, London)

Albert Chevalier was an actor and music-hall entertainer known as the "costers' laureate" because of his songs in Cockney dialect on London common life (a coster is a cart peddler).

An actor from 1877, he made his music-hall debut in 1891 at the London Pavillion, where he was an immediate hit, singing such songs as "The Coster's Serenade" and "It's the Nasty Way 'E Sez It." In 1896 he commenced a successful U.S. tour. Chevalier composed about 80 songs, of which the most popular was "My Old Dutch"; from 1920 he acted in a play of that name written by himself and Arthur Shirley. As he refused to introduce obscenity into his performances, Chevalier is credited with improving the general repute of music halls.

CECIL B. DEMILLE

(b. Aug. 12, 1881, Ashfield, Mass., U.S.–d. Jan. 21, 1959, Hollywood, Los Angeles, Calif., U.S.)

Cecil Blount DeMille was an American motion-picture producer-director whose use of spectacle attracted vast audiences and made him a dominant figure in Hollywood for almost five decades.

Long before he made his first sound picture, DeMille had become a cinema legend for his efforts in the development of silent movies from shorts to feature-length productions and in helping to establish Hollywood as the new centre of the filmmaking industry. Unlike such other great directors of the silents as D.W. Griffith and Mack Sennett, DeMille easily made the transition to sound pictures, continuing to be productive—and profitable—well into the 1950s.

EARLY LIFE AND SILENT FILMS: *THE SQUAW MAN* TO *THE GODLESS GIRL*

DeMille was the son of the cleric and playwright Henry Churchill DeMille. He was raised by his mother after his father died when he was 12, and he was later sent to the

Pennsylvania Military College. He enrolled in New York's American Academy of Dramatic Arts in 1898, and after graduating he debuted as an actor in 1900. He was soon collaborating with his brother, playwright William Churchill DeMille.

DeMille's theatrical career was marked by long strings of failures, and he was better known for being William's brother than for any of his own performances or plays. Seeking a change, in 1913 he joined his friend and collaborator producer Jesse Lasky, businessman (and Lasky's brother-in-law) Samuel Goldfish (later Goldwyn), and attorney Arthur Friend in forming the Jesse L. Lasky Feature Play Company. DeMille was director-general in the new film company. His first film was a western, *The Squaw Man* (1914), about the love between an English nobleman and the Indian woman who dies for him. It was one of the first full-length feature films produced in Hollywood. The film was an instant success, assuring the future of the Lasky Company. Five more features emerged in 1914 under DeMille's direction, including *The Virginian*; he had another 12 to his credit in 1915, including *Carmen* (the first of six films he made starring popular opera singer Geraldine Farrar) and *The Girl of the Golden West*.

The Cheat (1915) and *The Golden Chance* (1915) were shot simultaneously by DeMille. In *The Cheat*, a spendthrift socialite (Fannie Ward) turns to a Japanese businessman (Sessue Hayakawa) to recoup the charity money she has embezzled. In *The Golden Chance*, a poor seamstress (Cleo Ridgely) is given the opportunity to play the part of a rich woman. Both films were noted for their expressive use of lighting, with much of the screen in shadow.

The Lasky Company merged with Adolph Zukor's Famous Players in 1916 to form Famous Players–Lasky (later Paramount Pictures). There DeMille made his first historical epic, *Joan the Woman* (1916), with Farrar playing Joan of Arc, and a remake of *The Squaw Man* (1918).

DeMille's ability to give the public what it wanted soon made him a "name" director in the days when directors were virtually unknown. He made comedies and melodramas about married life that reflected the postwar freedom from moral restraint, beginning with *Old Wives for New* (1918). These films also made a star of Gloria Swanson, who made six films with DeMille, beginning with *Don't Change Your Husband* (1919), and featured the lavish costumes and opulent sets that marked his later epics.

Poster *for* The Ten Commandments *(1923), directed by Cecil B. DeMille.*

DeMille next produced his first biblical epics, which featured spectacular crowd scenes and sets. *The Ten Commandments* (1923) has two stories, the first being that of the *Exodus* and the second being about a conflict in modern times between two brothers, one who is a Christian and the other who rejects religion. Despite the commercial success of *The Ten Commandments*, budget overruns on it and other films strained DeMille's relations with Zukor and Paramount. He left Paramount in 1925 and formed his own production company, Cecil B. DeMille Pictures, where he made four movies. The most commercially successful was *The King of Kings* (1927), a life of Christ that was one of the most popular films of the silent era. The company's last film and his last silent film, *The Godless Girl* (1929), was about atheism sweeping through a high school and was also an indictment of the harsh conditions in juvenile reform schools.

TALKING PICTURES: *DYNAMITE* TO *UNION PACIFIC*

DeMille joined Metro-Goldwyn-Mayer (MGM) in 1928. In *Dynamite* (1929), his first talking picture, a frivolous society girl marries a poor death-row inmate to retain her inherited fortune, but her plans for a brief marriage are upset when he is proved innocent. *Madame Satan* (1930) boasted a typically extravagant DeMille finale: a costume party held on a zeppelin over New York is struck by a bolt of lightning, necessitating a mass exit via parachutes. However, the box-office receipts were weak, and they did not improve much for his third version of *The Squaw Man* (1931).

MGM and DeMille let their disappointing association dissolve, and he approached Paramount with an epic about the persecution of Christians under the dissolute emperor Nero, *The Sign of the Cross* (1932), for which he was willing to pay half of the $650,000 budget. The combination of lurid debauchery with religious uplift was enormously successful. The film grossed $2.9 million, and he remained at Paramount for the rest of his career.

This Day and Age (1933) was an original turn on the gangster saga, with a killer dealt justice for his crimes by a group of intrepid high-school vigilantes. *Four Frightened People* (1934) was also atypical for DeMille—a survival story in which four Americans (Claudette Colbert,

Herbert Marshall, Mary Boland, and William Gargan) flee a plague outbreak on their ship only to try to survive the rigours of the Malayan jungle (filmed on location in Hawaii).

With *Cleopatra* (1934) DeMille returned to the historical spectacular with which he would forever after be associated. Here Cleopatra (Colbert) exercises her wiles on Marc Antony (Henry Wilcoxon) and *Julius Caesar* (Warren William). *The Crusades* (1935) was another lavish spectacle, with Loretta Young as Berangaria of Navarre and Wilcoxon as Richard the Lionheart, but it was a box-office disappointment.

DeMille turned to American history for his next films. In *The Plainsman* (1936), Gary Cooper and Jean Arthur starred as the romantically involved Wild Bill Hickok and Calamity Jane. It was DeMille's biggest box-office success since returning to Paramount. *The Buccaneer* (1938) was about privateer Jean Lafitte (Frederic March) and the Battle of New Orleans. *Union Pacific* (1939) was an account of the building of the transcontinental railroad and starred Joel McCrea and Barbara Stanwyck.

FILMS OF THE 1940S AND 1950S: *NORTH WEST MOUNTED POLICE* TO *THE TEN COMMANDMENTS*

North West Mounted Police (1940) was DeMille's first colour film. Gary Cooper played a Texas Ranger who travels to Canada to hunt a fugitive, and it was Paramount's biggest hit of 1940. *Reap the Wild Wind* (1942) was another smash; John Wayne and Raymond Massey starred as competing salvagers in the Florida Keys (circa 1840) who battle storms, shipwrecks, and a giant squid.

In *The Story of Dr. Wassell* (1944) a navy doctor (Cooper) saves nine wounded men during World War II by sneaking them past the Japanese to the safety of Australia. DeMille invited Cooper back for *Unconquered* (1947) to play a militia captain during the French and Indian War who rescues a convict (Paulette Goddard) from indentured servitude while readying for the attack of the Seneca nation on Fort Pitt. The $4 million epic incurred a huge loss for Paramount.

DeMille rebounded with *Samson and Delilah* (1949), a profitable epic whose $11 million gross ignited a mania in Hollywood for biblical films. After appearing as himself with his former protégée Gloria Swanson in the memorable finale to Billy Wilder's *Sunset Boulevard,* he made *The Greatest Show on Earth* (1952), a salute to the circus starring Charlton Heston and James Stewart. It received the Academy Award for best picture, and DeMille received his only Oscar nomination for best director.

DeMille's final movie, *The Ten Commandments* (1956), was a remake of his 1923 film but without the modern-day story. Heston starred (in his best-known role) as Moses and Yul Brynner as his foe the Pharaoh Ramses. The vast scale of *The Ten Commandments* (particularly in the scenes of the Israelites leaving Egypt and the parting of the Red Sea), the Oscar-winning special effects, and the larger-than-life performances have made it the film for which DeMille is best remembered.

DeMille's *Autobiography* was published in 1959. It acknowledged the strong and assertive personality for which he was known: he was the first director to use a megaphone on the set and the first to install a loudspeaker system for issuing orders. Apart from his film work, from 1936 to 1945 he appeared on radio in *Lux Radio Theatre*, a popular weekly series of adaptations of recent motion pictures. He was also noted for his right-wing political views and strenuous opposition to labour unions.

Although critics often dismissed DeMille's films as devoid of artistic merit, he was conspicuously successful in a genre—the epic—that he made distinctively his own. His honours included a special Academy Award (1949) for "brilliant showmanship" and the Irving G. Thalberg Award (1952).

SOPHIE TUCKER

(b. Jan. 13, 1884, Russia–d. Feb. 9, 1966, New York, N.Y., U.S.)

Sophie Tucker (born Sophie Kalish) was an American singer whose 62-year stage career included American burlesque, vaudeville, and nightclub and English music hall appearances.

Born somewhere in Russia as her mother was on her way to join her father in the United States, Sophie Kalish grew up in Boston and then in Hartford, Connecticut, where her mother ran a restaurant. Her father had changed the family name to Abuza after his arrival in the United States. From her childhood she wanted to be an entertainer, and she began by singing in the family restaurant, in part to escape waiting on tables and dishwashing. In 1906 she changed her name to Sophie Tucker and landed a few singing jobs.

Her professional career began in 1906 when, after a successful amateur appearance, she opened in a blackface routine at the old Music Hall in New York City. (Intended as comic entertainment, blackface minstrelsy was performed by a group of white minstrels with black-painted faces, whose material caricatured the singing and dancing of slaves. Today it is generally accepted to be offensive and in poor taste.) In 1909 she appeared with the *Ziegfeld Follies*. Tucker traveled the vaudeville circuits from coast to coast for more than 20 years and also made occasional appearances in England, where she gained a substantial following. Her brassy, flamboyant style, set off by her warm and ample presence, was perfectly suited to both sentimental ballads and risqué songs, and she became a great favourite of audiences. In 1911 she first sang "Some of These Days," which became her trademark. Tucker's first appearance at the Palace Theater in New

York City, which was considered the summit of success in vaudeville, came in August 1914. It was in 1928, at the Palace, that she was first billed as "The Last of the Red-Hot Mamas." She also appeared in numerous editions of Earl Carroll's *Vanities* and the Shuberts' *Gaieties* and in such shows as *Louisiana Lou* (1911), *Round in Fifty in London* (1922), *Charlot's Revue* (1925), with Gertrude Lawrence, and Cole Porter's hit *Leave It to Me* (1938). For a time in the 1920s she operated her own New York club, Sophie Tucker's Playground.

In the early 1930s, when vaudeville was beginning to seem passé, Tucker turned to nightclubs, while many of her fellow vaudevillians either attempted the movies or slid into oblivion. She made several films, including *Honky Tonk* (1929), *Broadway Melody of 1937* (1937), and *Follow the Boys* (1944), but she preferred live audiences, and she played to them with great success for more than 30 years. She also made occasional television appearances, mainly on *The Ed Sullivan Show*, during the 1950s and early '60s, and she was an active performer until 1965. Her autobiography, *Some of These Days*, was published in 1945.

CHARLIE CHAPLIN

(b. April 16, 1889, London, Eng.–d. Dec, 25, 1977, Corsier-sur-Vevey, Switz.)

Charlie Chaplin was the byname of Sir Charles Spencer Chaplin, a British comedian, producer, writer, director, and composer who is widely regarded as the greatest comic artist of the screen and one of the most important figures in motion-picture history.

EARLY LIFE AND CAREER

Chaplin was named after his father, a British music-hall entertainer. He spent his early childhood with his mother, the singer Hannah Hall, after she and his father separated, and he made his own stage debut at age five, filling in for his mother. The mentally unstable Hall was later confined to an asylum. Charlie and his half brother Sydney were sent to a series of bleak workhouses and residential schools.

Using his mother's show-business contacts, Charlie became a professional entertainer in 1897 when he joined the Eight Lancashire Lads, a clog-dancing act. His subsequent stage credits include a small role in William Gillette's *Sherlock Holmes* (1899) and a stint with the vaudeville act Casey's Court Circus. In 1908 he joined the Fred Karno pantomime troupe, quickly rising to star status as The Drunk in the ensemble sketch *A Night in an English Music Hall*.

While touring America with the Karno company in 1913, Chaplin was signed to appear in Mack Sennett's Keystone comedy films. Though his first Keystone one-reeler, *Making a Living* (1914), was not the failure that historians have claimed, Chaplin's initial screen character, a mercenary dandy, did not show him to best advantage. Ordered by Sennett to come up with a more-workable screen image, Chaplin improvised an outfit consisting of a too-small coat, too-large pants, floppy shoes, and a battered derby. As a finishing touch, he pasted on a postage-stamp mustache and adopted a cane as an all-purpose prop. It was in his second Keystone film, *Kid Auto Races at Venice* (1914), that Chaplin's immortal screen alter ego, "the Little Tramp," was born.

In truth, Chaplin did not always portray a tramp; in many of his films his character was employed as a waiter, store clerk, stagehand, fireman, and the like. His character might be better described as the quintessential misfit— shunned by polite society, unlucky in love, jack-of-all-trades but master of none. He was also a survivor, forever leaving past sorrows behind, jauntily shuffling off to new adventures. The Tramp's appeal was universal: audiences loved his cheekiness, his deflation of pomposity, his casual savagery, his unexpected gallantry, and his resilience in the face of adversity. Some historians have traced the Tramp's origins to Chaplin's Dickensian childhood, while others have suggested that the character had its roots in the motto of Chaplin's mentor, Fred Karno: "Keep it wistful, gentlemen, keep it wistful." Whatever the case, within months after his movie debut, Chaplin was the screen's biggest star.

His 35 Keystone comedies can be regarded as the Tramp's gestation period, during which a caricature became a character. The films improved steadily once Chaplin became his own director. In 1915 he left Sennett to accept a $1,250-weekly contract at Essanay Studios. It was there that he began to inject elements of pathos into his comedy, notably in such shorts as *The Tramp* (1915) and *Burlesque on Carmen* (1915). He moved on to an even more lucrative job ($670,000 per year) at the Mutual Company Film Corporation. There, during an 18-month period, he made the 12 two-reelers that many regard as his finest films, among them such gems as *One A.M.* (1916), *The Rink* (1916), *The Vagabond* (1916), and *Easy Street* (1917). It was then, in 1917, that Chaplin found himself attacked for the first (though hardly the last) time by the press. He was criticized for not enlisting to fight in World War I. To aid the war effort, Chaplin raised funds for the troops via bond drives.

In 1918 Chaplin jumped studios again, accepting a $1 million offer from the First National Film Corporation for eight shorts. That same year he married 16-year-old film extra Mildred Harris—the first in a procession of child brides. For his new studio he made shorts such as *Shoulder Arms* (1918) and *The Pilgrim* (1923) and his first starring

Charlie Chaplin (centre) and Jackie Coogan (bottom) in The Kid *(1921).*

feature, *The Kid* (1921), which starred the irresistible Jackie Coogan as the kid befriended and aided by the Little Tramp. Some have suggested that the increased dramatic content of those films is symptomatic of Chaplin's efforts to justify the praise lavished upon him by the critical intelligentsia. A painstaking perfectionist, he began spending more and more time on the preparation and production of each film. In his personal life too, Chaplin was particular. Having divorced Mildred in 1921, Chaplin married in 1924 16-year-old Lillita MacMurray, who shortly would become known to the world as film star Lita Grey. (They would be noisily divorced in 1927.)

From 1923 through 1929 Chaplin made only three features: *A Woman of Paris* (1923), which he directed but did not star in (and his only drama); *The Gold Rush* (1925), widely regarded as his masterpiece; and *The Circus* (1928), an underrated film that may rank as his funniest. All three were released by United Artists, the company cofounded in 1919 by Chaplin, husband-and-wife superstars Douglas Fairbanks and Mary Pickford, and director D.W. Griffith. Of the three films, *The Gold Rush* is one of the most-memorable films of the silent era. Chaplin placed the Little Tramp in the epic setting of the Yukon, amid bears, snowstorms, and a fearsome prospector (Mack Swain); his love interest was a beautiful dance-hall queen (Georgia Hale). The scene in which the Tramp must eat his shoe to stay alive epitomizes the film's blend of rich comedy and well-earned pathos.

THE SOUND ERA: *CITY LIGHTS* TO *LIMELIGHT*

As the Little Tramp, Chaplin had mastered the subtle art of pantomime, and the advent of sound gave him cause for alarm. After much hesitation, he released his 1931 feature

City Lights as a silent, despite the ubiquity of talkies (films with sound) after 1929. It was a sweet, unabashedly sentimental story in which the Little Tramp falls in love with a blind flower girl (Virginia Cherrill) and he vows to restore her sight. The musical score, the lone "sound" element the film offered, was composed by Chaplin, and he conducted its recording; no matter the lack of dialogue, it was a huge success.

In 1932 Chaplin began a relationship with young starlet Paulette Goddard. His next film, *Modern Times* (1936), was a hybrid, essentially a silent film with music, sound effects, and brief passages of dialogue. Chaplin also gave his Little Tramp a voice, as he performed a gibberish song. Chaplin played a nameless factory worker who has been dehumanized by the mindless task he has to perform—tightening bolts on parts that fly by on an assembly line; Goddard played "A Gamin," the stray who comes under his wing. It was the last silent feature to come out of Hollywood, but audiences still turned out to see it. Most significantly, it was the Little Tramp's final performance.

The Great Dictator (1940) was Chaplin's most overt political satire and his first sound picture. Chaplin starred in a dual role as a nameless Jewish barber and as Adenoid Hynkel, Dictator of Tomania—a dead-on parody of German dictator Adolf Hitler, to whom Chaplin bore a remarkable physical resemblance. Goddard played Hannah, the barber's Jewish friend, who flees Tomania after the barber is arrested and sent to a concentration camp, and Jack Oakie gave a hilarious impersonation of Italian dictator Benito Mussolini as Napaloni, Dictator of Bacteria. The japing tone of the picture's lampooning was a movement away from Chaplin's usual poetic approach; *The Great Dictator* was simply too bitter and too outraged to permit much in the way of gentle comedy. The film did well at the box office, and he received his only Academy Award nomination as best actor.

After making just three movies over a 10-year period, Chaplin would take seven more years before his next film. Problems in his personal life were again partly to blame. In 1942 he and Goddard divorced (despite likely never having officially married). In 1943 a paternity suit was brought against him by young would-be actress Joan Barry. That same year he married 18-year-old Oona O'Neill, daughter of playwright Eugene O'Neill; again he was accused of cradle robbing. In the Barry suit the courts ruled against Chaplin in 1944; he was named the father of Barry's child, although he was cleared of the more serious charges of violating the Mann Act, which prohibited interstate transportation of women for "immoral purposes."

His darkest comedy, *Monsieur Verdoux*, was released in 1947, and by then Chaplin was in the headlines again, as possibly being called before the House Un-American Activities Committee (HUAC) to testify about his relations with communists, especially exiled German composer Hanns Eisler. Chaplin starred in that "Comedy of Murders" (as *Monsieur Verdoux* was promoted) as Henri Verdoux, a happily married father and former bank clerk who becomes the scourge of 1930s Paris by romancing and then killing a series of rich widows and spinsters for their fortunes. (Chaplin's character was based on French murderer Henri Landru, who was known as the Bluebeard of France when he went on his killing spree during the 1910s.) *Monsieur Verdoux* was an utter failure commercially upon its release—his first since *A Woman of Paris* 24 years earlier—and critical opinion was divided, although Chaplin's screenplay was nominated for an Oscar. It is still difficult to determine whether *Monsieur Verdoux* would have been better received had he not been suffering from the attentions of HUAC. When Chaplin heard news that he would be summoned before the committee, he immediately accepted, saying, "I am not a communist. I am a peacemonger." He planned a rerelease of *Monsieur Verdoux* in Washington, D.C., for the week Eisler was to testify before HUAC, and he invited the committee members to the premiere. However, HUAC chairman J. Parnell Roberts canceled Chaplin's appearance and said he would not be a part of publicity for *Monsieur Verdoux*.

Chaplin took another five years to launch his next film, the melancholy *Limelight* (1952). He played Calvero, a music-hall idol whose day has passed, and British actress Claire Bloom (then 19) costarred as Terry, a ballet dancer whom Calvero saves from a suicide attempt; he shelters, encourages, and finally helps elevate her to the top of her profession, even as his own star dims and then blinks out. Chaplin's half brother Sydney and his son Charlie, Jr., both had small parts, and silent comedy star Buster Keaton had a key role as a theatre pianist who watches Calvero expire. (*Limelight* would be given an Oscar for its score, to which Chaplin contributed, in 1973, after the film finally received the requisite release in Los Angeles.)

For Chaplin, *Limelight*'s release was further tainted by the U.S. Immigration and Naturalization Service advising him (as he sailed on an ocean liner with Oona to the film's premiere in London) that he would be denied reentry to the United States unless he was willing to answer charges "of a political nature and of moral turpitude." The Chaplins continued on their way to England; she returned to the States to close out their business affairs, while he kept going, finally settling in Corsier-sur-Vevey, Switzerland, where he and Oona would live for the rest of their lives. He liquidated his interest in United Artists.

FINAL WORKS: *A KING IN NEW YORK* AND *A COUNTESS FROM HONG KONG*

Chaplin made use of his own experiences as a victim of McCarthyism in his next film, the British-made *A King in New York* (1957). Satirizing the very witch-hunts that had sent him into self-imposed exile, Chaplin fashioned a diatribe against the foibles of 1950s America that only occasionally managed to nail its target. (Ironically, the film was not released in the United States until 1973.)

While an anthology titled *The Chaplin Revue* (comprising the shorts *A Dog's Life* [1918], *Shoulder Arms* [1918], and *The Pilgrim* [1923]) was being given a theatrical release in the United States in 1959, Chaplin began work on his memoirs. *My Autobiography* (1964) provided a great deal of information about Chaplin's childhood and rise to stardom but was less forthcoming about his work and adult life. Nevertheless, the warm reception it was accorded made another film project viable.

The passing of a full decade since *A King in New York* and the radical change in the political climate of the United States ensured that there was much anticipation surrounding *A Countess from Hong Kong* (1967), a British-made romantic comedy starring Marlon Brando and Sophia Loren, the biggest names he had worked with since he himself was a premier box-office draw. However, it proved to be a critical and commercial disappointment.

In his last years Chaplin was accorded many of the honours that had been withheld from him for so long. In 1972 he returned to the United States for the first time in 20 years to accept a special Academy Award for "the incalculable effect he has had on making motion pictures the art form of this century." It was a bittersweet homecoming. Chaplin had come to deplore the United States, but he was visibly and deeply moved by the 12-minute standing ovation he received at the Oscar ceremonies. As Alistair Cooke described the events:

> He was very old and trembly and groping through the thickening fog of memory or a few simple sentences. A senile, harmless doll, he was now—as the song says—"easy to love," absolutely safe to admire.

Chaplin made one of his final public appearances in 1975, when he was knighted. Several months after his death, his body was briefly kidnapped from a Swiss cemetery by a pair of bungling thieves—a macabre coda that Chaplin might have concocted for one of his own two-reelers.

FRITZ LANG

(b. Dec. 5, 1890, Vienna, Austria-Hungary—d. Aug. 2, 1976, Los Angeles, Calif., U.S.)

Fritz Lang was an Austrian-born American motion-picture director whose films, dealing with fate and man's inevitable working out of his destiny, are considered masterpieces of visual composition and expressionistic suspense. Lang had already created an impressive body of work in the German cinema before coming to the United States in 1934. Although it took him some 21 years to fashion 22 Hollywood films, arguably at least half of them are noirish masterpieces of menace—tone poems of fear and fate that have stood the test of time.

EARLY LIFE AND GERMAN FILMS

Lang's father was a *Baumeister* (designer-contractor) and, as such, did not quite enjoy the status of an architect,

34

which Lang later claimed was his father's occupation. His mother, who may well have converted from Judaism to Roman Catholicism in response to growing anti-Semitism in Austria, raised her children in the Roman Catholic faith. Lang briefly studied civil engineering in Vienna but soon became enamoured of café life and painting (especially the works of Egon Schiele and Gustav Klimt). For several years he traveled in North Africa, Asia, and the South Seas and throughout Europe, studying painting in Munich and Paris. An exhibition of his paintings opened in Paris in 1914, just before he returned to Austria and was conscripted into the Austrian army for service in World War I. He was wounded four times (losing vision in his right eye), ultimately requiring a year's convalescence in a Vienna army hospital, where he tried his hand at writing screenplays. After his discharge he began acting on the Vienna stage. In Berlin he wrote screenplays for producer Joe May, and in 1919 he was given the opportunity to write and direct his first movie, *Halbblut* (*The Half-Caste*), the theme of which foreshadowed such triumphs from his Hollywood period as *The Woman in the Window* (1944) and *Scarlet Street* (1945). In 1920 he began working for producer Erich Pommer at Decla Biscop Studio, which became part of the German filmmaking giant UFA.

Through the 1920s Lang made evermore ambitious films, some of them so long and dense that they were exhibited in two parts. Among the best known are *Der müde Tod* (1921; *Destiny*), an allegorical melodrama; *Dr. Mabuse, der Spieler - Ein Bild der Zeit* (1922; *Dr. Mabuse: The Gambler*), a crime thriller; and *Die Nibelungen: Siegfried* (1924; *Siegfried*) and *Die Nibelungen: Kriemhilds Rache* (1924; *Kriemhild's Revenge*), both of which were based on a 13th-century epic saga. In 1920 Lang married novelist Thea von Harbou, with whom he had been collaborating on screenplays and would continue to do so through 1932. In 1924 he traveled to the United States for the first time, to observe moviemaking techniques in New York City and Hollywood.

Lang's first project upon his return to Germany was the futuristic masterpiece *Metropolis* (1927), which he spent most of 1925 and 1926 shooting for UFA, nearly exhausting the considerable resources of the studio. The film's plot, about a repressive society divided into exploited workers, indolent rulers, and emotionless robots, may have owed something to H.G. Wells, but the breathtaking visual scheme was like nothing ever attempted on screen. Lang planned and executed his films in exquisite visual detail, and his placement of people, places, and things within the frame (mise-en-scène) and his expressive use of lighting were calculated, exacting, and evocative. With *Metropolis* he was aided not just by the renowned cinematographer Karl Freund but also by special-effects innovator Eugen Schüfftan, who employed a camera process of his own invention that made it possible to blend shots of miniatures with live action by using a specially designed mirror. After self-producing the crime film *Spione* (*Spies*) in 1928, Lang returned to science fiction for the silent production *Frau im Mond* (1929; *Woman in the Moon*; also known as *By Rocket to the Moon*), which was released without even a score.

His first sound film, *M* (1931), a horrifying account of a child murderer (based on a true story), was Lang's greatest international success and, ultimately, his own personal favourite among his films. Anchored by Peter Lorre's chilling performance as the unhinged killer of young girls who is finally hunted down by the Berlin underworld, *M* is one of the cinema's enduring early talkies and a landmark of German Expressionism, the national artistic movement that employed distortion and exaggeration to depict subjective emotions and responses rather than objective reality and that was suffused in alienation and pessimism. Expressionism's cinematic development was bookended by Robert Wiene's *The Cabinet of Dr. Caligari* (1920) and *M*.

Less compelling was *Das Testament des Dr. Mabuse* (1933; *The Testament of Dr. Mabuse*), a crime thriller that was overtly the sequel to *Dr. Mabuse: The Gambler*; covertly, it was intended by Lang as an anti-Nazi statement that equated the state and German dictator Adolph Hitler with criminality. Joseph Goebbels, Hitler's minister of propaganda, banned the film but summoned Lang to a meeting in which he informed the filmmaker of Hitler's admiration for *M* and offered him the post of artistic director of UFA, the leading position in the German film industry. Wanting no part of that and fearful of what might ultimately happen to him as result of his half-Jewish background, Lang fled to Paris (though he would return to Germany again briefly on a couple of occasions). He left behind his bank accounts, personal belongings, and wife, van Harbou, who was already a member of the Nazi Party; she divorced Lang and became one of the Third Reich's most-accomplished writers and directors of propaganda films.

FIRST FILMS IN HOLLYWOOD

Lang made one film while in France, *Liliom* (1934), and then accepted David O. Selznick's offer to make a motion picture in Hollywood for Metro-Goldwyn-Mayer, Inc., (MGM). That film, *Fury* (1936), which starred Spencer Tracy and Sylvia Sidney, was a powerful, unforgiving study of mob violence but met with only moderate box-office success, prompting MGM to not extend Lang's contract with the studio. He next found work with independent producer Walter Wanger on the equally grim *You Only Live Once* (1937). Based partly on the story of real-life fugitives

Bonnie and Clyde, it starred Henry Fonda as an ex-convict who is unjustly sentenced to death for murder. Unaware that he has been pardoned, he breaks out of jail and heads for the Canadian border with his wife (Sidney), one step ahead of a nightmarish manhunt, the intractable jaws of fate, and death. *You and Me* (1938), the eccentric tale of a couple (Sidney and George Raft) who get married without realizing that they both have a criminal past, is less well remembered than the critically acclaimed *You Only Live Once*.

FILMS OF THE 1940S

Lang then moved to Twentieth Century-Fox, beginning his tenure there with a pair of Technicolor westerns—*The Return of Frank James* (1940), a fine sequel to Henry King's *Jesse James* (1939), with Fonda repeating his role as Frank James, now attempting to avenge Jesse's death; and *Western Union* (1941), a handsome, meticulously researched staging of the company's bold expansion west.

Lang's next effort, *Man Hunt* (1941), based on Geoffrey Household's complicated but thrilling suspense novel *Rogue Male* (1939), became one of his masterpieces. Walter Pidgeon starred in the taut drama as an English hunter in pre-World War II Germany who by chance finds himself with an opportunity to assassinate Hitler. Lang's clashes with producer Darryl F. Zanuck at that time resulted in the director's departure from Fox. He then collaborated with Bertolt Brecht on the independent production *Hangmen Also Die!* (1943), another World War II-related film, this time an account of the assassination of SS leader Reinhard Heydrich in Prague.

Although Lang had begun incorporating thematic and visual elements of film noir into his work as early as *You*

Only Live Once, his full embrace of that influential film-making style coincided with the flourishing of its golden age in the mid-1940s. Given German Expressionism's huge influence on film noir, it is unsurprising that Lang would become one of its most-gifted practitioners. Like German Expressionism, film noir was steeped in pessimism and presented a dark view of human nature. Visually, both styles employed dramatic high-contrast lighting, shafts of light and shadows, and odd perspectives. All those elements were much on display in Lang's films noir of the mid-1940s.

The Woman in the Window (1944) was one of his most nightmarish dramas. Skillfully adapted by Nunnally Johnson from an obscure novel, it starred Edward G. Robinson as a married college professor who becomes involved with the woman (Joan Bennett) who is the subject of a painting with which he has become infatuated. Bad luck leads him inexorably on the path to blackmail, murder, and the ever-tightening net of the law. Very loosely based on a Graham Greene novel, Lang's next project, the gripping *Ministry of Fear* (1944), featured Ray Milland as a recently discharged mental patient whose life is mysteriously endangered by a motley assortment of spies, double agents, and bogus mediums. Lang then assembled the principal actors from *The Woman in the Window* for *Scarlet Street* (1945), a remake of Jean Renoir's *La Chienne* (1931). Robinson delivered another extraordinary performance as the appropriately named Chris Cross, a milquetoast department-store cashier whose shrewish wife (Rosalind Ivan) denies him every pleasure except the one he finds as a weekend painter. He falls for a younger woman (Bennett) whose true romantic interest lies with a con man (Dan Duryea). Both Chris and his beloved artworks are exploited by the conscienceless pair until he finally snaps.

On the heels of that triumph, Lang's career entered a prolonged slump. *Cloak and Dagger* (1946) was a less-than-consistently engaging espionage film. Even more disappointing was the psychological drama *Secret Beyond the Door* (1947).

FILMS OF THE 1950S

House by the River (1950), an atmospheric Southern Gothic melodrama made for Poverty Row studio Republic Pictures, was followed by *American Guerrilla in the Philippines* (1950), a rousing if conventional World War II adventure starring Tyrone Power as a stranded U.S. Navy officer leading native Filipinos in their fight against superior Japanese forces. With *Rancho Notorious* (1952) Lang hit his stride again. Made for RKO, the quirky noirish western starred Marlene Dietrich as the hard-boiled owner (and chanteuse) of an outlaw hideout. A revenge-driven cowboy (Arthur Kennedy) wangles an invitation to the hideout from a gunslinger (Mel Ferrer), leading to romance and then violence.

Lang then deftly directed a high-profile cast that included Barbara Stanwyck, Robert Ryan, Paul Douglas, and Marilyn Monroe in the hyperemotional melodrama *Clash by Night* (1952), which was based on a play by Clifford Odets. *The Blue Gardenia* (1953), featuring Anne Baxter as a woman accused of murdering a lecher (Raymond Burr), was a neatly plotted film noir, but it caused much less of a stir than Lang's other film of 1953, *The Big Heat*. That film unleashed the raw fury of Glenn Ford as a rogue police officer whose wife is killed by a mob, but Gloria Grahame provided the movie's moral centre and peculiar resonance. The critics were largely unimpressed by the reteaming of Ford and Grahame in *Human Desire* (1954), Lang's remake for Columbia of Renoir's 1938 adaptation of Émile Zola's novel *La Bête humaine* (1890; *The Human Beast*). The anomalous *Moonfleet* (1955), a period buccaneer film, followed to little notice.

While the City Sleeps (1956) presented Lang with more familiar material, a frantic manhunt for the psychopathic "Lipstick Killer" (John Drew Barrymore) by a pack of amoral journalists (Dana Andrews, Vincent Price, Thomas Mitchell, and George Sanders). Lang's second picture for RKO in 1956 was *Beyond a Reasonable Doubt*, a paranoid thriller with Andrews portraying a man who pretends to be guilty of murder, only to find that he cannot extricate himself from the web of deceit he has woven. The film's dramatization of fate's implacable vortex was a fitting conclusion to Lang's Hollywood career.

LAST FILMS

Lang made a pair of related films in India—*Tiger of Bengal* and *The Tomb of Love* (also known as *The Indian Tomb*), both released in 1959—that were edited into a single film, *Journey to the Lost City* (1960), for release in the United States. He then returned to Germany, where he directed his final film, the third installment of the Dr. Mabuse series, *Die 1000 Augen des Dr. Mabuse* (1960; *The Thousand Eyes of Dr. Mabuse*), before retiring in California.

MARY PICKFORD

(b. April 9, 1893, Toronto, Ont., Can.–d. May 28, 1979, Santa Monica, Calif., U.S.)

Gladys Mary Smith, better known by her byname Mary Pickford, was a Canadian-born U.S. motion-picture actress, "America's sweetheart" of the silent screen, and one of the first film stars. At the height of her career, she was one of the richest and most famous women in the United States.

Gladys Mary Smith was the daughter of actors. Soon after the death of her father she began taking child's roles in productions in which her mother was playing. She made her first stage appearance in a Toronto stock company at the age of five. At eight she went on tour, and within 10 years she was playing on Broadway. From 1906 the family adopted the name Pickford. She made her New York debut in David Belasco's *The Warrens of Virginia* in December 1907. At age 14 she had already learned more of stagecraft than many older actors, and her winsome face, framed by a mass of golden curls, made her appeal virtually irresistible.

Pickford began working as a motion-picture extra at D.W. Griffith's Biograph Studio, starring in his 1909 film *The Lonely Villa*. By 1913 she had turned permanently to the screen, rising to first rank with Adolph Zukor's Famous Players Company. Her meteoric rise from an anonymous player to a star with her own production company (Mary Pickford Studios, created by Famous Players) was attributable not only to the phenomenal popularity of her films but also to her dedication to her craft and her meticulous care in creating quality entertainments. The ringleted ingenue with an expression of sweet sincerity and invincible innocence that she played in such silent films as *Hearts Adrift* (1914), *Poor Little Rich Girl* (1917), *Rebecca of Sunnybrook Farm* (1917), and *Johanna Enlists* (1918) fascinated audiences everywhere. She was known at first as the "Biograph Girl with the Curls" and then as "Our Mary" when that much of her name was revealed; with the release of *Tess of the Storm Country* in 1914, she was firmly established as "America's Sweetheart." In 1917 First National Films paid her $350,000 for each of three films, including the very successful *Daddy Long Legs* (1919).

In 1919 Pickford took the lead in organizing the United Artists Corporation with Griffith, Charlie Chaplin, and Douglas Fairbanks. In 1920, after the dissolution of her first marriage (1911–19) to actor Owen Moore, she married Fairbanks (divorced 1935). Pickford's popularity continued unabated in *Pollyanna* (1920), *Little Lord Fauntleroy* (1921), *Little Annie Rooney* (1925), *My Best Girl* (1927), *Coquette* (1929; her first talking picture, for which she won an Academy Award for best actress), *The Taming of the Shrew* (1929; her only film with Fairbanks), and *Kiki* (1931).

With *Secrets* (1933), her 194th film, Pickford retired from the screen. Thereafter she devoted herself to United Artists, of which she was first vice president from 1935 and for which she produced several films. She also wrote *Why Not Try God* (1934), *The Demi-Widow* (1935), and *My Rendezvous with Life* (1935), and in the 1930s she appeared on radio. In 1937 she married actor Charles ("Buddy") Rogers. Her later years were spent on business and civic and charitable activities, and she eventually became a recluse at Pickfair, the lavish estate she had built with Fairbanks. *Sunshine and Shadow*, her autobiography, was published in 1955.

HAROLD LLOYD

(b. April 20, 1893, Burchard, Neb., U.S.–d. March 8, 1971, Hollywood, Calif., U.S.)

Harold Lloyd was a U.S. motion-picture comedian who was the highest paid star of the 1920s and one of the cinema's most popular personalities.

The son of an itinerant commercial photographer, Lloyd finally settled in San Diego, Calif., where in 1913 he started playing minor parts in one-reel comedies. He mastered the art of the comic chase in the short time he was a member of Mack Sennett's Keystone comedy troupe. In

1915 Lloyd joined the new acting company formed by Hal Roach, a former actor who had turned producer. During this period he experimented with a comic character, the bewhiskered Willie Work. The most consistently successful of his early films, however, were those of the Lonesome Luke series. Beginning with *Just Nuts* (1915), Luke quickly became a popular U.S. screen character.

By 1918 the figure of the ordinary white-faced man in round glasses had replaced Luke as Lloyd's screen trademark. He developed his humour from plot and situation and was the first comedian to use physical danger as a source of laughter. Lloyd performed his own stunts and was known as the screen's most daring comedian. In *Safety Last!* (1923), an outstanding success, he hung from the hands of a clock several stories above a city street; in *Girl Shy* (1924) he took a thrilling ride atop a runaway streetcar; in *The Freshman* (1925), one of the most successful of all silent pictures, he stood in for the football tackling dummy.

Lloyd's peak of popularity was reached during the period of silent films, when emphasis was on visual rather than verbal humour, although he made many films after the coming of sound. His last was *Mad Wednesday* (1947). He was honoured with a special Academy Award in 1952 for his contribution to motion-picture comedy. In 1962 Lloyd released *Harold Lloyd's World of Comedy,* a compilation of scenes from his old movies, and *Harold Lloyd's Funny Side of Life.* The reception given to both demonstrated the timelessness of Lloyd's silent comedy.

RUDOLPH VALENTINO

(b. May 6, 1895, Castellaneta, Italy–d. Aug. 23, 1926, New York, N.Y., U.S.)

Rudolph Valentino was the byname of Rodolfo Alfonso Raffaello Pierre Filibert Guglielmi di Valentina d'Antonguolla, an Italian-born American motion-picture actor, who was idolized as the "Great Lover" of the 1920s.

Valentino immigrated to the United States in 1913 and worked for a time as a gardener, as a dishwasher, and later as a dancer in vaudeville. In 1918 he went to Hollywood, where he played small parts in films until he was given the role of Julio in *The Four Horsemen of the Apocalypse* (1921). He immediately became a star, his popularity being managed by skillful Hollywood press agents. Valentino's films, which were usually romantic dramas, include *The Sheik* (1921), *Blood and Sand* (1922), *The Eagle* (1925), and *The Son of the Sheik* (1926).

Valentino's sudden death from a ruptured ulcer at age 31 caused worldwide hysteria, several suicides, and riots at his lying in state, which attracted a crowd that stretched for 11 blocks. Each year after his death a mysterious "Woman in Black," sometimes several "Women in Black," appeared at his tomb.

THE GERSHWINS

IRA GERSHWIN
(B. DEC. 6, 1896, MANHATTAN, NEW YORK, N.Y., U.S.—D. AUG. 17, 1983, BEVERLY HILLS, CALIF., U.S.)

Ira Gershwin (original name Israel Gershvin) was an American lyricist who collaborated with his younger brother, George Gershwin, on more than 20 Broadway musicals and motion pictures until George's death (1937) and who later collaborated on films and plays with others—Moss Hart, Kurt Weill, Jerome Kern, Harry Warren, and Harold Arlen—and contributed to Gershwin revivals.

Gershwin was born on New York's Lower East Side of Russian-Jewish immigrant parents. He early showed literary talent and attended City College of New York for two years (1914–16). Thereafter, he did odd jobs until his brother, already becoming known as a composer and musician, asked him to write lyrics; their first song of collaboration was "The Real American Folk Song," which appeared in *Ladies First* (1918). During the early years, Ira Gershwin used a pseudonym, Arthur Francis, in order not to capitalize on his brother's reputation.

Over the years he wrote many brilliant lyrics for such Gershwin songs as "The Man I Love," "'S Wonderful," "I Got Rhythm," "Embraceable You," "A Foggy Day," and "Fascinating Rhythm" and prepared the lyrics for *Porgy and Bess* (1935), with such songs as "Summertime," "I Got Plenty o' Nuttin'," and "It Ain't Necessarily So." His later credits include "My Ship" with Kurt Weill (1940), "Long Ago and Far Away" with Jerome Kern (1944), and "The Man That Got Away" with Harold Arlen (1954), written for Judy Garland. He collected all the lyrics of his best-known songs and wrote commentaries on each in *Lyrics on Several Occasions* (1959). Ira Gershwin continued writing until the last year of his life, rewriting lyrics for Gershwin tunes used in the musical *My One and Only* (1983).

GEORGE GERSHWIN

(B. SEPT. 26, 1898, BROOKLYN, NEW YORK, N.Y., U.S.—D. JULY 11, 1937, HOLLYWOOD, CALIF., U.S.)

George Gershwin (original named Jacob Gershvin) was one of the most significant and popular American composers of all time. He wrote primarily for the Broadway musical theatre, but important as well are his orchestral and piano compositions in which he blended, in varying degrees, the techniques and forms of classical music with the stylistic nuances and techniques of popular music and jazz.

EARLY CAREER AND INFLUENCES

Gershwin was the son of Russian-Jewish immigrants. Although his family and friends were not musically inclined, Gershwin developed an early interest in music through his exposure to the popular and classical compositions he heard at school and in penny arcades. He began his musical education at age 11, when his family bought a second-hand upright piano, ostensibly so that George's older sibling, Ira, could learn the instrument. When George surprised everyone with his fluid playing of a popular song, which he had taught himself by following the keys on a neighbor's player piano, his parents decided that George would be the family member to receive lessons. He studied piano with the noted instructor Charles Hambitzer, who introduced his young student to the works of the great classical composers. Hambitzer was so impressed with Gershwin's potential that he refused payment for the lessons; as he wrote in a letter to his sister, "I have a new pupil who will make his mark if anybody will. The boy is a genius..."

Gershwin continued to broaden his musical knowledge and compositional technique throughout his career with such disparate mentors as the idiosyncratic American composers Henry Cowell and Wallingford Riegger, the distinguished traditionalist Edward Kilenyi, and Joseph Schillinger, a musical theorist known for his mathematically grounded approach to composition. After dropping out of school at age 15, Gershwin earned an income by making piano rolls for player pianos and by playing in New York nightclubs. His most important job in this period was his stint as a song plugger (probably the youngest in Tin Pan Alley), demonstrating sheet music for the Jerome Remick music-publishing company. In an era when sheet-music sales determined the popularity of a song, song pluggers such as Gershwin worked long hours pounding out tunes on the piano for potential customers. Although Gershwin's burgeoning creativity was hampered by his three-year stint in "plugger's purgatory" (as Gershwin biographer Isaac Goldberg termed it), it was nevertheless an experience that greatly improved his dexterity and increased his skills at improvisation and transposing. While still in his teens, Gershwin was known as one of the most talented pianists in the New York area and worked as an accompanist for popular singers and as a rehearsal pianist for Broadway musicals. In 1916 he composed his first published song, "When You Want 'Em You Can't Get 'Em (When You've Got 'Em You Don't Want 'Em)," as well as his first solo piano composition, "Rialto Ripples." He began to attract the attention of some Broadway luminaries, and the operetta composer Sigmund Romberg included one of Gershwin's songs in *The Passing Show of 1916*.

These early experiences greatly increased Gershwin's knowledge of jazz and popular music. He enjoyed especially the songs of Irving Berlin and Jerome Kern—referring to Berlin as "America's Franz Schubert" and stating that Kern was "the first composer who made me conscious that most popular music was of inferior quality, and that musical comedy was made of better material"—and he was inspired by their work to compose for the Broadway stage. In 1919 entertainer Al Jolson performed the Gershwin song "Swanee" in the musical *Sinbad*; it became an enormous success, selling more than two million recordings and a million copies of sheet music, and making Gershwin an overnight celebrity. That same year, *La, La Lucille*, the first show for which Gershwin composed the entire score, premiered; its most popular songs included "The Best of Everything," "Nobody but You," and "Tee-Oodle-Um-Bum-Bo." Also in 1919, Gershwin composed his first "serious" work, the *Lullaby* for string quartet. A study in harmony that Gershwin composed as an exercise for Kilenyi, *Lullaby*'s delicate beauty transcends its academic origins. Ira Gershwin published the work several years after George's death, and it has gone on to become a favourite with string quartets and with symphony orchestras, for which it was subsequently scored.

RHAPSODY IN BLUE

During the next few years, Gershwin contributed songs to various Broadway shows and revues. From 1920 to 1924 he composed scores for the annual productions of George White's *Scandals*, the popular variety revue, producing such standards as "(I'll Build a) Stairway to Paradise" and "Somebody Loves Me." For the *Scandals* production of 1922, Gershwin convinced producer White to incorporate a one-act jazz opera. This work, *Blue Monday* (later reworked and retitled as *135th Street*), was poorly received and was removed from the show after one performance. Bandleader Paul Whiteman, who had conducted the pit orchestra for the show, was nevertheless impressed by the piece. He and Gershwin shared the common goal of bringing respectability to jazz music, which in 1922 was still being regarded, as evidenced in a *New York American* editorial, as "degrading, pathological, nerve-irritating, sex-exciting music." To this end, in late 1923 Whiteman asked Gershwin to compose a piece for an upcoming concert—entitled "An Experiment in Modern Music"—at

New York's Aeolian Concert Hall. Legend has it that Gershwin forgot about the request until early January 1924, when he read a newspaper article announcing that the Whiteman concert on February 12 would feature a major new Gershwin composition. Writing at a furious pace in order to meet the deadline, Gershwin composed *Rhapsody in Blue*, perhaps his best-known work, in three weeks' time.

Owing to the haste in which it was written, *Rhapsody in Blue* was somewhat unfinished at its premiere. Gershwin improvised much of the piano solo during the performance, and conductor Whiteman had to rely on a nod from Gershwin to cue the orchestra at the end of the solo. Nevertheless, the piece was a resounding success and brought Gershwin worldwide fame. The revolutionary work incorporated trademarks of the jazz idiom (blue notes, syncopated rhythms, onomatopoeic instrumental effects) into a symphonic context. Gershwin himself later reflected on the work:

> *There had been so much chatter about the limitations of jazz, not to speak of the manifest misunderstandings of its function. Jazz, they said, had to be in strict time. It had to cling to dance rhythms. I resolved, if possible, to kill that misconception with one sturdy blow...No set plan was in my mind, no structure to which my music would conform. The Rhapsody, you see, began as a purpose, not a plan.*

The work, arranged by Ferde Grofé (composer of the *Grand Canyon Suite*) for either symphony orchestra or jazz band, is perhaps the most-performed and most-recorded orchestral composition of the 20th century. It is the only one of Gershwin's major works that Gershwin himself did not orchestrate.

POPULAR SONGS

For the remainder of his career, Gershwin devoted himself to both popular songs and orchestral compositions. His Broadway shows from the 1920s and '30s featured numerous songs that became standards: "Fascinating Rhythm," "Oh, Lady Be Good," "Sweet and Low-Down," "Do, Do, Do," "Someone to Watch over Me," "Strike Up the Band," "The Man I Love," "'S Wonderful," "I've Got a Crush on You," "Bidin' My Time," "Embraceable You," "But Not for Me," "Of Thee I Sing," and "Isn't It a Pity." He also composed several songs for Hollywood films, such as "Let's Call the Whole Thing Off," "They All Laughed," "They Can't Take That Away from Me," "A Foggy Day," "Nice Work if You Can Get It," "Love Walked In," and "Love Is Here to Stay." His lyricist for nearly all of these tunes was his older brother, Ira, whose glib, witty lyrics—often punctuated with slang, puns, and wordplay—received nearly as much acclaim as George's compositions. The Gershwin brothers comprised a somewhat unique song-writing partnership in that George's melodies usually came first—a reverse of the process employed by most composing teams. (When asked by interviewers, "Which comes first, the words or the music?", Ira's standard response was, "The contract.") So facile was George's musical imagination that quality songs were often composed within a few minutes of improvisation; other times, he dipped into his notebooks of song sketches that he accumulated over time (he once said, "I have more tunes in my head than I could put down on paper in a hundred years") and embellished an old melody he had labeled "g.t." (for "good tune"). Ira would then spend a week or more fitting words to the tune, polishing each line (to the extent that he was nicknamed "The Jeweller" by other songwriters) until he was satisfied. Songwriter Arthur Schwartz regarded Ira's efforts to be "a truly phenomenal feat, when one considers he was required to be brilliant within the most confining rhythms and accents."

One of the Gershwins' best-known collaborations, "I Got Rhythm," was introduced by Ethel Merman in the musical *Girl Crazy* (1930). The following year, Gershwin scored a lengthy, elaborate piano arrangement of the song, and in late 1933 he arranged the piece into a set of variations for piano and orchestra; *"I Got Rhythm" Variations* has since become one of Gershwin's most-performed orchestral works. In addition, the 32-bar structure of "I Got Rhythm" has become the second-most frequently used harmonic progression in jazz improvisation, next to that of the traditional 12-bar blues.

Gershwin's piano score for "I Got Rhythm" was part of a larger project begun in 1931, *George Gershwin's Songbook*. A collection of Gershwin's personal favourites among his many hit tunes, it featured the composer's own adaptations designed "for the above-average pianist." Offering valuable insight into Gershwin's use of rhythm and harmony, as well as his own piano style, the *Songbook* selections have become concert staples for several noted pianists throughout the years and have occasionally been adapted into full orchestra arrangements.

OTHER WORKS FOR ORCHESTRA

In 1925 Gershwin was commissioned by the Symphony Society of New York to write a concerto, prompting the composer to comment, "This showed great confidence on their part as I had never written anything for symphony before...I started to write the concerto in London, after buying four or five books on musical structure to find out what the concerto form actually was!" The resulting work, *Concerto in F* (1925), was Gershwin's lengthiest

composition and was divided into three traditional concerto movements. The first movement loosely follows a
sonata structure of exposition, development, and recapit-
ulation, and it appropriates themes and rhythms from the
popular "Charleston." The second movement—the "high
water mark of [Gershwin's] talent," according to conductor Walter Damrosch, who conducted the work's premiere
performance—is a slow, meditative adaptation of blues
progressions, and the third movement—"an orgy of
rhythms," according to Gershwin—introduces new
themes and returns, rondo-like, to the themes of the first.
Although not as well received at the time as *Rhapsody in
Blue*, the *Concerto in F* eventually came to be regarded as
one of Gershwin's most important works as well as perhaps the most popular American piano concerto.

An American in Paris (1928), Gershwin's second-most
famous orchestral composition, was inspired by the composer's trips to Paris throughout the 1920s. His stated
intention with the work was to "portray the impressions
of an American visitor in Paris as he strolls about the city,
listens to various street noises, and absorbs the French
atmosphere"; for this purpose, Gershwin incorporated
such touches of verisimilitude as real French taxi horns. It
is this piece that perhaps best represents Gershwin's
employment of both jazz and classical forms. The harmonic structure of *An American in Paris* is rooted in blues
traditions (particularly the "Homesick Blues" middle section), and soloists are often required to bend, slide, and
growl certain notes and passages, in the style of jazz musicians of the 1920s. The melodies that are repeated and
embellished throughout the work, however, are never subject to alteration—the antithesis of the jazz philosophy
that regards melody as a mere loose outline for imaginative decoration. With its varied rhythms and free structure

("Five sections held together more or less by intuition," according to one critic), *An American in Paris* seemed more balletic than symphonic and, indeed, the piece gained its most lasting fame 23 years after its premiere, when it was used by Gene Kelly for the closing ballet sequence of the classic, eponymous film musical in 1951.

Gershwin's other major orchestral compositions have grown in stature and popularity throughout the years. His *Second Rhapsody* (1931) began life under the working titles "Manhattan Rhapsody" and "Rhapsody in Rivets" and was featured, in embryonic form, as incidental music in the film *Delicious* (1931). Perhaps the most experimental of Gershwin's major works, it has been praised as his most perfect composition in terms of structure and orchestration. Gershwin's *Cuban Overture* (1932), which he stated was inspired by "two hysterical weeks in Cuba where no sleep was had," employed rhumba rhythms and such percussion instruments as claves, maracas, bongo drums, and gourds, all of which were generally unknown at the time in the United States. It is a work frequently revived by symphony conductors, who find its brash, festival-like mood to be a rousing concert-opener.

PORGY AND BESS

Throughout his career, Gershwin had major successes on Broadway with shows such as *Lady, Be Good!* (1924), *Oh, Kay!* (1926), *Strike Up the Band* (1930), *Girl Crazy* (1930), and, especially, the daring political satire *Of Thee I Sing* (1931), for which Ira and librettists George S. Kaufman and Morrie Ryskind shared a Pulitzer Prize. (Rules of the Pulitzer committee at the time did not allow for composers to share in a drama award. Ira objected that George was not a corecipient, but George insisted that the rules be obeyed. In protest, Ira hung his Pulitzer certificate in his bathroom.) These shows, smash hits in their time, are (save for Gershwin's music) largely forgotten today; ironically, his most enduring and respected Broadway work, *Porgy and Bess*, was lukewarmly received upon its premiere in 1935. Gershwin's "American Folk Opera" was inspired by the DuBose Heyward novel *Porgy* (1925) and featured a libretto and lyrics by Ira and the husband-wife team of DuBose and Dorothy Heyward. In preparation for the show, Gershwin spent time in the rural South, studying firsthand the music and lifestyle of impoverished African Americans. Theatre critics received the premiere production enthusiastically, but highbrow music critics were derisive, distressed that "lowly" popular music should be incorporated into an opera structure. Black audiences throughout the years have criticized the work for its condescending depiction of stereotyped characters and for Gershwin's inauthentic appropriation of black musical forms. Nevertheless, Gershwin's music—including such standards as "Summertime," "It Ain't Necessarily So," "Bess, You Is My Woman Now," and "I Got Plenty O' Nuttin'"—transcended early criticism to attain a revered niche in the musical world, largely because it successfully amalgamates various musical cultures to evoke something uniquely American and wholly Gershwin. *Porgy and Bess* received overdue recognition in the years 1952–54 when the U.S. State Department selected it to represent the United States on an international tour, during which it became the first opera by an American composer to be performed at the La Scala opera house in Milan. While it still raises political issues, contemporary attitudes towards the work are reflected in a statement by Grace Bumbry, who portrayed Bess in the Metropolitan Opera's widely praised revival in 1985: "I resented the role at first, possibly because I really didn't know the score, and I think because of the racial aspect. I thought it beneath me, I felt I had worked far too hard, that we had come too far to regress to 1935. My way of dealing with it was to see that it really was a piece of Americana, of American history." Many now consider the score from *Porgy and Bess* to be Gershwin's greatest masterpiece.

Aftermath and Assessment

Gershwin was known as a gregarious man whose huge ego was tempered by a genuinely magnetic personality. He loved his work and approached every assignment with enthusiasm, never suffering from "composer's block." Throughout the first half of 1937, Gershwin began experiencing severe headaches and brief memory blackouts, although medical tests showed him to be in good health. By July, Gershwin exhibited impaired motor skills and drastic weight loss, and he required assistance in walking. He lapsed into a coma on July 9, and a spinal tap revealed the presence of a brain tumor. Gershwin never regained consciousness and died during surgery two days later. He was at the peak of his powers with several unrealized projects ahead of him (among them, some sketches for a new string quartet and a new symphony, a proposed ballet score, and musical comedy collaborations with George S. Kaufman and DuBose Heyward). His death stunned the nation, whose collective feelings can be summed up in a famous statement from novelist John O'Hara: "George Gershwin died on July 11, 1937, but I don't have to believe it if I don't want to."

Ira Gershwin, so devastated that he could not work for more than a year after George's death, became the keeper of his brother's legacy. In later years, he supervised the release of several unpublished Gershwin compositions, including several works for piano, the

Lullaby for string quartet, and the *Catfish Row Suite* from *Porgy and Bess* (a work cobbled together after the show had closed and now considered to be the last orchestral work to be composed and scored by Gershwin). Ira also put lyrics to tunes from George's notebooks, creating "new" Gershwin songs for the films *The Shocking Miss Pilgrim* (1947) and *Kiss Me, Stupid* (1964). He had continued success with other collaborators, including Kurt Weill, Jerome Kern, and Harold Arlen.

Gershwin's music remains a subject of debate among prominent international conductors, composers, and music scholars, some of whom find his works for orchestra to be naively structured, little more than catchy melodies strung together by the barest of musical links. In 1954, Leonard Bernstein summed up the feelings of many classical musicians, saying, "The themes are terrific—inspired, God-given. I don't think there has been such an inspired melodist on this earth since Tchaikovsky. But if you want to speak of a composer, that's another matter." Nevertheless, Gershwin's accomplishments are considerable: he ranks (along with Irving Berlin, Cole Porter, and Richard Rodgers) as one of the four greatest composers for the American musical theatre, as well as the only popular composer of the 20th century to have made a significant and lasting dent in the classical music world. He had great admirers in the classical field, including such luminaries as Arturo Toscanini, Fritz Reiner, Arnold Schoenberg, Maurice Ravel, Sergey Prokofiev, and Alban Berg, all of whom cited Gershwin's genius for melody and harmony. His orchestral works, now performed by most of the world's prestigious symphony orchestras, have attained a status for which Gershwin longed during his lifetime. Aaron Copland and Charles Ives may rival Gershwin for the title of "great American composer," but their works tend to be admired, whereas

Gershwin's are beloved. As the noted musicologist Hans Keller stated, "Gershwin is a genius, in fact, whose style hides the wealth and complexity of his invention. There are indeed weak spots, but who cares about them when there is greatness?"

FRED ASTAIRE

(b. May 10, 1899, Omaha, Neb., U.S.—d. June 22, 1987, Los Angeles, Calif., U.S.)

Fred Astaire (original name Frederick Austerlitz) was an American dancer of stage and motion pictures who is best known for a number of highly successful musical comedy films in which he starred with Ginger Rogers. He is regarded by many as the greatest popular-music dancer of all time.

Astaire was born into a wealthy family. He studied dancing from the age of four and in 1906 formed an act with his sister, Adele, that became a popular vaudeville attraction. The two appeared briefly in the Mary Pickford film *Fanchon the Cricket* (1915) and made their Broadway debut in *Over the Top* (1917). They achieved international fame with stage hits that included *For Goodness Sake* (1922), *Funny Face* (1927), and *The Band Wagon* (1931). When Adele retired after marrying Lord Charles Cavendish in 1932, Astaire made a screen test, receiving the verdict from executives: "Can't act, can't sing. Balding. Can dance a little." He was nevertheless cast as a featured dancer in the Metro-Goldwyn-Mayer production *Dancing Lady* (1933), which starred Joan Crawford, Clark Gable, and the Three Stooges.

Also in 1933 Astaire was paired with Ginger Rogers in the RKO Radio Pictures production *Flying Down to Rio*. They were a sensation, stealing the picture from stars

Delores del Rio and Gene Raymond, and public demand compelled RKO to feature the pair in a classic series of starring vehicles throughout the 1930s, with *The Gay Divorcee* (1934), *Top Hat* (1935), and *Swing Time* (1936) often cited as the best of the lot. Although Astaire worked well with several leading ladies throughout his career, his partnership with Rogers had a special chemistry. Their

Fred Astaire and Rita Hayworth in You'll Never Get Rich *(1941).*

respective elegance (Astaire) and earthiness (Rogers) rubbed off on one another, and it has often been said that he gave her class and she gave him sex appeal. Their dance routines, often in the midst of sumptuous Art Deco settings, were intricate tap or graceful ballroom numbers that served as sophisticated statements of romantic love. Only once—in *Carefree* (1938)—did Astaire and Rogers share an on-screen kiss, and then only in a dream sequence.

Astaire's immensely popular dancing style appeared relaxed, light, effortless, and largely improvised. In reality, he was a hard-working perfectionist who tirelessly rehearsed routines for hours on end. Working in collaboration with legendary choreographer Hermes Pan for his films with Rogers, Astaire eschewed the then-popular Busby Berkeley approach to filmed musicals and its emphasis on special effects, surreal settings, and chorus girls in ever-changing kaleidoscope patterns. Instead, Astaire revolutionized the movie musical by simplifying it: solo dancers or couples were shot in full-figure, and dances were filmed with a minimum of edits and camera angles. He is regarded as a pioneer in the serious presentation of dance on film.

After the last RKO Astaire-Rogers film, in 1939, Astaire appeared with various partners such as Eleanor Powell, Rita Hayworth (whom Astaire cited as his favourite on-screen partner), and Lucille Bremer. He retired temporarily in 1946 but returned to the screen in 1948 and appeared in a series of Technicolor musicals for MGM that, next to his films with Rogers, constitute his most highly regarded body of work. Several of Astaire's most-famous dance routines appear in these films, such as the slow-motion dance in *Easter Parade* (1948), the dance with empty shoes in *The Barkleys of Broadway* (1949, his only reunion with Ginger Rogers), the ceiling dance and the duet with a hat rack in *Royal Wedding* (1951), and the dance on air in *The Belle of New York* (1952). The best of Astaire's films during this period was *The Band Wagon* (1953), often cited as one of the greatest of film musicals; it featured Astaire's memorable duet with Cyd Charisse to the song "Dancing in the Dark." Astaire's run of classic MGM musicals ended with *Silk Stockings* (1957), after which his screen appearances were mostly in nondancing character roles. He continued to dance with new partner Barrie Chase for several Emmy Award-winning television specials throughout the 1950s and '60s, and he danced again on-screen in *Finian's Rainbow* (1968) and for a few steps with Gene Kelly in *That's Entertainment, Part II* (1976).

In addition to Astaire's immeasurable contributions to the art of dance, he was noted for his quintessentially American vocal style. Although possessing a rather thin-toned tenor voice, Astaire received much praise from jazz critics for his innate sense of swing and his conversational way with a song. Several compilations have been issued of Astaire songs from film sound tracks, but his best vocal recordings were those he undertook in the early 1950s with jazz combos led by pianist Oscar Peterson. They have been released under several titles on various LP and CD collections over the years.

Astaire's most notable dramatic roles were in *On the Beach* (1959); *The Pleasure of His Company* (1962); *The Towering Inferno* (1974), for which he received an Oscar nomination for best supporting actor; and *Ghost Story* (1981), his final film. He was awarded an honorary Academy Award for his contributions to film in 1950, and he received a Life Achievement Award from the American Film Institute in 1981. Despite the many accolades for his unquestionable greatness, Astaire remained as modest and elegant as the characters he portrayed. As he said in his autobiography, *Steps in Time* (1959), "I have no desire to prove anything by it. I just dance."

SIR ALFRED HITCHCOCK

(b. Aug. 13, 1899, London, Eng.–d. April 29, 1980, Bel Air, Calif., U.S.)

S ir Alfred Hitchcock was an English-born American motion-picture director whose suspenseful films and television programs won immense popularity and critical acclaim over a long and tremendously productive career. His films are marked by a macabre sense of humour and a somewhat bleak view of the human condition.

EARLY LIFE

Hitchcock grew up in London's East End in a milieu once haunted by the notorious serial killer known as Jack the Ripper, talk of whom was still current in Hitchcock's youth two decades later. Although he had two siblings, he recalled his youth as a lonely one, with a father who was a stern disciplinarian; it is said that he once ordered Alfred to appear at the local police station with a note saying that he had been misbehaving, whereupon the sergeant on duty (at the request of Hitchcock's father) locked him up for a few minutes, a sufficient length of time to give Alfred a fear of enclosed spaces and a strong concern for wrongful imprisonment, both of which would figure in his later work. When he was not being disciplined, he was cosseted by an overly watchful mother, who used food as a balm — to which he would later trace his trademark paunch.

Hitchcock went to St. Ignatius College before attending the London County Council School of Marine Engineering and Navigation in 1913–14. He worked in the sales department at W.T. Henley's Telegraph Works Company until 1918, when he moved to the advertising department. Giving in to his artistic side, Hitchcock enrolled at the University of London in 1916 to take drawing and design classes. His facility in that field in 1920 helped land him a spot designing title cards (which silent films required) for the American film company Famous Players–Lasky, which had opened a British branch in Islington. When Famous Players closed down its British branch in 1922, he stayed on at Islington. He worked on films for independent producers and came to assume more responsibility, working as an art director, production designer, editor, assistant director, and writer.

FIRST FILM

Hitchcock's first film as a director was the comedy *Mrs. Peabody* (1922; also called *Number 13*), which was not completed, for lack of funding. His first released film was *Always Tell Your Wife* (1923), which he codirected with its star Seymour Hicks, but he did not receive credit. Solo credit did not come for another two years, with the melodrama *The Pleasure Garden* (1925). That was followed by *The Mountain Eagle* (1926), a drama set in the Kentucky mountains. But it was *The Lodger: A Story of the London Fog* (1927) that both he and students of the cinema would come to regard as his first "real" work—and one that very much drew on his youthful surroundings. Adapted from a popular novel by Marie Belloc Lowndes, the suspenseful story introduces the structure of many Hitchcock films to come: a London man (Ivor Novello) is accused of being a Jack the Ripper–like killer and finds it nearly impossible to prove his innocence. The film became his first hit and also was the first film in which he made his trademark cameo appearance.

In 1926 Hitchcock married his film editor and script supervisor, Alma Reville. The following year he made the melodrama *Downhill, Easy Virtue* (from a Noel Coward play), and the boxing drama *The Ring*, which was a critical success. The comedies *The Farmer's Wife* and *Champagne* (both 1928) were followed by the tragic romance (and box-office hit) *The Manxman* (1929).

Hitchcock's first talking picture was the thriller *Blackmail* (1929). One of the year's biggest hits in England, it became the first British film to make use of synchronized sound only after the completed silent version was postdubbed and partly reshot. Polish actress Anny Ondra (who had starred in *The Manxman*) played a would-be model who stabs an artist when he tries to assault her. The murder investigation is headed by the model's fiancé, but she is being blackmailed for the killing and is afraid to confide in him. The film's most memorable sequence is a chase through the British Museum and across its roof, but Hitchcock builds the mood of encroaching menace throughout. *Juno and the Paycock* (1929) was adapted from Sean O'Casey's popular play, while *Elstree Calling* (1930) was a collection of musical and comedy sketches that Hitchcock codirected with three others.

Murder! (1930) provided Hitchcock with another opportunity to explore cinematic suspense. Shot simultaneously in a German-language version (*Mary*, 1931), it stars Herbert Marshall as Sir John Menier, a gentleman knight and famed actor who turns amateur sleuth in order to save from the gallows an actress who has been convicted of murder. Though light in tone, the film is distinguished by its dramatic camera work, colourful theatrical setting, and groundbreaking use of voice-over narration. Neither *The Skin Game* (1931) nor *Rich and Strange* (1931; also called *East of Shanghai*), an odd comedy, made much of an impact at the time of release, but *Number Seventeen* (1932) offered a thrilling chase finale. The musical *Waltzes from Vienna* (1934; also called *Strauss's Great Waltz*) was Hitchcock's last foray into that genre.

FIRST INTERNATIONAL RELEASES: *THE MAN WHO KNEW TOO MUCH* TO *JAMAICA INN*

Hitchcock signed with Gaumont-British in 1934, and his first film for that company, *The Man Who Knew Too Much* (1934), was also his first international success. Leslie Banks and Edna Best star as the Lawrences, a married couple on vacation in Switzerland with their daughter Betty (Nova Pilbeam). They inadvertently become enmeshed in a plot to assassinate a diplomat when the conspirators kidnap Betty to ensure the Lawrences' silence until the deed is accomplished by the lethal Abbott (German actor Peter Lorre in his first English-speaking role). In just 75 minutes, culminating with the classic Royal Albert Hall finale, Hitchcock established himself as the new master of the sinister.

Hitchcock built on that foundation with *The 39 Steps* (1935), an adaptation of John Buchan's thriller. Robert Donat played the archetypal Hitchcock protagonist: an innocent vacationer unwillingly drawn into an elaborate scheme hatched by a nest of spies. On the run, handcuffed to a young woman (Madeleine Carroll) whom he has just met, they are hunted while they try to decipher the meaning of the film's mysterious title. This was a premier example of a genre Hitchcock virtually invented—the romantic thriller. *Secret Agent* (1936) offers Carroll, John Gielgud, and Lorre as undercover agents for British intelligence, traipsing through the Swiss Alps on the trail of hostile spies. Based on W. Somerset Maugham's *Ashenden*, the film subsumes romantic byplay in favour of plentiful mordant humour.

Sabotage (1936) was far less playful, as might be expected of an adaptation of Joseph Conrad's novel about terrorism, *The Secret Agent*. Sylvia Sidney played Winnie Verloc, who is married to a terrorist (Oscar Homolka) who gives her young brother (Desmond Tester) a bomb-laden suitcase to deliver without telling him of its contents; the lad dallies while delivering it, and the suitcase explodes in an intensely suspenseful sequence.

Young and Innocent (1937) was considerably more charming and still offered much in the way of suspense. Derrick de Marney starred as a young man who (once again) has been unjustly accused of murder; Pilbeam played the local constable's teenage daughter who decides to help the accused, and they quickly fall in love.

The Lady Vanishes (1938) is a deft thriller that finds a traveller (Margaret Lockwood) riding a train across Europe; she wonders at the sudden—and apparently unnoticed—disappearance of another fellow traveller (Dame May Whitty), but no one else on the train seems to remember her. This was Hitchcock's biggest hit—in both England and the United States—since *The 39 Steps*, and its masterful synthesis of comedy and suspense inspired American producer David O. Selznick to sign Hitchcock to a long-term contract. Before moving to Hollywood, however, Hitchcock made one last picture in England, the Gothic costumer *Jamaica Inn* (1939), from a popular novel by Daphne du Maurier; Charles Laughton played a country squire who secretly heads a band of pirates.

THE HOLLYWOOD YEARS: *REBECCA* TO *DIAL M FOR MURDER*

The British film industry's loss was Hollywood's gain, as *Rebecca* (1940) made abundantly clear. Du Maurier's novel *Rebecca* was a property Selznick had acquired at great cost to follow his production of *Gone with the Wind* (1939), and the potentate bequeathed Hitchcock a star-filled cast: Laurence Olivier as the brooding Maxim de Winter, Joan

Fontaine as his trembling bride, and Judith Anderson as the threatening Mrs. Danvers. The film was an enormous success both commercially and critically. It won the Academy Award for best picture, and Hitchcock earned his first Oscar nomination for best director.

Foreign Correspondent (1940) starred Joel McCrea as a newspaper reporter who becomes involved with assassinations, Nazis, and a kidnapped Dutch diplomat. The film is filled with stunning set pieces — such as an assassination in a crowd of umbrellas and a climactic plane crash.

The screwball comedy *Mr. and Mrs. Smith* (1941) was Hitchcock's first change of pace since coming to Hollywood. The film starred Carole Lombard and Robert Montgomery as the eponymous bickerers who discover that their marriage is legally invalid. It was a box-office success but was Hitchcock's last comedy without any suspense elements.

Suspicion (1941) seemed to promise a return to form. Fontaine played Lina, the timid wife of Johnnie (Cary Grant), a cad who may be trying to kill her. Hitchcock originally intended for the film to end with Lina's suicide. However, suicide was discouraged under the strictures of Hollywood's Production Code, which governed what could be depicted in movies, and the film ended with Lina's suspicions about Johnnie's character proving utterly groundless. The film made little sense without a legitimate payoff, and Hitchcock later admitted that he had not played fair with his audience.

In *Saboteur* (1942) Robert Cummings played a patriotic factory worker framed for murder and sabotage, and Priscilla Lane played the trusting woman who aids and abets his crosscountry flight. The film has its share of exciting moments, including a charity ball where the couple are trapped in a crowd and the climax on top of the Statue of Liberty.

The chilling *Shadow of a Doubt* (1943) was a darker and more psychologically complex work. Hitchcock worked out the script with Thornton Wilder. Joseph Cotten gave one of his most-noted performances as the charming, utterly psychopathic Uncle Charlie, who drops in to visit his relatives in quiet Santa Rosa after murdering a woman; Teresa Wright played his devoted niece (also named Charlie), who fights against her growing realization that her beloved uncle is a misogynistic serial killer of whom the entire country is terrified.

The claustrophobic *Lifeboat* (1944) was a heavily allegorical tale about eight survivors of a ship torpedoed by a German U-boat. The challenge of a film set entirely in a lifeboat attracted Hitchcock. The film alternates between suspense and philosophical debate; the story was written for the screen by John Steinbeck. Hitchcock received his second Academy Award nomination for best director.

Hitchcock went to England in 1944 to make two patriotic short films for the British Ministry of Information lauding the French Resistance, *Bon voyage* and *Aventure malgache*. They were intended for distribution in liberated France and its colonies but were little seen prior to their 1994 release on video. He then returned to Hollywood to make *Spellbound* (1945). A psychological (and psychiatric) mystery adapted by Ben Hecht from a Francis Beeding novel, it starred Ingrid Bergman as an analyst who finds herself falling in love with the new director of the asylum (Gregory Peck), whom she begins treating after realizing that he is suffering from amnesia apparently brought on by feelings of guilt over committing murder. The film also contains what was a highly publicized two-minute Salvador Dalí dream sequence, but it was actually filmed by William Cameron Menzies after the sequence Hitchcock and Dalí had planned proved too complex. Hitchcock was dissatisfied with the film, which he summarized as "just another manhunt story wrapped in pseudo-psychoanalysis." He earned his third Oscar nomination for best director.

Notorious (1946) was much more polished. Written for the screen by Hecht, the espionage plot of Nazis in Rio de Janeiro and a hidden cache of uranium was secondary to the romance story. Alicia Huberman (Bergman), the dissolute daughter of a convicted Nazi spy, is recruited by American spy Devlin (Grant) to infiltrate a Nazi stronghold in Rio by seducing and marrying Nazi operative Sebastian (Claude Rains). Devlin loves Huberman passionately but does not interfere when she is asked to sacrifice herself on the altar of patriotism; she loves him passionately and despairs at his callousness.

The Paradine Case (1947) was Hitchcock's last film for Selznick. A courtroom drama set in England, it starred Peck as a married barrister whose ethics are compromised when he falls in love with a defendant (Alida Valli).

Hitchcock formed his own production company, Transatlantic Pictures, which would make films in America and England. Its first film was also his first colour film, *Rope* (1948), which was based on the sensational 1924 Leopold-Loeb murder case. Jimmy Stewart starred as the vainglorious protagonist, a former professor whose dangerously amoral philosophizing has inspired two students (John Dall and Farley Granger) to strangle a friend just to experience the thrill of the kill; they then throw a cocktail party to gloat over his corpse, which has been stuffed into a trunk standing in plain view of the guests. *Rope* is best known for Hitchcock's audacious attempt to make the picture look as if it had been shot in one continuous take. (A movie camera could only hold 10 minutes of film, so *Rope*'s 80 minutes is actually eight 10-minute takes, with the breaks cleverly disguised.)

Under Capricorn (1949) was one of Hitchcock's least typical and least popular films at the box office. A melodrama set in 1830s Australia (though shot in England), it starred Bergman as an upper-crust Englishwoman who violates society's taboos by eloping with her groom (Cotten) and following him to Australia after he is sentenced for the murder of her brother. The box-office failure of *Under Capricorn* ended Transatlantic Pictures.

Hitchcock signed a contract with Warner Brothers, and his first film there, the comic thriller *Stage Fright* (1950), was one of his lighter works. Marlene Dietrich played Charlotte Inwood, an actress who may have murdered her husband. Her young lover Jonathan Cooper (Richard Todd) is accused of the crime, and drama student Eve Gill (Jane Wyman) takes a job with Inwood in the hopes of clearing Cooper, her former boyfriend. The theatrical setting and Dietrich's performance are regarded as highlights of this film.

Strangers on a Train (1951) was an engrossing thriller based on a Patricia Highsmith novel. Unhappily married tennis pro Guy Haines (Granger) has the bad fortune one day to be riding a train with charming psychopath Bruno Antony (Robert Walker). Bruno suggests that he and Guy "exchange" murders, so that neither can be traced to the crime. Guy humours Bruno and laughs off the proposal, little dreaming that Bruno will demonstrate his good faith by strangling Guy's wife and then demanding that Guy complete the bargain by killing Bruno's father. The homoerotic underpinnings and Walker's performance contribute to the film's great appeal.

Stranger's mordant humour does not appear in *I Confess* (1953), in which Montgomery Clift played a priest in Quebec (where the picture was largely filmed) who is being blackmailed by a murderer whose confession, which the priest cannot reveal, shields him from exposure. *Dial M for Murder* (1954) was much more commercial. Originally shot in 3D toward the end of that short-lived craze, the film is an adaptation of a Frederick Knott play that maintained the boundaries of the London flat presented onstage. Grace Kelly starred as a straying rich wife whose jealous husband (Ray Milland) first tries to have her killed and then attempts to frame her for stabbing her would-be assassin in self-defense.

THE PARAMOUNT YEARS: *REAR WINDOW* TO *NORTH BY NORTHWEST*

Moving to Paramount, Hitchcock entered his third phase of sustained brilliance—one with a maturity of theme and a mastery of technique that make even the great periods of 1934–38 and 1940–46 almost pale in comparison. In *Rear Window* (1954) Jeff, a wheelchair-bound press photographer (Stewart), spends his invalid days peering into the windows of the many apartments across the courtyard from him. He and his girlfriend Lisa (Kelly) suspect that in one of those apartments a man has murdered his wife. *Rear Window*, like *Rope* and *Lifeboat*, was another technical challenge for Hitchcock. Although Jeff and the camera never leave his apartment, the story required the construction of a gigantic courtyard set. The subtext about invading the privacy of others implicates moviegoers as a band of easily seduced voyeurs. Hitchcock was again Oscar-nominated for best director.

Kelly also appeared in *To Catch a Thief* (1955), a romantic thriller shot on the French Riviera, in which she was paired with the debonair Cary Grant, who played a former jewel thief who may have returned to his old ways. Hitchcock came to regret this production, since it was on location that Kelly met Monaco's Prince Rainier, who would take her away from the movies, and him, forever.

If *Thief* was lightweight, *The Trouble with Harry* (1955) was downright irreverent. A black comedy about a

Vermont town's problems with a corpse that just will not stay buried, it had the virtues of amusing performances by Edmund Gwenn and (in her screen debut) Shirley MacLaine, but the film attracted little box-office business.

Hitchcock was lured into television with the promise of a much wider audience. His droll introductions for *Alfred Hitchcock Presents* (1955–62; later *The Alfred Hitchcock Hour*, 1962–65) gradually but inevitably converted him into America's—perhaps even the world's—best-known director. He still concentrated on motion pictures but approved which scripts and directors would be used; he also directed 20 episodes.

Hitchcock returned to serious work with *The Man Who Knew Too Much* (1956), a big-budget remake of his humble 1934 thriller. It starred Stewart and Doris Day as the parents whose son is kidnapped when the father accidentally acquires information about an assassination. The film advanced Day's career as a singer, incidentally, with the song "Que Sera, Sera," which climbed high on the pop charts.

The bleak *The Wrong Man* (1956) was based on the Kafkaesque but true (and nationally publicized) story of Queens musician Manny Balestrero (Henry Fonda), who was wrongfully arrested in 1953 for robbing an insurance company and had great difficulty proving his innocence. Shot in many of the New York City locales where the case unfolded, the film has verisimilitude to spare with its respectful, quasidocumentary approach.

Considered by many to be his masterpiece and by some to be the greatest of all films, *Vertigo* (1958) was a challenging, sometimes obscure, and painful exploration of identity, fantasy, and compulsion. Stewart starred as Scottie, a former San Francisco policeman who has taken early retirement because of his fear of heights. A rich friend asks him to shadow his wife Madeleine (Kim Novak), who has been prone to taking mysterious leaves of absence. But Scottie's detecting soon metamorphoses into a kind of voyeurism, as his observation of Madeleine turns into love, then obsession, and finally agony. *Vertigo* is a brave dramatization of the themes closest to Hitchcock. It failed to attract contemporary audiences and was almost entirely overlooked in the Academy Award nominations; even Bernard Herrmann's chilling score was passed by.

Hitchcock retreated from the naked trauma of *Vertigo* to make the entertaining *North by Northwest* (1959), a romantic thriller reminiscent of *The 39 Steps* and *Saboteur*. Grant is the consummate Hitchcock protagonist, New York ad man Roger Thornhill, who is mistaken for George Kaplan, a government agent who has become the target of a very persistent group of international spies. But Thornhill/Kaplan proves to be quite resourceful himself, even with the serious disadvantage of never remotely knowing what is going on.

PSYCHO AND THE 1960S

After the commercial success of *North by Northwest*, Hitchcock made his most shocking movie, *Psycho* (1960). Critics were uncertain what to make of it; moviegoers, on the other hand, were immediately avid for it. In the beginning it seems that the beautiful Marion Crane (Janet Leigh) is the protagonist, but Hitchcock resolves her peril halfway through the picture by killing her off in the famous shower scene, leaving the audience alone with the lunacy of Norman Bates (Anthony Perkins). The long-term effects of *Psycho* on both the grammar of the cinema and the implicit trust between an audience and a director— which Hitchcock had now forevermore compromised with this shocking plotline—were enormous. So were the picture's box-office receipts: the controversy helped it become the year's second highest grosser. Hitchcock received his final Academy Award nomination for best director for *Psycho*.

By the time Hitchcock made *The Birds* (1963) for Universal (which would release his last six films), the media had been trained to respond to his every signal. There were cover stories in national magazines and countless features extolling Hitchcock's latest blond discovery, model Tippi Hedren. The story itself—millions of birds settle in and finally attack the residents of a small town in coastal California—was based on a novelette by Daphne du Maurier; screenwriter Evan Hunter expanded it considerably to incorporate all sorts of Freudian byplay among

Scene from the film The Birds *(1963)*.

social butterfly Melanie Daniels (Hedren); lawyer Mitch Brenner (Rod Taylor), her romantic interest; school-teacher Annie Hayworth (Suzanne Pleshette), his former romantic interest; and icy Lydia Brenner (Jessica Tandy), Taylor's possessive mother. *The Birds* unfolds with a dream logic in which the birds are a punishment for Daniels.

When Grace Kelly refused to come out of retirement to take the part, Hedren starred in *Marnie* (1964) as a compulsive liar suffering from kleptomania. Her handsome employer (Sean Connery) is attracted to her and wants to help her discover the roots of her emotional difficulties — including fear of sex, thunderstorms, and the colour red—and so marries her, little realizing just how severely she has been traumatized. *Marnie* proved to be a divisive film, with some seeing it as an refined embodiment of Hitchcock's obsessions but others regarding it as a mere indulgent catalogue of those obsessions that is unsupported by an interesting story.

Hitchcock's next two films, the Cold War thrillers *Torn Curtain* (1966) and *Topaz* (1969), were neither commercially nor critically successful.

Final Productions

It appeared that Hitchcock's powers had waned, but they returned in *Frenzy* (1972), the first movie he made in England since *Stage Fright.* Jon Finch played the hallowed role of the man wrongly accused of murder, and Barry Foster played the sadistic "sex killer" who revels in his freedom while the wrong man is being hunted by Scotland Yard. *Frenzy* was Hitchcock shorn of the big budgets, stars, and media attention that had combined, in the opinion of some, to make him lazy and smug.

Hitchcock made *Family Plot* (1976) as his swan song. Scripted by Ernest Lehman in the comic vein of *The*

Trouble with Harry, Family Plot followed a colourful, rather endearing collection of psychic frauds, scalawags, and jewel thieves.

REPUTATION AND GENERAL THEMES

Hitchcock has been called by some the greatest of all directors, the most adroit, and the most admired, and the case has been made that he was all of these. His many classics are widely acknowledged—including *The 39 Steps, The Lady Vanishes, Rebecca, Shadow of a Doubt, Notorious, Strangers on a Train, Rear Window, Vertigo, North by Northwest, Psycho,* and *The Birds*—and in these films Hitchcock's genius as both filmmaker and storyteller is abundantly evident.

Hitchcock's films usually centre on either murder or espionage, with deception, mistaken identities, and chase sequences complicating and enlivening the plots. Wry touches of humour and occasional intrusions of the macabre complete this mixture of cinematic elements. Three main themes predominate in Hitchcock's films. The most common is that of the innocent man who is mistakenly suspected or accused of a crime and who must then track down the real perpetrator in order to clear himself (e.g., *The Lodger* and *North by Northwest*). The second theme is that of the guilty woman who enmeshes a male protagonist and ends up either destroying him or being saved by him (e.g., *Vertigo* and *Marnie*). The third theme is that of the (frequently psychopathic) murderer whose identity is established during the working out of the plot (e.g., *Shadow of a Doubt* and *Psycho*).

Hitchcock's greatest gift was his mastery of the technical means to build and maintain suspense. To this end he used innovative camera viewpoints and movements, elaborate editing techniques, and effective soundtrack music, often supplied in his best films by Bernard Herrmann. He had a sound grasp of human psychology, as manifested both in his credible treatment of everyday life and in the tense and nightmarish situations encountered in his more-chilling films. His ability to convincingly evoke human menace, subterfuge, and fear gave his psychological thrillers great impact while maintaining their subtlety and believability. He was also a master of something he called the "MacGuffin"—that is, the use of an object or person who, for storytelling purposes, keeps the plot moving along even though that thing or person is not really central to the story. (Examples include the titular steps in Hitchcock's *The 39 Steps* and the microfilm in *North by Northwest*.)

Among the honours Hitchcock received are the Irving G. Thalberg Award from the Academy of Motion Picture Arts and Sciences (1968) and the Life Achievement Award from the American Film Institute (1979). Hitchcock was knighted in 1980.

HUMPHREY BOGART

(b. Dec. 25, 1899, New York, N.Y., U.S.—d. Jan. 14, 1957, Hollywood, Calif., U.S.)

Humphrey Bogart (full name Humphrey DeForest Bogart) was an American actor who became a preeminent motion picture "tough guy" and was a top box office attraction during the 1940s and '50s. In his performances he projected the image of a worldly wise, individualistic adventurer with a touch of idealism hidden beneath a hardened exterior. Offscreen he gave the carefully crafted appearance of being a cynical loner, granting only minimal concessions to Hollywood conventions. He became a cult hero of the American cinema.

Bogart was the son of a prominent surgeon and a commercial artist. He served in the United States Navy at the end of World War I, and after the war he began a stage career in New York City playing juvenile roles in drawing-room and country-house comedies. By the mid-1920s he had won a leading role in the comedy *Cradle Snatchers* (1925) and other plays, and the young actor with the distinctive lisp began receiving good notices from critics. He often played the ascot-wearing playboy or country-club fixture who seemingly frolicked through life in dinner jacket and tails, which is the ultimate irony in light of his later screen persona as the hard-bitten, world-weary man of few words. He is reported to have originated the classic line of the mindless society fellow: "Tennis, anyone?"

Bogart's Broadway success led to roles in two film shorts — *The Dancing Town* (1928) and *Broadway's Like That* (1930) — and a contract with the Fox Film Corporation. His supporting roles in some 10 films made between 1930 and 1934 failed to make an impact, and the disillusioned Bogart returned to the Broadway stage. He scored his biggest triumph to date as the ruthless killer Duke Mantee in Robert Sherwood's *The Petrified Forest* (1936). He finally garnered some serious attention in Hollywood when Warner Bros. adapted the play for the screen the following year. Bogart spent the next five years playing numerous supporting roles — mostly gangster types — and occasional leading roles in B-films. His best pictures of this period are such films as *Black Legion* (1936), *Marked Woman* (1937), *Dead End* (1937), *The Roaring Twenties* (1939), and *They Drive by Night* (1940).

Two films in 1941 marked the turning point of Bogart's career. In *High Sierra* he played a killer with a tortured soul and a sense of morality—a departure from the one-dimensional thugs he had portrayed earlier. His performance as detective Sam Spade in *The Maltese Falcon*

(1941), John Huston's adaptation of the Dashiell Hammett detective thriller, helped make the film a classic. He followed this with leading roles in such well-regarded films as *All Through the Night* and *Across the Pacific* (both 1942) before he was cast in what is perhaps his quintessential screen characterization, that of cabaret owner Rick Blaine in *Casablanca* (1942). Despite its hurried, chaotic production, begun when the script was only half-finished, *Casablanca* is one of the best in moviemaking history; it ranked third—following *Citizen Kane* (1941) and *The Godfather* (1972)—on the American Film Institute's 2007 list of the top 100 American films. Released just after America's entrance into World War II, *Casablanca*'s topicality and sentimental cynicism helped to make it an enormous success. The film won the Oscar for best picture, and Bogart's Oscar-nominated performance secured his newfound status as Warners' top male star.

From this success Bogart went on to compile an impressive list of screen credits. Few actors can match his track record for quality films: *To Have and Have Not* (1944), *The Big Sleep* (1946), *The Treasure of the Sierra Madre* (1948), *Key Largo* (1948), *In a Lonely Place* (1950), *The African Queen* (1951; Academy Award for best actor), *Sabrina* (1954), and *The Caine Mutiny* (1954) are all regarded as screen classics. He seldom appeared in a truly bad picture, and his legend helped such minor films as *Sahara* (1943), *Passage to Marseilles* (1944), *Dark Passage* (1947), *Beat the Devil* (1953), and *The Barefoot Contessa* (1954) to achieve cult status.

Bogart's screen persona was that of laconic reserve with the suggestion of complex underlying emotions. It was this duality that distinguished Bogart from other "tough guy" actors, who relied on swagger and bravado to convey their anger with the world; Bogart, conversely, employed cool detachment to suggest world-weariness. He often gave his most ruthless characters a slight hint of decency, whereas the heroes he portrayed often had a dark or vulnerable side. He succeeded in making cynicism an endearing quality.

After three troubled marriages, Bogart found lasting happiness when he wed actress Lauren Bacall in 1945. Their rapport was evident in their memorable onscreen pairings in *To Have and Have Not*, *The Big Sleep*, *Dark Passage*, and *Key Largo*. They teamed again for a well-received television adaptation of *The Petrified Forest* (1955) that also starred Henry Fonda and were planning another screen collaboration when Bogart died in 1957.

Although he was a popular actor during the 1940s and '50s, Bogart achieved the status of a legend after his death. In 1999 he was named the top male film star of the 20th century by the American Film Institute.

CLARK GABLE

(b. Feb. 1, 1901, Cadiz, Ohio, U.S.–d. Nov. 16, 1960, Hollywood, Calif., U.S.)

William Clark Gable, better known as simply Clark Gable, was an American film actor who epitomized the American ideal of masculinity and virility for three decades. An enormously popular star during his lifetime, Gable was dubbed the "King of Hollywood."

The only son of an itinerant oil-field worker, Gable embarked on an acting career while in his early 20s and soon found himself the protégé of veteran actress Josephine Dillon, who coached Gable in poise and elocution and paid for his orthodontic work. Although several years her junior, Gable married Dillon in 1924, about the same time he began to land small roles in silent films. His first big break came when he was cast in the lead of the Broadway play *Machinal* (1928).

In 1930 Gable's performance in a Los Angeles stage production of *The Last Mile* brought him to the attention of Hollywood producers. Although he failed his first screen test at Metro-Goldwyn-Mayer—in part because producers thought Gable's ears too big for a leading man—his supporting performance in the low-budget western *The Painted Desert* (1931) convinced MGM executives of Gable's talent and screen presence. The actor garnered public attention with his aggressive, masculine performances in such films as *A Free Soul* (1931) and *Night Nurse* (1931); this forceful persona—equal parts "man's man" and "ladies' man"—helped make him one of Hollywood's top stars within a year.

Among Gable's most successful films for MGM during this period were *Red Dust* (1932), *Strange Interlude* (1932), *Dancing Lady* (1933), *Hold Your Man* (1933), *Manhattan Melodrama* (1934), and *Men in White* (1934). Despite his macho persona in such films, Gable's screen presence was largely nonthreatening: his magnetic smile and playful winks rendered him a charming rogue who did not take himself too seriously. Although Gable himself maintained a self-deprecating attitude toward his own talent throughout the years, he often proved himself most competent in demanding roles and was equally deft at romantic comedy and epic drama.

As punishment for refusing a role, MGM lent Gable to Columbia Pictures—a studio then known derisively as "poverty row"—for the Frank Capra comedy *It Happened One Night* (1934). The punishment turned out to be a coup for Gable, as the film—the story of a spoiled, runaway heiress (portrayed by Claudette Colbert) and the newspaper reporter (Gable) who tries to exploit her story—swept the Academy Awards in all five major categories: best picture, actress, director, screenplay, and best actor for Gable. Many of Gable's best films of the period were either those he resisted doing or those that were made on loan-out to other studios. He did not feel himself right for the role of mutineer Fletcher Christian in *Mutiny on the Bounty* (1935), yet the film proved hugely popular and earned Gable another Academy Award nomination. He played Jack London's hero in *The Call of the Wild* (1935) for Twentieth Century Fox, before reluctantly accepting the role of rakish political boss Blackie Norton in *San Francisco* (1936), one of the most praised and popular films of Gable's career. It was also the first movie in which he costarred with Spencer Tracy; they would also team in the hit films *Test Pilot* (1938) and *Boom Town* (1940).

Wary of period films after flopping in the costume drama *Parnell* (1937), Gable at first declined the role of Rhett Butler in David O. Selznick's production of the Margaret Mitchell best-seller, *Gone with the Wind* (1939). As the book had been the best-selling novel of all time, Gable also felt that no screen adaptation could live up to the expectations of the general public. Studio coercion and widespread public demand compelled Gable to reconsider, and the resulting film was, and remains to this day, one of the most popular movies ever made. The grand, epic-scale, four-hour Civil War melodrama won the Oscar for best picture (during what many historians consider to be the benchmark year for Hollywood filmmaking), and Gable garnered his third Oscar nomination for the role with which he is most associated.

After two failed marriages, Gable found his perfect mate in actress Carole Lombard. The two were married in 1939, but Gable's happiness was short-lived when in 1942 the gifted comedienne was killed in a plane crash while returning home from a war-bond rally. The business of making movies suddenly seemed frivolous to the devastated Gable, who walked away from his Hollywood commitments to join the Army Air Corps, even though he was well past draft age. He served as a tail gunner during the war, making him a greater hero than ever in the eyes of his fans, and attained the rank of major. Gable returned to films upon his discharge, but the joyous insouciance of his earlier performances was largely absent in the films he made after Lombard's death.

Gable made several good films during the 1940s and '50s, but none rank as classics. With the possible exceptions of *The Hucksters* (1947) and *Mogambo* (1953), the best of Gable's later films were those he made near the end of his career, including *Band of Angels* (1957), a Civil War potboiler in which he played a plantation owner; *Run Silent, Run Deep* (1958), a tense submarine adventure in which Gable costarred with Burt Lancaster; and the romantic farces *Teacher's Pet* (1958) with Doris Day and *It Started in Naples* (1960) with Sophia Loren. His final film, *The Misfits* (1961), was his best in many years and features one of Gable's finest performances, but it is a film clouded by tragedy. It was the final film for both Gable and Marilyn Monroe, two of Hollywood's most enduring icons, and it was one of the last films for the gifted Montgomery Clift. Gable, who insisted on doing his own stunt work for grueling scenes involving the roping of wild horses, died of a heart attack within days of the film's completion. *The Misfits*, in which Gable portrays a cowboy out of place in the modern world, was a fitting final movie for an actor who epitomized Hollywood's Golden Age and who himself was something of a misfit in the era of television and method actors. Upon his death, several newspapers throughout the country displayed the same banner headline: "The King is Dead."

BING CROSBY

(b. May 3, 1903, Tacoma, Wash., U.S.–d. Oct. 14, 1977, near Madrid, Spain)

Harry Lillis Crosby, better known as Bing Crosby, was an American singer, actor, and songwriter who achieved great popularity in radio, recordings, and motion pictures. He became the archetypal crooner of a period when the advent of radio broadcasting and talking pictures and the refinement of sound-recording techniques made the climate ideal for the rise of such a figure. His casual stage manner and mellow, relaxed singing style influenced two generations of pop singers and made him the most successful entertainer of his day.

Crosby began to sing and to play the drums while studying law at Spokane, Wash. After a period spent singing with the Paul Whiteman orchestra in 1927, he appeared in the early sound film *King of Jazz* (1931). Crosby became a star after getting his own program on the CBS radio station in New York City in 1932. He began appearing in more films, and by the late 1930s his records were selling millions of copies. His songwriting activities included part-authorship of "A Ghost of a Chance" and "Where the Blue of the Night" (his radio theme song). His recording of "White Christmas" became one of the most popular songs of the century, exceeded in record sales only by his "Silent Night." In the 1940s he was the star of a popular radio variety show. Crosby won an Academy Award for best actor for his portrayal of Father O'Malley in the film *Going My Way* (1944).

Crosby's career took a new turn to comedy in the series of seven "Road" films in which he appeared with Bob Hope and Dorothy Lamour, beginning with *Road to Singapore* (1940). His other films include *The Bells of St.*

Mary's (1945), *White Christmas* (1954), and *The Country Girl* (1954). His autobiography, *Call Me Lucky*, appeared in 1953. Crosby ran a successful television production company in the 1960s. An astute businessman, he amassed one of the largest fortunes in Hollywood from his earnings as an entertainer and from shrewd investments. By the mid-1970s, 400 million copies of his records had been sold. He was a notable sportsman and died of a heart attack while on a golf course.

CARY GRANT

(b. Jan. 18, 1904, Bristol, Gloucestershire, Eng.–d. Nov. 29, 1986, Davenport, Iowa, U.S.)

Cary Grant (original name, Archibald Alexander Leach) was a British-born American film actor whose good looks, debonair style, and flair for romantic comedy made him one of Hollywood's most popular and enduring stars.

To escape poverty and a fractious family, Archie Leach ran away from home at age 13 to perform as a juggler with the Bob Pender Troupe of comedians and acrobats. He frequently worked in music halls in London, where he acquired a Cockney accent. Leach made the United States his home during the company's American tour of 1920, and for the next several years he honed his performing skills in such disparate pursuits as a barker at Coney Island, a stilt walker at Steeplechase Park, and a straight man in vaudeville shows. His performances throughout the country in numerous stage musicals and comedies during the late 1920s and early '30s led to a contract with Paramount Pictures in 1932. Studio executives thought "Archie Leach" was an unsuitable name for a leading man and rechristened the actor "Cary Grant," a name he would legally adopt in

1941. Grant first appeared in several short films and low-budget features for Paramount, and he attracted some attention with his role as a wealthy playboy in the Marlene Dietrich vehicle *Blonde Venus* (1932). The next year Grant became a star, when Mae West chose him for her leading man in two of her most successful films, *She Done Him Wrong* and *I'm No Angel* (both 1933).

Although he appears a bit reserved in these early films, Grant established a screen persona of debonair charm and an air of humorous intelligence. Widely regarded as one of the handsomest men in film history, Grant was an ingratiating and nonthreatening sex symbol. Adding to his appeal was his unique speaking voice: his not wholly successful efforts to rid himself of his natural Cockney accent resulted in a clipped, much-imitated speaking pattern. His screen success was helped in no small measure by the great number of classic films in which he appeared. Upon the expiration of his Paramount contract in 1935, Grant became one of the few top stars to freelance his services, allowing him control over his career and the freedom to choose his scripts carefully.

During the late 1930s and early '40s, Grant established himself in the genres of screwball comedy and action-adventure. Katharine Hepburn and Irene Dunne were his frequent and highly effective costars. With Hepburn he appeared in the drag comedy *Sylvia Scarlett* (1935), the classic screwball comedies *Holiday* (1938) and *Bringing Up Baby* (1938), and the upper-class satire *The Philadelphia Story* (1940), and with Dunne he made the madcap farces *The Awful Truth* (1937) and *My Favorite Wife* (1940) as well as the comic tearjerker *Penny Serenade* (1941). Grant also proved himself capable of rugged action roles, with well-regarded performances in the popular *Only Angels Have Wings* and *Gunga Din* (both 1939). Other Grant classics from this period include his turns as a whimsical poltergeist in *Topper* (1937) and as the charmingly conniving newspaper editor Walter Burns in *His Girl Friday* (1940), which is regarded as one of the greatest comedies in movie history. Howard Hawks, George Cukor, Leo McCarey, George Stevens, Garson Kanin, and Frank Capra were some of the renowned directors for whom Grant worked during this time.

Grant's association with Alfred Hitchcock resulted in some of the best work from both men. The director elicited some of the actor's best performances by casting him somewhat against type: the characters Grant portrays in the Hitchcock films have an underlying dark side that was compellingly juxtaposed with his characteristic suave demeanour. In their first collaboration, *Suspicion* (1941), Grant played an unsympathetic character who may or may not be a murderer. He gave a fascinating and appropriately disturbing performance as a callous American agent who uses the woman he loves (Ingrid Bergman) to his own advantage in *Notorious* (1946), one of Hitchcock's most-renowned films. In the next decade, Grant appeared in Hitchcock's lighthearted and stylish caper *To Catch a Thief* (1955), a film noted for its ad-libbed scenes, rife with double-entendres, between Grant and costar Grace Kelly. *North by Northwest* (1959) was a career milestone for both Grant and Hitchcock and is regarded as a masterful blend of suspense and humour.

Grant received Academy Award nominations twice — for *Penny Serenade* and *None but the Lonely Heart* (1944) — and received an honorary Oscar in 1970, but he and Edward G. Robinson share the dubious distinction of being Hollywood's most highly regarded actors never to have won Oscars for acting. His performances in such memorable films as *Mr. Lucky* (1943), *The Bishop's Wife* (1947), *Mr. Blandings Builds His Dream House* (1948), *I Was a Male War Bride* (1949), *Monkey Business* (1952), and *An Affair to*

Remember (1957) have nonetheless stood the test of time far better than the work of many of his award-winning contemporaries.

Grant's screen career extended into the 1960s, when he appeared in such films as the romantic farce *That Touch of Mink* (1962) with Doris Day and the stylish caper *Charade* (1963) with Audrey Hepburn. *Walk Don't Run* (1966) inadvertently became his final film, as he was enmeshed in divorce (from fourth wife Dyan Cannon) and child-custody proceedings that dragged on until 1969 and consumed his attention; it is said that he lost much of his interest in filmmaking during that period. One of the few stars for whom the term "screen icon" is not mere hyperbole, Grant in 1999 ranked second (next to Humphrey Bogart) on the American Film Institute's list of the 100 greatest film stars of all time.

KATHARINE HEPBURN

(b. May 12, 1907, Hartford, Conn., U.S.—d. June 29, 2003, Old Saybrook, Conn., U.S.)

Katharine Hepburn (full name Katharine Houghton Hepburn) was an indomitable American stage and film actress, known as a spirited performer with a touch of eccentricity. She introduced into her roles a strength of character previously considered to be undesirable in Hollywood leading ladies. As an actress she was noted for her brisk upper-class New England accent and tomboyish beauty.

Hepburn's father was a wealthy and prominent Connecticut surgeon, and her mother was a leader in the woman suffrage movement. From early childhood, Hepburn was continually encouraged to expand her intellectual horizons, speak nothing but the truth, and keep herself in top physical condition at all times. She would apply all of these ingrained values to her acting career, which began in earnest after her graduation from Bryn Mawr College in 1928. After scoring her first major Broadway success in *The Warrior's Husband* (1932), she was invited to Hollywood by RKO Radio Pictures.

Hepburn was an unlikely Hollywood star. Possessing a distinctive speech pattern and an abundance of quirky mannerisms, she earned unqualified praise from her admirers and unmerciful criticism from her detractors. Unabashedly outspoken and iconoclastic, she did as she pleased, refusing to grant interviews, wearing casual clothes at a time when actresses were expected to exude glamour 24 hours a day, and openly clashing with her more experienced coworkers whenever they failed to meet her standards. She nonetheless made an impressive movie debut in *A Bill of Divorcement* (1932) and went on to win an Academy Award for her third film, *Morning Glory* (1933). Her much-publicized return to Broadway, in *The Lake* (1933), proved to be a flop. And while moviegoers enjoyed Hepburn's performances in homespun entertainments such as *Little Women* (1933) and *Alice Adams* (1935), they were largely resistant to historical vehicles such as *Mary of Scotland* (1936), *A Woman Rebels* (1936), and *Quality Street* (1937). Hepburn recovered some lost ground with her sparkling performances in the comedies *Bringing Up Baby* (1938) and *Holiday* (1938), but it was too late: a group of leading film exhibitors had already written off Hepburn as "box office poison."

Undaunted, Hepburn accepted a role written specifically for her in Philip Barry's 1938 Broadway comedy *The Philadelphia Story*, which proved to be a hit. She purchased the motion picture rights to the play and was able to jumpstart her Hollywood career by starring in the 1940 film version. She continued to make periodic returns to the stage (notably as the title character in the 1969 Broadway musical *Coco*), but Hepburn remained essentially a film actor for the remainder of her career. Her stature increased as she chalked up such cinematic triumphs as *The African Queen* (1951), *Summertime* (1955), and *Long Day's Journey into Night* (1962). She won a second Academy Award for *Guess Who's Coming to Dinner* (1967), a third for *The Lion in Winter* (1968), and an unprecedented fourth Oscar for *On Golden Pond* (1981); her 12 Academy Award nominations also set a record, which stood until 2003, when broken by Meryl Streep. In addition, Hepburn appeared frequently on television in the 1970s and '80s. She was nominated for an Emmy Award for her memorable portrayal of Amanda Wingfield in Tennessee Williams's *The Glass Menagerie* (1973), and she won the award for her performance opposite Laurence Olivier in *Love Among the Ruins* (1975), which reunited her with her favourite director, George Cukor. Though hampered by a progressive neurological disease, she was nonetheless still active in the early '90s, appearing prominently in films such as *Love Affair* (1994) and writing several volumes of memoirs, including her autobiography, *Me: Stories of My Life* (1991).

Hepburn was married once, to Philadelphia broker Ludlow Ogden Smith, but the union was dissolved in 1934. While filming *Woman of the Year* in 1942, she began an enduring, intimate relationship with her costar, Spencer Tracy, with whom she would appear in films such as *Adam's Rib* (1949) and *Pat and Mike* (1952). Tracy and Hepburn never married—he was Roman Catholic and would not divorce his wife—but they remained close both personally and professionally until his death in 1967, just days after completing the filming of *Guess Who's Coming to Dinner*. Hepburn had suspended her own career for nearly five years to nurse Tracy through what turned out to be his final illness. In 1999 the American Film Institute named Hepburn the top female American screen legend of all time.

JOHN WAYNE

(b. May 26, 1907, Winterset, Iowa, U.S.—d. June 11, 1979, Los Angeles, Calif., U.S.)

John Wayne, nicknamed the Duke (original name Marion Michael Morrison was a major American motion-picture actor who embodied the image of the strong, taciturn cowboy or soldier and who in many ways personified the idealized American values of his era.

Marion Morrison was the son of an Iowa pharmacist; he acquired the nickname "Duke" during his youth and billed himself as Duke Morrison for one of his early films. In 1925 he enrolled at the University of Southern California (Los Angeles), where he played football. He worked summers at the Fox Film Corporation as a propman and developed a friendship with director John Ford, who cast

John Wayne in The Searchers *(1956).*

him in some small film roles starting in 1928. His first lead-ing role—and his first appearance as "John Wayne"—came in director Raoul Walsh's *The Big Trail* (1930). During the next eight years Wayne starred in more than 60 low-budget motion pictures, mostly in roles as cowboys, soldiers, and other rugged men of adventure. He reached genuine star stature when Ford cast him as the Ringo Kid in the classic western *Stagecoach* (1939). After that film his place in American cinema was established and grew with each successive year. Ford's *The Long Voyage Home* (1940), a film based on several Eugene O'Neill one-act plays, fea-tured one of Wayne's most-praised performances from the early years of his stardom and offered further evidence of his commanding screen presence.

Speculation exists as to whether Wayne purposely avoided military service during World War II, but evi-dence suggests that his attempts to enlist in the Navy were rejected because of his age, an old football injury, and a federal government directive to draft boards to go easy on actors whose talents could be used for building morale. He spent the war years entertaining troops overseas and mak-ing films such as the popular action-adventures *Flying Tigers* (1942), *The Fighting Seabees* (1944), *They Were Expendable* (1945), and *Back to Bataan* (1945), all of which featured Wayne as quintessentially American fighting men who overcome great odds. He also appeared during this period in melodramas such as *The Spoilers* (1942) and *Flame of the Barbary Coast* (1945). By the end of the war, Wayne was firmly established as one of Hollywood's top stars.

Wayne's screen image was permanently defined in the many classic films he made with directors Ford and Howard Hawks during the postwar years and into the early 1960s. For Ford, Wayne starred in what has come to be known as the "Cavalry Trilogy": *Fort Apache* (1948), *She Wore a Yellow Ribbon* (1949), and *Rio Grande* (1950), three

elegiac films in which Wayne portrays stoic cavalry offi-
cers of the Old West. Wayne's roles in these and other
films for Ford offer a somewhat complex representation
of the American character in that they exhibit unflagging
patriotism but are disillusioned by, and resigned to, the
inherent hypocrisies within America. In this manner the
Ford-Wayne films both honour and undermine the mythology of the Old West, nowhere more so than in *The Searchers*
(1956), a film considered by some to be the greatest western ever made. Wayne's character in this film pursues a
noble goal (rescuing his kidnapped niece from a renegade
Comanche tribe), but his obsessive behaviour and blatant
bigotry reveal him to be as mad as he is heroic. Ford's
exploration of the dark underbelly of Old West legends
culminated in *The Man Who Shot Liberty Valance* (1962), a
film that both questions and justifies the "when the truth
interferes with the legend, print the legend" philosophy of
19th-century journalists of the American West. In all, the
Ford-Wayne films present an Old West rendered obsolete
by the very society it helped to create. Wayne also appeared
in films for Ford that were not westerns, including stand-
outs such as *The Quiet Man* (1952) and *Donovan's Reef* (1963).

Howard Hawks's collaborations with Wayne are less
iconoclastic than Ford's, but no less revered. *Red River*
(1948), another candidate for the greatest western of all
time, features Wayne as an autocratic, monomaniacal cattle baron at odds with the orphan boy he has reared
(portrayed in adulthood by Montgomery Clift in his first
screen role) and the modern values he represents. Wayne
did not work with Hawks again until *Rio Bravo* (1959), a
film born of Hawks's and Wayne's dissatisfaction with the
popularity of *High Noon* (1952), the Gary Cooper western
in which citizens of a western community are portrayed as
weak-willed and cowardly when their sheriff asks their
help in forming a posse. The sheriff portrayed by Wayne in

Rio Bravo, conversely, is determined to do his duty with or without help from anyone. Although greeted with lukewarm reviews upon its release, *Rio Bravo* is now regarded as a classic western. Hawks and Wayne remade essentially the same story twice, in *El Dorado* (1967) and in *Rio Lobo* (1970), Hawks's final film.

Wayne's standout films for other directors include *Sands of Iwo Jima* (1949), in which his performance as an uncompromisingly tough Marine sergeant earned an Oscar nomination; *Hondo* (1953), perhaps the only classic western filmed in 3D; *The Alamo* (1960), an epic-length film that Wayne himself directed and in which he starred as Davy Crockett; *The Longest Day* (1962) and *In Harm's Way* (1965), two hugely successful World War II epics; and *McLintock!* (1963), a slapstick western farce that was his only successful comedy. After a screen career of more than 40 years, Wayne was honoured with an Academy Award for his portrayal of the drunken, cantankerous, but endearing U.S. Marshal Rooster Cogburn in *True Grit* (1969), a role he reprised opposite Katharine Hepburn in *Rooster Cogburn* (1975), a partial remake of the Hepburn–Humphrey Bogart classic *The African Queen* (1951). Wayne's final film, *The Shootist* (1976), in which he portrays an aging gunfighter who is dying of cancer, was praised by many as his best western since *Rio Bravo*. This role was a poignant screen farewell for an actor who himself would succumb to cancer three years later.

Wayne endured criticism throughout his career from those who questioned his versatility as an actor. His ability to convey quiet tenderness, however, and his capacity for multilayered portrayals of complex characters, as in *Red River* and *The Searchers*, was often overlooked. Wayne himself was also the subject of controversy: his outspoken right-wing politics were admired by conservatives but derided by liberals as being naively jingoistic. His politics notwithstanding, he is considered a towering cinematic icon and, to some, the greatest Hollywood star of all time. He was posthumously awarded the Congressional Gold Medal and the Presidential Medal of Freedom.

KUROSAWA AKIRA

(b. March 23, 1910, Tokyo, Japan—d. Sept. 6, 1998, Tokyo)

Kurosawa Akira was the first Japanese film director to win international acclaim, with such films as *Rashomon* (1950), *Ikiru* (1952), *Seven Samurai* (1954), *Throne of Blood* (1957), *Kagemusha* (1980), and *Ran* (1985).

Kurosawa's father, who had once been an army officer, was a teacher who contributed to the development of athletics instruction in Japan. After leaving secondary school, Kurosawa attended an art school and began painting in the Western style. Although he was awarded important art prizes, he gave up his ambition to become a painter and in 1936 became an assistant director in the PCL cinema studio. Until 1943 he worked there mainly as an assistant to Yamamoto Kajirō, one of Japan's major directors of World War II films. During this period Kurosawa became known as an excellent scenarist. Some of his best scenarios were never filmed but only published in journals; yet they were noticed by specialists for their freshness of representation and were awarded prizes.

In 1943 Kurosawa was promoted to director and made his first feature film, *Sanshiro Sugata*, from his own scenario; this story of Japanese judo masters of the 1880s scored a great popular success. In 1944 he made his second film, *Ichiban utsukushiku (The Most Beautiful)*, a story about girls at work in an arsenal. Immediately thereafter, he married the actress who had played the leading part in the

Kurosawa Akira during the filming of Kagemusha *(1980).*

picture, Yaguchi Yoko; they had two children, a son and a daughter. In August 1945, when Japan offered to surrender in World War II, he was shooting his picture *Tora no o fumu otokotachi* (*They Who Step on the Tiger's Tail*), a parody of a well-known Kabuki drama. The Allied occupation forces, however, prohibited the release of most films dealing with Japan's feudal past, and this outstanding comedy was not distributed until 1952.

Kurosawa's *Waga seishun ni kuinashi* (1946; *No Regrets for Our Youth*) portrays the history of Japanese militarism from 1933 through the end of the war in terms of a person executed on suspicion of espionage during the war. Of the many postwar films criticizing Japanese militarism, this was the most successful, both artistically and commercially. It was *Yoidore tenshi* (1948; *Drunken Angel*), however, that made Kurosawa's name famous. This story of a consumptive gangster and a drunken doctor living in the postwar desolation of downtown Tokyo is a melodrama intermingling desperation and hope, violence, and melancholy. The gangster was portrayed by a new actor, Mifune Toshirō, who became a star through this film and who subsequently appeared in most of Kurosawa's films.

Kurosawa's *Rashomon* was shown at the Venice Film Festival in 1951 and was awarded the Grand Prix. It also won the Academy Award for best foreign-language film. This was the first time a Japanese film had won such high international acclaim, and Japanese films now attracted serious attention all over the world. An adaptation of two short stories written by Akutagawa Ryūnosuke, the film deals with a samurai, his wife, a bandit, and a woodcutter in the 10th century; a rape and a murder are recollected by the four persons in distinctly different ways. This presentation of the same event as seen by different persons caught the imagination of the audience and advanced the idea of cinema as a means of probing a metaphysical problem.

Ikiru ("To Live") is regarded by many critics as one of the finest works in the history of the cinema. It concerns a petty governmental official who learns he has only half a year until he will die from cancer. He searches for solace in the affection of his family but is betrayed, then seeks enjoyment but becomes disillusioned, and, in the end, is redeemed by using his position to work for the poor. In this film, which abounds in strong moral messages, Kurosawa depicts in an extremely realistic manner the collapse of the family system, as well as the hypocritical aspects of officials in postwar Japanese society. The picture was an outstanding document of the life and the spiritual situation of Japanese people, who were then beginning to recover from the desperation caused by defeat in the war.

The epic *Shichinin no samurai* (*Seven Samurai*) is considered the most entertaining of Kurosawa's films and also his greatest commercial success. It depicts a village of peasants and a few leaderless samurai who fight for the village against a gang of marauding bandits; although it was inspired by his admiration of Hollywood Westerns, it was executed in an entirely Japanese style.

Ikimono no kiroku (1955; *I Live in Fear*, or *Record of a Living Being*) is a deeply honest film portraying a Japanese foundry owner's terror of the atomic tests conducted by the United States and the Soviet Union. Its pessimistic conclusion, however, made it a commercial failure.

Kurosawa was also noted for his adaptations of European literary classics into films with Japanese settings. *Hakuchi* (1951; *The Idiot*) is based upon Fyodor Dostoyevsky's novel of the same title, *Kumonosu-jo* (*Throne of Blood*) was adapted from Shakespeare's *Macbeth*, and *Donzoko* (1957; *The Lower Depths*) was from Maksim Gorky's drama: each of these films is skillfully Japanized. *Throne of Blood*, which reflects the style of the sets and acting of the Japanese Noh play and uses not a word of the original text, has been called the best film of all the countless cinematized Shakespearean dramas.

Kurosawa's pictures contributed a strong sense of style to the artistic Japanese film, which had been pursuing a naturalistic trend. The violent action of his more commercial works also exerted a powerful influence.

In 1960 he set up Kurosawa Productions, of which he became president, and began to produce his own works. As producer, however, he was continually embarrassed by economic difficulties. Throughout the 1960s, Kurosawa made a number of entertainment films, mainly with samurai as leading characters; *Yojimbo* (1961; "The Bodyguard") is a representative work. *Akahige* (1965; *Red Beard*) combines elements of entertainment with a sentimental humanism. In the 1960s, however, Japanese cinema fell into an economic depression, and Kurosawa's plans, in most cases, were found by film companies to be too expensive. As a result, Kurosawa attempted to work with Hollywood producers, but each of the projects ended in failure. At the Kyōto studio in 1968, for 20th Century Fox, he started shooting *Tora, Tora, Tora!*, a war film dealing with the air attack on Pearl Harbor. The work progressed slowly, however, and the producer, fearing an excess in estimated cost, dismissed Kurosawa and replaced him with another director. After a six-year interval, Kurosawa at last managed to present another of his films, *Dodesukaden* (1970; *Dodeskaden*). His first work in colour, a comedy of poor people living in slums, it recaptured much of the poignancy of his best works but failed financially. The period of personal despondency and artistic silence that followed ended in the mid-1970s when Kurosawa filmed *Dersu Uzala* (1975) in Siberia at the invitation of the Soviet government. This story of a Siberian hermit won wide acclaim.

Kagemusha ("The Shadow Warrior"), released in 1980, was the director's first samurai film in 14 years. It concerns a petty thief who is chosen to impersonate a powerful feudal lord killed in battle. This film was notable for its powerful battle scenes. Kurosawa's next film, *Ran* (1985; "Chaos"), was an even more successful samurai epic. An adaptation of Shakespeare's *King Lear* set in 16th-century Japan, the film uses sons instead of daughters as the aging monarch's ungrateful children. *Ran* was acclaimed as one of Kurosawa's greatest films in the grandeur of its imagery, the intellectual depth of its screen adaptation, and the intensity of its dramatic performances. His last three films—*Dreams* (1990), *Rhapsody in August* (1990), and *Madadayo* (1993)—were not as well received.

Although other Japanese filmmakers acquired substantial international followings after the pioneering success of *Rashomon*, Kurosawa's films continue to command great interest in the West. They represent a unique combination of elements of Japanese art—in the subtlety of their feeling and philosophy, the brilliance of their visual composition, and their treatment of samurai and other historic Japanese themes—with a distinctly Western feeling for action and drama and a frequent use of stories from Western sources, both literary classics and popular thrillers.

LUCILLE BALL

(b. Aug. 6, 1911, Celoron, near Jamestown, N.Y., U.S.–d. April 26, 1989, Los Angeles, Calif., U.S.)

Lucille Désirée Ball was a radio and motion-picture actress and longtime comedy star of American television, best remembered for her classic television comedy series *I Love Lucy*.

Ball determined at an early age to become an actress and left high school at age 15 to enroll in a drama school in New York City. Her early attempts to find a place in the theatre all met with rebuffs, and she took a job as a model under the name Diane Belmont. She was moderately successful as a model, and a poster on which she appeared brought her to the attention of the Hollywood studios and won her spots in *Roman Scandals* (1933), *Blood Money* (1933), *Kid Millions* (1934), and other movies.

Ball remained in Hollywood and appeared in increasingly larger roles in a succession of movies—*Carnival* (1935), *Stage Door* (1937), *Room Service* (1938), *Five Came Back* (1939), and *Too Many Girls* (1940), in which she starred and which also featured the popular Cuban bandleader and actor Desi Arnaz, whom she married in 1940. For 10 years they conducted separate careers, he as a bandleader and she as a movie actress who was usually seen in B-grade comedies. She won major roles in *The Big Street* (1942) with Henry Fonda, *Du Barry Was a Lady* (1943), *Without Love* (1945), *Ziegfeld Follies* (1946), and *Sorrowful Jones* (1949) and *Fancy Pants* (1950), both with Bob Hope. All of her comedies were box office successes, but they failed to make the most of her wide-ranging talents.

In 1950 Ball and her husband formed Desilu Productions, which, after experimenting with a radio program, launched in October 1951 a television comedy series entitled *I Love Lucy*. Starring the two of them in a comedy version of their real lives, the show was an instant hit, and, for the six years (1951–56 and, under the title *The Lucille Ball–Desi Arnaz Show*, 1957–58) during which fresh episodes were produced, it remained at or near the top of the TV ratings. *I Love Lucy* proved to be an outstanding vehicle for Ball's exceptional comedic talents. As the character Lucy, a wisecracking housewife who regularly concocted schemes to get herself out of the house, Ball showcased her expertise for timing, physical comedy, and range of characterization. The show also introduced several technical innovations to television broadcasting (notably the use of three cameras to film the show) and set the standard for situation comedies, thriving in reruns for decades.

Lucille Ball and Desi Arnaz.

Meanwhile Desilu acquired RKO Pictures, began producing other shows for television, and became one of the major companies in a highly competitive field. Ball and Arnaz were divorced in 1960, and two years later she succeeded him as president of Desilu, becoming the only woman at that time to lead a major Hollywood production company. She starred in the Broadway show *Wildcat* in 1961 and returned to television in *The Lucy Show* (1962–68). She resumed movie work with *Yours, Mine and Ours* (1968) and *Mame* (1974). In 1967 Ball sold Desilu and formed her own company, Lucille Ball Productions, which produced her third television series, *Here's Lucy* (1968–74). She continued to appear thereafter in special productions and as a guest star. In 1985 she played a Manhattan bag lady in the television film *Stone Pillow*. Her fourth and final television series, *Life with Lucy*, aired for two months in 1986. Ball died three years later.

Ball influenced generations of comedians, and her popularity continued into the 21st century. The Lucille Ball–Desi Arnaz Center, which includes a museum dedicated to *I Love Lucy*, is a popular tourist attraction in Jamestown, N.Y..

GENE KELLY

(b. Aug. 23, 1912, Pittsburgh, Penn., U.S.—d. Feb. 2, 1996, Beverly Hills, Calif., U.S.)

Gene Kelly (full name Eugene Curran Kelly) was an American dancer, actor, choreographer, and motion-picture director whose athletic style of dancing, combined with classical ballet technique, transformed the movie musical and did much to change the American public's conception of male dancers.

One of five children born to a record company sales executive and a former actress, Kelly dreamed of becoming a professional athlete but was redirected into dancing by his mother. He majored in journalism at Pennsylvania State College (now University) and economics at the University of Pittsburgh (A.B., 1933), but the allure of performing proved too strong to resist. He toured in vaudeville with his brother Fred (later a prolific stage and television director), and for several years he ran a successful dancing school in Pittsburgh.

In 1938 he moved to New York City and won a role as a chorus member in Cole Porter's *Leave It to Me*, figuring prominently in star Mary Martin's showstopping number "My Heart Belongs to Daddy." The following year he was cast in the flashy role of Harry the Hoofer in William Saroyan's Pulitzer Prize-winning play *The Time of Your Life*, and in 1940 he achieved stardom with his likeable interpretation of the raffish protagonist in the Richard Rodgers and Lorenz Hart musical drama *Pal Joey*. On seeing the play, film producer David O. Selznick offered Kelly a Hollywood contract, and Kelly accepted, doing so because Selznick did not require a screen test of him. Before leaving New York in 1941, Kelly choreographed the hit musical *Best Foot Forward* (1941).

FILMS OF THE 1940S: *COVER GIRL*, *ANCHORS AWEIGH*, *THE PIRATE*, AND *ON THE TOWN*

Kelly made his film debut opposite Judy Garland in *For Me and My Gal* (1942), immediately endearing himself to moviegoers with his carefree acting and spontaneous athletic dancing style. It was not until he was loaned to Columbia Pictures to costar in the Rita Hayworth musical *Cover Girl* (1944) that he was able to bring his own special artistic vision to the big screen. Before Kelly's arrival, the movie musical had been divided into essentially two basic styles: the splashy, impersonal, girl-filled extravaganzas of Busby

Berkeley and the intimate personality vehicles of Fred Astaire. Kelly adroitly bridged the gap between Berkeley's cinematic pyrotechnics and Astaire's straightforward theatrical approach with *Cover Girl*'s "Alter Ego" number, in which, with the aid of meticulously timed special-effects work, he performed a two-man "challenge dance" with himself. He introduced another innovation in *Anchors Aweigh* (1945), when he danced with an animated-cartoon mouse (Jerry, of the Tom and Jerry cartoons), and in *The Pirate* (1948) he staged the first of his many filmed ballets, boldly blending solo dancing, mass movement, offbeat camera angles, and vibrant colours to tell a story in purely visual terms. Kelly also performed several dramatic roles during that period, most notably as D'Artagnan in the swashbuckler *The Three Musketeers* (1948).

On the Town (1949), codirected by Kelly and his longtime assistant Stanley Donen, further transcended the limits of the Hollywood soundstage with an unforgettable opening musical number filmed entirely on location in the streets of New York City.

FILMS OF THE 1950S: *AN AMERICAN IN PARIS*, *SINGIN' IN THE RAIN*, AND *BRIGADOON*

Kelly surpassed that triumph two years later with the Academy Award-winning *An American in Paris* (1951). Climaxed by a spectacular 13-minute ballet that incorporated visual motifs of French Post-Impressionism, the film was singled out by critics and filmgoers alike as Kelly's masterpiece. Since the mid-1970s, however, its reputation has been eclipsed by *Singin' in the Rain* (1952), a witty and upbeat spoof of Hollywood during the talkie revolution. With its perfectly balanced mixture of singing, dancing, comedy, and romance, *Singin' in the Rain* is now widely regarded as the greatest film musical ever made. His next released musical, *Brigadoon* (1954), directed by Vincente Minnelli and based on the Alan Jay Lerner and Frederick Loewe Broadway hit, was not a critical or commercial success. Kelly's decision to drop Agnes de Mille's stage choreography for new staging of his own designed for the wide-screen Cinemascope format proved particularly controversial.

Kelly subsequently codirected with Donen and starred in *It's Always Fair Weather* (1955), a loose follow-up to *On the Town*, which showcased Kelly's creative choreography for Cinemascope. Equally praiseworthy (though a flop with the public) was his first solo directorial effort, the wordless concert feature *Invitation to the Dance* (filmed in 1952, released in 1956). But as the 1950s wore on, the movie musical genre fell victim to mounting production costs and diminishing box-office returns. Consequently, Kelly's film career lost much of its momentum, though he made several credible dramatic appearances in such films as *Crest of the Wave* (1954).

FILMS OF THE 1960S AND BEYOND

After turning in a fine dramatic performance in *Inherit the Wind* (1960), Kelly directed *Gigot* (1962), a heart-tugging story filmed in Paris and starring Jackie Gleason as a deaf man who takes a waif under his wing. Kelly also directed the comedy *A Guide for the Married Man* (1967), which starred Walter Matthau as the title character being tutored on how to efficiently cheat on his wife. That same year Kelly returned to France to play an American piano player in Jacques Demy's tribute to Hollywood musicals *Les Demoiselles de Rochefort* (1967; *The Young Girls of Rochefort*).

Hello, Dolly! (1969) was Kelly's adaptation of the Broadway hit starring Barbra Streisand, Matthau, and Louis Armstrong. The western comedy *The Cheyenne Social*

Club (1970) starred Henry Fonda and James Stewart as two cowboys who unwittingly inherit management of a brothel. Kelly's final directing credit was as codirector (with Jack Haley, Jr.) of *That's Entertainment, Part 2* (1976), the follow-up to the 1974 original's compilation of highlights from MGM musicals. He hosted the film with onetime costar Astaire.

Kelly's final film as an actor was the cult favourite *Xanadu* (1980), a musical starring pop sensation Olivia Newton-John. Before retiring, his last roles were in the television miniseries *North and South* (1985) and *Sins* (1986).

During the last three decades of his life, Kelly received dozens of awards and honours, among them the French Legion of Honour for his choreography of the Paris Opéra Ballet "Pas de Deux" (1960) and a Life Achievement Award from the American Film Institute.

ORSON WELLES

(b. May 6, 1915, Kenosha, Wis., U.S.–d. Oct. 10, 1985, Los Angeles, Calif., U.S.)

George Orson Welles was an American motion-picture actor, director, producer, and writer. His innovative narrative techniques and use of photography, dramatic lighting, and music to further the dramatic line and to create mood made his *Citizen Kane* (1941)—which he wrote, directed, produced, and acted in—one of the most-influential films in the history of the art.

EARLY WORK

Welles was born to a mother, Beatrice Ives, who was a concert pianist and a crack rifle shot and a father, Richard Welles, who was an inventor and a businessman. Welles was a child prodigy, adept at the piano and violin, acting, drawing, painting, and writing verse; he also entertained his friends by performing magic tricks and staging mini-productions of William Shakespeare's plays.

Welles's parents separated when he was four years old, and his mother died when he was nine. In 1926 Welles entered the exclusive Todd School in Woodstock, Illinois. There his gifts found fertile ground, and he dazzled the teachers and students with stagings of both modern and classical plays. His father died in 1930, and Welles became the ward of a family friend, Chicago doctor Maurice Bernstein. In 1931 he graduated from Todd, but, instead of attending college, he studied briefly at the Art Institute of Chicago before traveling to Dublin, where he success-fully auditioned at the Gate Theatre for the part of the Duke of Württemberg in a stage adaptation of Lion Feuchtwanger's novel *Jew Süss*.

Welles remained in Ireland for a year, acting with the company at the Abbey Theatre as well as at the Gate; he also designed sets, wrote a newspaper column, and began directing plays. In 1932 Welles left Dublin and tried to get work on the stages of London and New York; unsuccess-ful, he instead traveled for a year in Morocco and Spain. In 1933 in the United States, he was introduced to actress Katharine Cornell by author Thornton Wilder and was hired to act in Cornell's road company, playing Mercutio in Shakespeare's *Romeo and Juliet*, Marchbanks in George Bernard Shaw's *Candida*, and Octavius Barrett in Rudolf Besier's *The Barretts of Wimpole Street*. In 1934 Welles orga-nized a summer drama festival at the Todd School, where he played Svengali in an adaptation of George du Maurier's *Trilby* and Claudius in *Hamlet*. At the end of the festival, he made his first film, the short *The Hearts of Age*. With Todd School headmaster Roger Hill, he prepared *Everybody's Shakespeare* (1934), editions for performance of *Twelfth Night*, *The Merchant of Venice*, and *Julius Caesar*, with introductions by Hill and Welles and illustrations by Welles. He made his New York debut as Tybalt in Cornell's production of *Romeo and Juliet* in December 1934.

THEATRE AND RADIO IN THE 1930S

When Welles was performing in *Romeo and Juliet*, he met producer John Houseman, who immediately cast him as the lead in Archibald MacLeish's verse play *Panic*, which premiered in 1935 for Houseman's Phoenix Theatre Group. They then moved on in 1936 to mounting productions for the Works Progress Administration's (WPA's) Federal Theatre Project. Their first effort, for the Federal Theatre's Negro Division, was *Macbeth*, with an all African American cast and the setting changed from Scotland to Haiti. They began 1937 with Christopher Marlowe's *The Tragicall History of Doctor Faustus* (starring Welles). Their most (in)famous effort was Marc Blitzstein's proletarian musical play *The Cradle Will Rock*. WPA guards shut down the theatre the night before its opening. (The shutdown was ostensibly for budgetary reasons; however, the political nature of the play was considered too radical.) Welles and Houseman quickly rented another theatre, and on opening night the play was presented with the actors performing their roles from seats in the audience. That same year they formed the Mercury Theatre, which presented a renowned modern-dress version of Shakespeare's *Julius Caesar*. In 1938 the Mercury Theatre presented William Gillette's comedy *Too Much Johnson*. Welles shot three short silent films to precede each act of the play; however, the films were never finished. (The *Too Much Johnson* footage was believed to have been destroyed by fire in 1970; however, it was rediscovered, restored, and premiered in 2013.)

At the same time, Welles was making inroads in radio. His radio career began early in 1934 with an excerpt from

Panic. In 1935 he began appearing regularly on *The March of Time* news series, and subsequent radio roles included the part of Lamont Cranston in the mystery series *The Shadow*. In 1938 the Mercury players undertook a series of radio dramas adapted from famous novels. They attained national notoriety with a program based on H.G. Wells's *The War of the Worlds*; the performance on October 30, using the format of a simulated news broadcast narrated by Welles, announced an attack on New Jersey by invaders from Mars. (However, contemporary reports that the program caused a nationwide panic were exaggerated.)

The national coverage that resulted from his theatre and radio work brought Welles's name before Hollywood. In 1939 he signed an extraordinary contract with RKO that guaranteed him near-total autonomy and final cut on any film he made. For his first film, Welles chose Joseph Conrad's *Heart of Darkness*, which was to be filmed entirely from the point of view of the narrator Marlow. However, despite months of preparation, the film never got off the ground. Welles narrated *Swiss Family Robinson* (1940) while waiting for another project to evolve.

At RKO: *Citizen Kane* and *The Magnificent Ambersons*

Citizen Kane (1941) is arguably the greatest movie ever to come out of Hollywood, and it is surely one of the most-impressive debuts by any director. Welles also produced and coscripted the film with Herman J. Mankiewicz. Welles submitted a joyfully energetic performance as Charles Foster Kane, the newspaper magnate (clearly based on newspaper publisher William Randolph Hearst) who rises from a poor background to amass uncountable millions—none of which he is able to enjoy, thanks to his epic ambitions.

Citizen Kane featured an ensemble cast in support of Welles, composed mostly of Mercury actors, and included Joseph Cotten, Agnes Moorehead, Everett Sloane, Paul Stewart, and Ruth Warrick. Shot with an array of classic and experimental techniques by Gregg Toland, evocatively scored by Bernard Herrmann, and edited brilliantly by Robert Wise, *Citizen Kane* was a masterpiece of moviemaking. It was also the last time Welles made a Hollywood movie that reached the screen intact.

Although it initially received rave reviews, *Citizen Kane* was not a financial success. RKO found the film—with its complex flashback structure and lack of an appealing protagonist—difficult to market, and its box office was also

Orson Welles in Citizen Kane *(1941)*.

hindered by the Hearst newspapers' using their power to limit its commercial prospects. Nevertheless, *Citizen Kane* received nine Academy Award nominations, of which Welles received three (best actor, director, and original screenplay), but only the screenplay won an Oscar.

The Magnificent Ambersons (1942) was produced, written, and directed by Welles, and to some critics it represents the peak of his artistry—even though it was taken out of his hands by RKO after poor test screenings. It was heavily reedited by Wise (44 minutes were cut), and a new ending was tacked on. *The Magnificent Ambersons* was adapted from Booth Tarkington's novel about the declining fortunes of a wealthy 19th-century Indianapolis family whose smugness (and inability to comprehend the significance of industrialization and the automobile) leads to their downfall. The ensemble cast featured Tim Holt as the spoiled scion whose arrogance finally earns him a well-deserved comeuppance that nonetheless carries the weight of tragedy. Mercury actors (and *Citizen Kane* veterans) Cotten, Moorehead, and Ray Collins all delivered fine performances, and former silent star Dolores Costello and young Anne Baxter demonstrated Welles's attention to his female actors. Photographed brilliantly by Stanley Cortez, *The Magnificent Ambersons* was nominated for a best picture Oscar.

Even while Wise was cutting *The Magnificent Ambersons*, Welles was in South America filming his quasi-documentary *It's All True*, an anthology of three short films: *The Story of Samba (Carnaval)*, about Rio de Janeiro's annual Carnival; *My Friend Bonito*, about bullfighting; and *Four Men on a Raft*, about four humble fishermen who become national heroes after a daring voyage. RKO canceled the project midway, leaving Welles stranded in Rio. (The legendary project, never released, resurfaced when the mostly extant footage from *Four Men on a Raft* was assembled by

Richard Wilson, Bill Krohn, and Myron Meisel as part of the documentary *It's All True: Based on an Unfinished Film by Orson Welles* [1993].)

Welles had started work on *Journey into Fear* (1943) before leaving for Brazil, and he returned to find that RKO had begun meddling with it, as it had with *The Magnificent Ambersons*. This time, though, Welles was able to intercede and restore at least some of the brutal editing, but it was released at 69 minutes, having been cut down from 91. *Journey into Fear* was officially credited to Norman Foster, a director who also assisted Welles on *It's All True*, but it was produced, coscripted, and acted in by Welles, who played the supporting part of Colonel Haki of Turkish intelligence. The hand of Welles is clearly evident, although Welles later said that he "designed the film but can't properly be called its director." A gripping (if sometimes confusing) adaptation of Eric Ambler's thriller about espionage and munitions smuggling, *Journey into Fear* starred Welles's then paramour, Dolores Del Rio, as the mysterious Josette, and *Citizen Kane* veterans Cotten (who cowrote the screenplay), Warrick, Moorehead, and Sloane enhanced the production. However, RKO was unimpressed, and its new executives kicked Welles and his Mercury Productions off the lot.

FILMS OF THE LATER 1940S: *THE STRANGER*, *THE LADY FROM SHANGHAI*, AND *MACBETH*

Welles spent the rest of 1943 making two radio series, entertaining American troops fighting in World War II with a touring magic show with the assistance of Rita Hayworth (whom he married), Marlene Dietrich, Cotten, and Moorehead, giving speeches on behalf of the war effort, and even substituting for Jack Benny on his radio show. He also played the mysterious Rochester in Robert

Stevenson's *Jane Eyre* (1943) opposite Joan Fontaine. But none of the studios was rushing to sign him as a director. He starred opposite Claudette Colbert in Irving Pichel's melodrama *Tomorrow Is Forever* (1946) before finally being given a chance by producer Sam Spiegel.

The Stranger (1946) was a thriller about a Nazi, Franz Kindler (Welles), who is hiding out as a schoolteacher in a small New England town. His impending nuptials with a fellow teacher (Loretta Young) are interrupted when a war-crimes investigator (Edward G. Robinson) tracks him down and then waits for Kindler to give himself away. Welles was not happy with his work—he was trying to adhere to a strict schedule and budget to repair his reputation and so could ill afford any of his trademark flourishes—and *The Stranger* was thus his most-conventional film.

Heavily in debt from the failure of a colossal stage version of Jules Verne's *Around the World in Eighty Days*, Welles began shooting the film noir *The Lady from Shanghai* in 1946 for Columbia Pictures. The story, based on a pot-boiler by Sherwood King, was reimagined by Welles as a feverishly intricate meditation on the nature of evil, with Welles as the philosophic protagonist, sailor Michael O'Hara. Hayworth (temporarily reunited with Welles after having been separated for a year) was the treacherous Elsa Bannister, and Mercury veteran Sloane played her crippled but poisonous husband, the corrupt lawyer Arthur Bannister. It was released in 1948.

In a typical display of mordant humour, Welles had Hayworth shorn of her trademark red tresses and dyed a platinum blond, one of many points of contention between Welles and Columbia's president, Harry Cohn. The expensive (and rather complex) picture, shot in a variety of colourful Mexican locations, was a box-office failure. Today *The Lady from Shanghai* is regarded as one of Welles's masterpieces, a triumph of style especially in its climactic shootout in a hall of mirrors, even though Welles was unable to oversee its final, heavily truncated cut.

In 1947 Welles then made a loose but strikingly original film adaptation, *Macbeth* (1948), which he shot in 23 days at genre factory Republic Pictures. He had prepared for the low-budget shoot by directing a stage production in Salt Lake City, Utah, with most of the cast. Welles summarized his low-budget achievement by describing it as "a kind of violently sketched charcoal drawing of a great play." He used stylized sets and long takes to support his vision. (Although it was originally released at 107 minutes, the film was for many years seen only in an 86-minute version with the cast's original Scottish accents redubbed.)

After finishing shooting *Macbeth*, Welles went to Italy, where he acted as the 18th-century charlatan and magician Cagliostro (and directed a few scenes) in Gregory Ratoff's *Black Magic* (1949). He starred in other films, including Henry King's *Prince of Foxes* (1949), as a colourful Cesare Borgia, and most famously Carol Reed's classic thriller *The Third Man* (1949), as the amoral Harry Lime. Welles would spend much of the next 25 years in Europe.

FILMS OF THE 1950S: *OTHELLO*, *MR. ARKADIN*, AND *TOUCH OF EVIL*

Welles next played a 13th-century warlord in Henry Hathaway's *The Black Rose* (1950). He had begun shooting *Othello* in 1948 in Venice. Over the next three years, Welles fitfully continued filming it on location in Italy and Morocco and in a Rome studio, stopping whenever funds ran low to take on another acting assignment. Since the actors were not always all available, some scenes of conversations were edited together out of close-ups shot years apart. The result was finally shown at Cannes in 1952, winning the top prize. The nearly unknown cast—aside from Welles as *Othello*, it starred Canadian actress Suzanne Cloutier as Desdemona and Irish actor Micheál MacLiammóir (whom Welles had known since his time at the Gate Theatre) as Iago—ensured that its commercial prospects would remain modest. However, the film contains some of Welles's greatest camerawork and is regarded by some as one of his greatest achievements.

Mr. Arkadin (1955; also called *Confidential Report*) was based on an original story by Welles and was financed by European investors, who removed him from the film during editing. It is a *Citizen Kane*–like story with a different but equally tragic ending: the wealthy and powerful Arkadin (Welles) hires a shady young American (Robert Arden) to reassemble his past history, which the tycoon claims to have forgotten but actually fears will be so rife with scandal that his beloved daughter (Paolo Mori) will turn away from him in horror. During Welles's lifetime the film circulated in at least three versions, each with slightly different material, and it was not until 2006 that a "comprehensive version" was assembled. As with so many of Welles's later works, the picture's merits wrestle fiercely with its production deficiencies.

In 1955 Welles also began shooting *Don Quixote*, a contemporary reworking of the Miguel de Cervantes tale that he also produced, narrated, and coscripted. He worked on and off on *Don Quixote* until his death. At one point he even said the film would be called *When Are You Going to Finish Don Quixote*. The film was never completed. A fragmentary form of *Don Quixote* was assembled by Spanish filmmakers Patxi Irigoyen and Jesús Franco in 1992, but it was disparaged by film critics.

Welles accepted many film acting assignments in England, France, and Italy. He made two series of short documentaries for British television, *Orson Welles' Sketch*

Book and *Around the World with Orson Welles* (both 1955), and that same year he also produced *Moby Dick—Rehearsed* for the London stage, an adaptation of Herman Melville's novel in which he appeared as Captain Ahab and Father Mapple. American audiences saw him as Father Mapple in John Huston's *Moby Dick* (1956) and as the imposing Varner in Martin Ritt's *The Long, Hot Summer* (1958). He then returned to Hollywood for the first time in 10 years to make what is considered one of his finest, and most personal, films.

Touch of Evil (1958) was based on a detective novel by Whit Masterson. Welles took its plot about a crooked police chief and embroidered it with themes close to his heart—guilt and redemption, situational ethics versus absolute morality, relative versus utter evil—and some of his most-dazzling camera work. (The picture's opening tracking shot is one of Welles's most famous.) Charlton Heston and Janet Leigh starred as a Mexican police officer and his American wife caught in a maze of corruption just over the Mexican border, but it is really Welles as the crooked police chief Hank Quinlan and Dietrich as a hard-boiled madam who steal the show. Welles delivered a rough cut to Universal and then went to Mexico to shoot some scenes for *Don Quixote*. When he returned, Universal had added some footage and cut it down to 93 minutes. Welles wrote an extensive memo detailing his preferred changes. He was ignored, but in 1998 Universal released a 111-minute cut following Welles's memo. *Touch of Evil* was Welles's last Hollywood film.

LATER FILMS: *THE TRIAL*, *CHIMES AT MIDNIGHT*, AND *F FOR FAKE*

Welles acted in such films as Huston's *The Roots of Heaven* (1958) and Richard Fleischer's *Compulsion* (1959). He also used his famous mellifluous baritone in narrating films, such as Fleischer's *The Vikings* (1958) and Nicholas Ray's *King of Kings* (1961). He made *The Trial* (1962) in Europe. Franz Kafka's novel of existential dread was a good match for Welles's baroque pessimism, and, indeed, Welles considered it one of his best. Anthony Perkins (convincingly anguished as Joseph K.), Welles (formidable as Hastler, the advocate), Jeanne Moreau, and Romy Schneider made for an exceptional cast.

Casting himself as Shakespeare's buffoon Sir John Falstaff and borrowing elements from *Henry IV, Part 1*, *Henry IV, Part 2*, *The Merry Wives of Windsor*, *Henry V*, and *Richard II*, Welles assembled an impressionistic and often moving tribute to the grandeur of Shakespeare in *Chimes at Midnight* (1965; also called *Falstaff*). Welles struggled against budgetary and technical limitations — much of the picture was poorly dubbed — but he skillfully used Spanish locations and an excellent cast that included John Gielgud, Margaret Rutherford, Moreau, and Fernando Rey. The Battle of Shrewsbury sequence toward the end of the film has been lauded as one of Welles's best. But it is Welles's shambling, stumbling Falstaff who is rightly the film's centerpiece, and justice is done to his tragic fate.

After roles in René Clément's *Is Paris Burning?* (1966), Fred Zinnemann's *A Man for All Seasons* (1966), and the James Bond spoof *Casino Royale* (1967), Welles made *Histoire immortelle* (1968; *The Immortal Story*), an hour-long film for French television based on an Isak Dinesen novella. He also shot the thriller *The Deep* between 1967 and 1969; however, the film was never completed. Many more acting appearances followed, including roles in Huston's *The Kremlin Letter* (1970), Mike Nichols's *Catch-22* (1970, as General Dreedle), and Brian De Palma's *Get to Know Your Rabbit* (1972). From 1970 to 1976 he also shot and partially edited *The Other Side of the Wind*, a satire of

Hollywood about a director (played by Huston) who struggles to get his films financed and produced. However, money ran out before postproduction was completed, and the film was caught in a legal battle that lasted long after Welles's death.

F for Fake (1973) was an "essay film" (as Welles called it) about the nature of truth in art. The film had its basis in documentary footage shot by François-Arnold Reichenbach of art forger Elmyr de Hory and his biographer Clifford Irving. As Welles started working on Reichenbach's footage, Irving himself was unmasked as the forger of a fake autobiography of reclusive businessman Howard Hughes. Welles supplemented Reichenbach's footage with much new additional material, drawing on his own fakes, such as the *The War of the Worlds* broadcast and his love of magic. *F for Fake* was probably his most-intricate film and required one year of editing to complete.

Welles returned to the United States in 1975. His final completed film was *Filming "Othello"* (1979), made for West German television about the making of his *Othello*. In addition to acting in and providing voice-over narration for many films and television programs, in his final years Welles shot footage for several projects, including *Filming "The Trial"*, about the making of that film; *The Dreamers*, based on two short stories by Dinesen; *Orson Welles Solo*, an autobiographical film; and *The Magic Show*, with Welles performing magic tricks.

INGRID BERGMAN
(b. Aug. 29, 1915, Stockholm, Swed.–d. Aug. 29, 1982, London, Eng.)

Ingrid Bergman was one of the most popular motion-picture actresses in the United States from the 1940s until her death and an international star in Swedish, French, German, Italian, and British films. Her natural charm, freshness, intelligence, and vitality made her the image of sincerity and ideal womanhood.

Despite shyness and the resistance of her family, Bergman worked assiduously for admission to the Royal Dramatic Theatre School in Stockholm, where she studied for a year. Her screen debut in *Munkbrogreven* (1935; *The Count of the Monk's Bridge*), was followed by challenging roles in such Swedish films as the original *Intermezzo* (1936) and *En kvinnas ansikte* (1938; *A Woman's Face*). Taken to the United States to star in the Hollywood version of *Intermezzo* (1939; released in Great Britain as *Escape to Happiness*), Bergman achieved tremendous popularity through a series of critical and commercial successes that included *Casablanca* (1942); *For Whom the Bell Tolls* (1943); *Gaslight* (1944), for which she won the Academy Award for best actress; *Saratoga Trunk* (1945); *The Bells of St. Mary's* (1945); and two thrillers directed by Alfred Hitchcock, *Spellbound* (1945) and *Notorious* (1946).

Bergman's love affair with the Italian director Roberto Rossellini, during the filming of *Stromboli* (1950), led her first husband to divorce her. The scandal forced her to return to Europe, where she appeared in Italian and French films, such as *Europa '51* (1952; *The Greatest Love,* 1954) and *Un viaggio in Italia* (1954; *Journey to Italy,* 1955). After her marriage to Rossellini in 1950 ended in divorce, she made a triumphant Hollywood comeback in *Anastasia* (1956), for which she won her second Academy Award. She continued to appear in Hollywood productions, including *The Inn of the Sixth Happiness* (1958), as well as in European films. She won her third Oscar, for best supporting actress, for her role in the highly successful film *Murder on the Orient Express* (1974), but most agree that her greatest performance in her later years was as a concert pianist in the Swedish film *Autumn Sonata* (1978), directed by Ingmar Bergman. Her last role was that of Golda Meir, the Israeli prime minister, in the television play *A Woman Called Golda* (1981). For this role she was posthumously awarded an Emmy Award in 1982.

On the stage from 1940, when she starred in *Liliom,* Bergman appeared in critically acclaimed plays such as *Hedda Gabler* (Paris, 1962), *A Month in the Country* (Great Britain, 1965), *Captain Brassbound's Conversion* (London, 1971), and *The Constant Wife* (New York, 1975). She also starred in the television plays *The Turn of the Screw* (1959) and *Hedda Gabler* (1963).

My Story (1980) is her autobiography with alternating sections by Alan Burgess.

INGMAR BERGMAN

(b. July 14, 1918, Uppsala, Swed.–d. July 30, 2007, Fårö, Swed.)

I ngmar Bergman was a Swedish film writer-director, who achieved world fame with such films as *Det sjunde inseglet* (1957; *The Seventh Seal*); *Smultronstället* (1957; *Wild Strawberries*); the trilogy *Såsom i en spegel* (1961; *Through a Glass Darkly*), *Nattsvardsgästerna* (1961; *The Communicants*, or *Winter Light*), *Tystnaden* (1963; *The Silence*); and *Viskingar och rop* (1972; *Cries and Whispers*). He is noted for his versatile camera work and for his fragmented narrative style, which contribute to his bleak depiction of human loneliness, vulnerability, and torment.

LIFE

Bergman was the son of a Lutheran pastor and frequently remarked on the importance of his childhood background in the development of his ideas and moral preoccupations. Even when the context of his film characters' sufferings is not overtly religious, they are always implicitly engaged in a search for moral standards of judgment, a rigorous examination of action and motive, in terms of good and bad, right and wrong, which seems particularly appropriate to someone brought up in a strictly religious home. Another important influence in his childhood was the religious art Bergman encountered, particularly the primitive yet graphic representations of Bible stories and parables found in rustic Swedish churches, which fascinated him and gave him a vital interest in the visual presentation of ideas, especially the idea of evil as embodied in the devil.

Bergman attended Stockholm University, where he studied art, history, and literature. There for the first time he became passionately involved in the theatre and began writing and acting in plays and directing student productions. From these he went on to become a trainee director at the Mäster Olofsgården Theatre and the Sagas Theatre, where he produced a spectacularly unconventional and disastrous production of the Swedish playwright August Strindberg's *Ghost Sonata*. In 1944 he was given his first full-time job as a director, at Helsingborg's municipal theatre. Also, and more importantly, he met Carl-Anders Dymling, the head of the Svensk Filmindustri. Dymling was sufficiently impressed by him to commission an original screenplay, *Hets* (1944; *Frenzy*, or *Torment*). This was directed by Alf Sjöberg, then Sweden's leading film director, and had an enormous success, both at home and abroad. Largely as a result of this success, Bergman was, in 1945, given a chance to write and direct a film of his own, *Kris* (*Crisis*), and from this point on, his career was under way.

The films that Bergman wrote or directed, or both, in the next five years were, if not directly autobiographical, at least very much concerned with the sort of problems that he himself was encountering at that time: the role of the young in a changing society, ill-fated young love, and military service. At the end of 1948 he directed his first film based on an original screenplay of his own, *Fängelse* (1949; *Prison*, or *The Devil's Wanton*). It recapitulated all the themes of his previous films in a complex, perhaps overambitious story, built around the romantic and professional problems of a young film director who considers making a film based on the idea that the devil rules the world. While this is not to be taken without qualification as Bergman's message in his early work, it may at least be said that his imaginative world is divided very sharply between the worlds of good and evil, the latter always overshadowing the former, the devil lying in wait at the end of each idyll.

In 1951 Bergman's career in films, like nearly the whole of Swedish filmmaking, came to an abrupt halt as the result of a major economic crisis in Sweden. But in 1952 he returned with two films, *Kvinnors väntan* (*Waiting Women*, or *Secrets of Women*) and *Sommaren med Monika* (*Summer with Monika*, or *Monika*), that marked the beginning of his mature work. He was also appointed director of the Malmö municipal theatre, where he remained until 1959. This new phase introduced two markedly new characteristics in his work. In subject matter, Bergman, now himself married, returned again and again to the question of marriage. Viewing it from many angles, he examined the ways by which two people adjust to living together, their motives for being faithful or unfaithful to each other, and their reactions to bringing children into the world. At this time Bergman began to gather around him, in his film and stage productions, a faithful "stock company" of actors with whom he worked regularly to give his work and their interpretation of it a manifest consistency and style.

In 1955 Bergman had his first great international success with *Sommernattens leende* (*Smiles of a Summer Night*), a bittersweet romantic comedy-drama in a period setting. In the next few years, a kind of Bergman fever swept over the international film scene: concurrently with the succession of his new films, which included two masterpieces, *The Seventh Seal* (1957), a medieval morality play, and *Wild Strawberries* (1957), a meditation on old age, all of his early work was shown, and Bergman was universally recognized as one of the most important figures in cinema. Indeed, a far wider section of the cultured public became aware of his work than of that of any previous filmmaker; for the first time a filmmaker was as widely and as highly regarded as artists in any of the more traditional media.

Inevitably, a reaction set in, though Bergman continued to make films and direct plays with undiminished activity; and his trilogy of films, *Through a Glass Darkly*, *Winter Light,* and *The Silence,* dealing with the border line between sanity and madness and that between human contact and total withdrawal, was regarded by many as his crowning achievement. *Through a Glass Darkly* won an Academy Award for best foreign film.

About this time, Bergman acquired a country home on the bleak island of Fårö; and the island provided a characteristic stage for the dramas of a whole series of films that included *Persona* (1966), *Vargtimmen* (1968; *Hour of the Wolf*), *Skammen* (1968; *Shame*), and *En passion* (1969; *The Passion*, or *The Passion of Anna*), all dramas of inner conflicts involving a small, closely knit group of characters. With *Beröringen* (1971; *The Touch*), his first English-language film, Bergman returned to an urban setting and more romantic subject matter, though fundamentally the characters in the film's marital triangle are no less mixed up than any in the Fårö cycle of films; and then *Viskingar och rop* (1972; *Cries and Whispers*), *Scener ur ett aktenskap* (1974; *Scenes from a Marriage*), and *Herbstsonate* (1978; *Autumn Sonata*), all dealing compassionately with intimate family relationships, won popular as well as critical fame. Throughout the years, Bergman continued to direct for the stage, most notably at

Stockholm's Royal Dramatic Theatre. In 1977 he received the Swedish Academy of Letters Great Gold Medal, and in the following year the Swedish Film Institute established a prize for excellence in filmmaking in his name. *Fanny och Alexander* (1983; *Fanny and Alexander*), in which the fortunes and misfortunes of a wealthy theatrical family in turn-of-the-century Sweden are portrayed through the eyes of a young boy, earned an Academy Award for best foreign film.

Bergman also directed a number of television movies, notably the critically acclaimed *Saraband* (2003), which featured the main characters from *Scenes from a Marriage*; the movie received a theatrical release. In addition, he wrote several novels, including *Söndagsbarn* (1993; *Sunday's Children*) and *Enskilda samtal* (1996; *Private Confessions*), that were made into films. His memoir, *Laterna magica* (*The Magic Lantern*), was published in 1987.

ASSESSMENT

Bergman established a worldwide reputation for writing and directing films that, in an unmistakably individual style, examine the issues of morality by exploring man's relationship to himself, to others, and to God. His work and the worldwide vogue it enjoyed in the late 1950s and early 1960s introduced many people for the first time to the idea of the total filmmaker, the writer-director who throughout a sizable body of work uses the medium of film to express his own ideas and perceptions, with as much ease and conviction as artists in earlier generations used the novel or the symphony or the fresco. In addition, the immense international popularity of his films has tended to ensure that Bergman's picture of Sweden and the Swedish temperament is the first and often the only impression received by the outside world; and when other Swedish films seem to present much the same image, it is usually because the influence of Bergman on his Swedish colleagues is so pervasive rather than because his highly personal vision should be taken as an objectively true portrait of his country.

Bergman's anguished appraisal of the human situation lost nothing of its intensity through the years; rather, he progressively stripped away the distracting decorations in his films to create an abstract drama of man's relation with man and perhaps with God (if he exists). He dealt with man's attempt to define his own personality by removing his masks to see if there is a face underneath. The images of the creator as actor and the creator as magician recur throughout Bergman's work. He himself embodied elements of both the thinker and the actor, the preacher and the charlatan; in Bergman they all fused to create an artist of great force and individuality whose work is always unmistakably his own.

FEDERICO FELLINI

(b. Jan. 20, 1920, Rimini, Italy—d. Oct.31, 1993, Rome, Italy)

Federico Fellini was an Italian film director who was one of the most celebrated and distinctive filmmakers of the period after World War II. Early in his career he helped inaugurate the Neorealist cinema movement, but he soon developed his own distinctive style of typically autobiographical films that imposed dreamlike or hallucinatory imagery upon ordinary situations and portrayed people at their most bizarre.

EARLY LIFE AND INFLUENCES

After an uneventful provincial childhood during which he developed a talent as a cartoonist, Fellini at age 19 moved to Rome, where he contributed cartoons, gags, and stories to the humour magazine *Marc'Aurelio*. During World War II, Fellini worked as a scriptwriter for the radio program *Cico e Pallina*, starring Giulietta Masina, the actress who became Fellini's wife in 1943 and who went on to star in several of the director's greatest films during the course of their 50-year marriage. In 1944 Fellini met director Roberto Rossellini, who engaged him as one of a team of writers who created *Roma, città aperta* (1945; *Open City* or *Rome, Open City*), often cited as the seminal film of the Italian Neorealist movement. Fellini's contribution to the screenplay earned him his first Oscar nomination.

Fellini quickly became one of Italy's most successful screenwriters. Although he wrote a number of important scripts for such directors as Pietro Germi (*Il cammino della speranza* [1950; *The Path of Hope*]), Alberto Lattuada (*Senza pietá* [1948; *Without Pity*]), and Luigi Comencini (*Persiane chiuse* [1951; *Drawn Shutters*]), his scripts for Rossellini are most important to the history of the Italian cinema. These include *Paisà* (1946; *Paisan*), perhaps the purest example of Italian Neorealism; *Il miracolo* (1948; "The Miracle," an episode of the film *L'Amore*), a controversial work on the meaning of sainthood; and *Europa '51* (1952; *The Greatest Love*), one of the first films in postwar Italy that began to move beyond the documentary realism of the Neorealist period toward an examination of psychological problems and Existentialist themes.

Fellini made his debut as director in collaboration with Lattuada on *Luci del varietà* (1951; *Variety Lights*). This was the first in a series of works dealing with provincial life and was followed by *Lo sceicco bianco* (1951; *The White Sheik*) and *I vitelloni* (1953; *Spivs* or *The Young and the Passionate*), his first critically and commercially successful work. This film, a bitterly sarcastic look at the idle "mama's boys" of the provinces, is still considered by some critics to be Fellini's masterpiece.

MAJOR WORKS

Fellini's next films formed a trilogy that dealt with salvation and the fate of innocence in a cruel and unsentimental world. One of Fellini's best-known works, the heavily symbolic *La strada* (1954; "The Road"), stars Anthony Quinn as a cruel, animalistic circus strongman and Masina as the pathetic waif who loves him. The film was shot on location in the desolate countryside between Viterbo and Abruzzo, with the great empty spaces reflecting the virtual inhumanity of the relationship between the principal characters. Although it was criticized by the left-wing press in Italy, the film was highly praised abroad, winning an Academy Award for best foreign film. *Il bidone* (1955; *The Swindle*), which starred Broderick Crawford in a role intended for Humphrey Bogart, was a rather unpleasant tale of petty swindlers who disguise themselves as priests in order to rob the peasantry. Garnering a second foreign film Oscar for Fellini was the more successful *Le notti di Cabiria* (1957; *The Nights of Cabiria*), again starring Masina, this time as a simple, eternally optimistic Roman prostitute. Although not usually considered among Fellini's greatest works, *Le notti de Cabiria* (upon which the Broadway musical comedy *Sweet Charity* was based)

Fellini's next film, *La dolce vita* (1960; "The Sweet Life"), was his first collaboration with Marcello Mastroianni, the actor who would come to represent Fellini's alter ego in several films throughout the next two decades. The film—for which Fellini had Rome's main thoroughfare, the Via Veneto, rebuilt as a set—proved to be a panorama of the times, rife with surreal imagery, and a compelling indictment of popular media, decadent intellectuals, and aristocrats. Immediately hailed as one of the most important films ever made, *La dolce vita* contributed the word *paparazzi* (unscrupulous yellow-press photographers) to the English language and the adjective "Felliniesque" to the lexicon of film critics.

Regarded as a perfect blend of symbolism and realism, *Otto e mezzo* (1963; *8 1/2*), is perhaps Fellini's most widely praised film and earned the director his third Oscar for best foreign film. Entitled *8 1/2* for the number of films Fellini had made to that time (seven features and three shorts), the work shows the plight of a famous director (based on Fellini, portrayed by Mastroianni) in creative paralysis. The high modernist aesthetics of the film became emblematic of the very notion of free, uninhibited artistic creativity, and in 1987 a panel of motion picture scholars from 18 European nations named *8 1/2* the best European film ever made.

In the wake of *8 1/2* Fellini's name became firmly linked to the vogue of the postwar European art film. He began to deal with the myth of Rome, the cinema, and, especially, the director's own life and fantasy world, all of which Fellini considered interrelated themes in his works. His films of the late 1960s combine dreamlike images with original uses of colour photography. *Satyricon* (1969), inspired by such ancient Roman writers as Petronius and Apuleius, tells of the wanderings of a group of aimless young men in the world of antiquity. Fellini, who was unconcerned with historical accuracy, attempted to explore the human condition in an age before Christianity and the concept of original sin. A bizarre, flamboyant work, *Satyricon* remains a film on which critical opinion is heatedly divided. *Roma* (1971; *Fellini's Roma*) is the director's personal portrait of the Eternal City, and *Amarcord* (1973), which won Fellini a fourth Oscar for best foreign film, offers a nostalgic remembrance of Fellini's provincial adolescence during the Fascist period.

MATURE YEARS

Many of Fellini's later films were less successful commercially and encountered critical resistance. The sumptuous *Casanova* (1976), praised by some as a visual masterpiece and derided by others as a hollow confection, was a brooding, melancholy meditation on the meaning of sex and death. Such works as *La città delle donne* (1980; *City of Women*), *E la nave va* (1983; *And the Ship Sails On*), *Ginger e Fred* (1985; *Ginger and Fred*), *Intervista* (1987; *Interview*), and *La voce della luna* (1989; *The Voice of the Moon*), his last feature film, reflect the complex evolution of Fellini's mature cinematic style and treat a variety of postmodern topics: the role of the male in an increasingly feminist society, the effects of television on contemporary life, the nature of artistic creativity, and the growing homogenization of popular culture. During the last years of his life, Fellini produced television commercials for Barilla pasta, Campari Soda, and the Banco di Roma that are regarded as extraordinary lessons in cinematography revealing the director's deep grasp of popular culture. He also exhibited his sketches and cartoons, many of which were taken from his private dream notebooks, thus uncovering the source of much of his artistic creativity, the unconscious.

ASSESSMENT

Although the subject of derision from some revisionist critics, Fellini assured for himself a place of prime importance in the history of filmmaking. His best films, all of which were partially written by him, are freely structured tales in which dream and reality, as well as autobiography and fantasy, mingle in a world of symbolism. Breaking with traditional techniques of motion picture production, he succeeded in making the film such a personal medium that his own creative and personal problems became legendary. He received numerous honours during his lifetime, including 8 Oscars, 23 Oscar nominations, a career achievement Oscar in 1993, the Golden Lion career award from the Venice Film Festival in 1985, and dozens of prizes from the world's most prestigious film festivals. A poll of international film directors conducted in 1992 by *Sight and Sound* magazine ranked Fellini as the most significant film director of all time and cited two of Fellini's works (*La strada* and *8 1/2*) in a list of the 10 most influential films of all time.

SATYAJIT RAY

(b. May 2, 1921, Calcutta, India—d. April 23, 1992, Calcutta)

S atyajit Ray was a Bengali motion-picture director, writer, and illustrator who brought the Indian cinema to world recognition with *Pather Panchali* (1955; *The Song of the Road*) and its two sequels, known as the Apu Trilogy. As a director Ray was noted for his humanism, his versatility, and his detailed control over his films and their music. He was one of the greatest filmmakers of the 20th century.

Ray was an only child whose father died in 1923. His grandfather was a writer and illustrator, and his father, Sukumar Ray, was a writer and illustrator of Bengali nonsense verse. Ray grew up in Calcutta and was looked after by his mother. He entered a government school, where he was taught chiefly in Bengali, and then studied at Presidency College, Calcutta's leading college, where he was taught in English. By the time he graduated in 1940, he was fluent in both languages. In 1940 his mother persuaded him to attend art school at Santiniketan, Rabindranath Tagore's rural university northwest of Calcutta. There Ray, whose interests had been exclusively urban and Western-oriented, was exposed to Indian and other Eastern art and gained a deeper appreciation of both Eastern and Western culture, a harmonious combination that is evident in his films.

Returning to Calcutta, Ray in 1943 got a job in a British-owned advertising agency, became its art director within a few years, and also worked for a publishing house as a commercial illustrator, becoming a leading Indian typographer and book-jacket designer. Among the books he illustrated (1944) was the novel *Pather Panchali* by Bibhuti Bhushan Banarjee, the cinematic possibilities of which began to intrigue him. Ray had long been an avid filmgoer, and his deepening interest in the medium inspired his first attempts to write screenplays and his cofounding (1947) of the Calcutta Film Society. In 1949 Ray was encouraged in his cinematic ambitions by the French director Jean Renoir, who was then in Bengal to shoot *The River*. The success of Vittorio De Sica's *The Bicycle Thief* (1948), with its downbeat story and its economy of means—location shooting with nonprofessional actors—convinced Ray that he should attempt to film *Pather Panchali*.

But Ray was unable to raise money from skeptical Bengali producers, who distrusted a first-time director with such unconventional ideas. Shooting could not begin until late 1952, using Ray's own money, with the rest eventually coming from a grudging West Bengal government. The film took two-and-a-half years to complete, with the crew, most of whom lacked any experience whatsoever in motion pictures, working on an unpaid basis. *Pather Panchali* was completed in 1955 and turned out to be both a commercial and a tremendous critical success, first in Bengal and then in the West following a major award at the 1956 Cannes International Film Festival. This assured Ray the financial backing he needed to make the other two films of the trilogy: *Aparajito* (1956; *The Unvanquished*) and *Apur Sansar* (1959; *The World of Apu*). *Pather Panchali* and its sequels tell the story of Apu, the poor son of a Brahman priest, as he grows from childhood to manhood in a setting that shifts from a small village to the city of Calcutta. Western influences impinge more and more on Apu, who, instead of being satisfied to be a rustic priest, conceives troubling ambitions to be a novelist. The conflict between tradition and modernity is the great theme spanning all three films, which in a sense portray the awakening of India in the first half of the 20th century.

Ray never returned to this saga form, his subsequent films becoming more and more concentrated in time, with an emphasis on psychology rather than conventional narrative. He also consciously avoided repeating himself. As a result, his films span an unusually wide gamut of mood, milieu, period, and genre, with comedies, tragedies, romances, musicals, and detective stories treating all classes of Bengali society from the mid-19th to the late 20th century. Most of Ray's characters are, however, of average ability and talents—unlike the subjects of his documentary films, which include *Rabindranath Tagore* (1961) and *The Inner Eye* (1972). It was the inner struggle and corruption of the conscience-stricken person that fascinated Ray; his films primarily concern thought and feeling, rather than action and plot.

Some of Ray's finest films were based on novels or other works by Rabindranath Tagore, who was the principal creative influence on the director. Among such works, *Charulata* (1964; *The Lonely Wife*), a tragic love triangle set within a wealthy, Western-influenced Bengali family in 1879, is perhaps Ray's most accomplished film. *Teen Kanya* (1961; "Three Daughters," English-language title *Two Daughters*) is a varied trilogy of short films about women, while *Ghare Baire* (1984; *The Home and the World*) is a sombre study of Bengal's first revolutionary movement, set in 1907–08 during the period of British rule.

Ray's major films about Hindu orthodoxy and feudal values (and their potential clash with modern Western-inspired reforms) include *Jalsaghar* (1958; *The Music Room*), an impassioned evocation of a man's obsession with music; *Devi* (1960; *The Goddess*), in which the obsession is with a girl's divine incarnation; *Sadgati* (1981; *Deliverance*), a powerful indictment of caste; and *Kanchenjungha* (1962), Ray's first original screenplay and first colour film, a subtle exploration of arranged marriage among wealthy, westernized Bengalis. *Shatranj ke Khilari* (1977; *The Chess Players*), Ray's first film made in the Hindi language, with a comparatively large budget, is an even subtler probing of the impact of the West on India. Set in Lucknow in 1856, just before the Indian Mutiny, it depicts the downfall of the ruler Wajid Ali at the hands of the British with exquisite irony and pathos.

Although humour is evident in almost all of Ray's films, it is particularly marked in the comedy *Parash Pathar* (1957; *The Philosopher's Stone*) and in the musical *Goopy Gyne Bagha Byne* (1969; *The Adventures of Goopy and Bagha*), based on a story by his grandfather. The songs composed by Ray for the latter are among his best-known contributions to Bengali culture.

The rest of Ray's major work—with the exception of his moving story of the Bengal Famine of 1943–44, *Ahsani Sanket* (1973; *Distant Thunder*)—chiefly concerns Calcutta and modern Calcuttans. *Aranyer Din Ratri* (1970; *Days and Nights in the Forest*) observes the adventures of four young men trying to escape urban mores on a trip to the country, and failing. *Mahanagar* (1963; *The Big City*) and a trilogy of films made in the 1970s—*Pratidwandi* (1970; *The Adversary*), *Seemabaddha* (1971; *Company Limited*), and *Jana*

Aranya (1975; *The Middleman*)—examine the struggle for employment of the middle class against a background (from 1970) of revolutionary, Maoist-inspired violence, government repression, and insidious corruption. After a gap in which Ray made *Pikoo* (1980) and then fell ill with heart disease, he returned to the subject of corruption in society. *Ganashatru* (1989; *An Enemy of the People*), an Indianized version of Henrik Ibsen's play, *Shakha Prashakha* (1990; *Branches of the Tree*), and the sublime *Agantuk* (1991; *The Stranger*), with their strong male central characters, each represent a facet of Ray's own personality, defiantly protesting against the intellectual and moral decay of his beloved Bengal.

The motion-picture director also established a parallel career in Bengal as a writer and an illustrator, chiefly for young people. He revived the children's magazine *Sandesh* (which his grandfather had started in 1913) and edited it until his death in 1992. Ray was the author of numerous short stories and novellas, and in fact writing, rather than filmmaking, became his main source of income. His stories have been translated and published in Europe, the United States, and elsewhere. Some of Ray's writings on cinema are collected in *Our Films, Their Films* (1976). His other works include the memoir *Yakhana chota chilama* (1982; *Childhood Days*).

JUDY GARLAND

(b. June 10, 1922, Grand Rapids, Minn., U.S.–d. June 22, 1969, London, Eng.)

Frances Ethel Gumm, better known by her byname Judy Garland, was an American singer and actress whose exceptional talents and vulnerabilities combined to make her one of the most enduringly popular Hollywood icons of the 20th century.

Frances Gumm was the daughter of former vaudevillians Frank Gumm and Ethel Gumm, who operated the New Grand Theatre in Grand Rapids, Minn., where on Dec. 26, 1924, at age 2 ½, Frances made her debut. In 1932 — by that time a 10-year-old singing sensation — she received her first rave review from the entertainment news magazine *Variety*, and two years later, at the suggestion of the comedian George Jessel, she adopted the surname Garland. (She chose the first name Judy shortly thereafter, from the popular 1934 Hoagy Carmichael song of that name.) In September 1935, Judy Garland was signed by the world's largest motion-picture studio, Metro-Goldwyn-Mayer (MGM), without a screen test.

Her first film appearance as a contract player for MGM was in the short *Every Sunday* (1936). Her other early films include *Pigskin Parade* (which she made while on loan to Twentieth Century-Fox in 1936) and *Broadway Melody of 1938* (1937), in which she sang "You Made Me Love You." That was the first of many trademark songs. She began her popular screen partnership with Mickey Rooney in *Thoroughbreds Don't Cry* (1937); the pairing continued through *Love Finds Andy Hardy* (1938), *Babes in Arms* (1939), *Strike Up the Band* (1940), *Babes on Broadway* (1941), and *Girl Crazy* (1943).

Garland's winning combination of youth, innocence, pluck, and emotional openness is seen to good advantage in two of her best-known films: *The Wizard of Oz* (1939) and *Meet Me in St. Louis* (1944). In the former, her heartfelt expression of vulnerability and youthful longing in what would become another signature song, "Over the Rainbow," helped make the film one of the most beloved movie classics. It also brought Garland her first and only Academy Award, a special award with a miniature statuette for "outstanding performance by a screen juvenile." She played her last juvenile role in *Meet Me in St. Louis*, directed by her future husband Vincente Minnelli (with whom she had a daughter, Liza). In it she sang such hits as "Have Yourself a Merry Little Christmas" and "The Boy Next Door."

Of the 21 additional films she made in the 1940s, perhaps *The Harvey Girls* (1946) and *Easter Parade* (1948) are the best known. Despite placing in the Top Ten box office three times during the 1940s, making more than $100 million for the studio, and being considered the studio's greatest asset, Garland was granted an early release from her MGM contract in September 1950, following completion of *Summer Stock* (1950). The following year she returned to the stage, with triumphant performances at the London Palladium and New York's Palace Theatre. Her comeback was capped with the Warner Bros. musical *A Star Is Born* (1954), a three-hour showcase for all of Garland's talents. It was in this film, the last of the three with which she is most associated, that Garland's persona achieved maturity. Pitted against Dorothy Dandridge (*Carmen Jones*), Audrey Hepburn (*Sabrina*), Jane Wyman (*Magnificent Obsession*), and Grace Kelly (*The Country Girl*) for the best actress Oscar that year, Garland was favoured to win, but she lost to Grace Kelly in what comedian Groucho Marx called "the greatest robbery since Brinks" (a reference to the 1950 robbery of the Brinks Building in Boston, which was then the largest U.S. armed robbery).

Garland appeared in five more films, including *Judgment at Nuremberg* (1961), for which she garnered an Oscar nomination for best supporting actress, and the somewhat autobiographical *I Could Go On Singing* (1963), her only movie shot outside the United States.

Her film career has long overshadowed her success as a recording artist, but from 1936 to 1947 she cut more than 90 tracks for Decca Records, and she made a dozen record albums for Capitol Records between 1955 and 1965. She frequently made the best-seller charts from 1939 to 1967, working with such top arrangers as Mort Lindsey, Nelson Riddle, Jack Marshall, and Gordon Jenkins. These recordings reveal her sensitivity and intelligence as an interpreter of popular song.

After doctors told her in 1959 that decades of stress from overwork would prevent her from further performance, Garland staged her greatest comeback ever, with a 1960–61 series of one-woman concerts around the world, culminating in New York's Carnegie Hall. The two-record recording of this concert, *Judy at Carnegie Hall* (1961), revealed her intense connection to her audiences and proved to be her biggest-selling album. It won five Grammy Awards—including album of the year and best female vocal performance—and spent about a year and a half on the charts, staying at number one for 13 weeks. The album has never gone out of print, and a Fortieth Anniversary Edition was issued on compact disc by Capitol Records in 2001. Further, in 2003 the album was deemed "culturally, historically, or aesthetically" significant and placed on the National Recording Registry.

In the early 1960s Garland appeared often on television, hosting a weekly hour-long variety series, *The Judy Garland Show*, for 26 episodes during the 1963–64 season. Although she had been signed for a record amount of money, and the show revealed a concert artist at her peak, it was canceled after half a year.

During the mid- to late 1960s, Garland concentrated on concert performances and made appearances on the top television variety and talk shows of the day. A month-long third engagement at the Palace Theatre resulted in another popular album, *At Home at the Palace* (1967). Garland continued working until her death at age 47 by accidental barbiturate overdose. Her funeral in New York City drew 22,000 mourners.

Over the decades since her death and as the star of *The Wizard of Oz*, the movie seen by more people than any other in film history, Garland has remained an iconic American entertainer. Singer Frank Sinatra expressed the feelings of countless fans when he said, "She will have a mystic survival. She was the greatest. The rest of us will be forgotten, but never Judy."

MARLON BRANDO
(b. April 3, 1924, Omaha, Neb., U.S.–d. July 1, 2004, Los Angeles, Calif., U.S.)

Marlon Brando, Jr. was an American motion picture and stage actor known for his visceral, brooding characterizations. Brando was the most celebrated of the method actors, and his slurred, mumbling delivery marked his rejection of classical dramatic training. His true and passionate performances proved him one of the greatest actors of his generation.

Brando, the son of a salesman and an actress, grew up in Nebraska, California, and Illinois. After he was expelled from the Shattuck Military Academy in Faribault, Minnesota, for insubordination, he moved in 1943 to New York City, where he studied acting under Stella Adler at the Dramatic Workshop. He made his stage debut in 1944 as Jesus Christ in the Workshop production of Gerhart Hauptmann's *Hannele*, and in that same year he first appeared on Broadway in *I Remember Mama*. After that play's successful two-year run, Brando appeared in Maxwell Anderson's *Truckline Cafe*, George Bernard Shaw's *Candida*, and Ben Hecht's *A Flag Is Born* (all 1946) and was voted "Broadway's most promising actor" by New York critics. In 1947 he attained stage stardom with his astonishingly brutal, emotionally charged performance as Stanley Kowalski in the Elia Kazan-directed

Marlon Brando in A Streetcar Named Desire *(1951)*.

production of Tennessee Williams's *A Streetcar Named Desire* (1947).

Brando made his motion picture debut in *The Men* (1950), a powerfully realistic study of disabled World War II veterans. In preparation for his role, he spent a month in a hospital paraplegic ward. He received his first Oscar nomination for his performance in *A Streetcar Named Desire* (1951), Kazan's highly praised screen adaptation of the play, and went on to receive nominations for his performances in *Viva Zapata!* (1952) and *Julius Caesar* (1953). Also from this period is *The Wild One* (1953), a low-budget drama in which he played the leader of an outlaw motorcycle gang. The film became one of Brando's most famous and served to enhance his iconoclastic image. It also contains one of Brando's most oft-quoted lines; when asked what it is he is rebelling against, his character responds, "Whaddya got?"

Brando's sensitive portrayal of a union muscleman who testifies against his gangster boss in Kazan's *On the Waterfront* (1954) won for him the best-actor Oscar and firmly established him as one of Hollywood's most-admired actors. In 1954 he also portrayed Napoleon Bonaparte in *Desiree*, and in 1955 he sang and danced in the musical comedy *Guys and Dolls*. He had continued success with such films as *The Teahouse of the August Moon* (1956), *Sayonara* (1957; Oscar nomination), and *The Young Lions* (1958). In the 1960s, however, his career went into a long period of decline. He starred in the only film he ever directed, the western *One-Eyed Jacks* (1961); now a cult favourite, it was notorious at the time for Brando's excessive expenditure of time and money. A lavish remake of *Mutiny on the Bounty* (1962) was another expensive flop, and Brando's recalcitrant behaviour during its filming added to his growing reputation as a troublesome and demanding actor. Most of his remaining films of the '60s, including Charlie Chaplin's final film, *A Countess from Hong Kong* (1967), are forgettable.

Francis Ford Coppola's *The Godfather* (1972) rejuvenated Brando's career. As organized-crime boss Don Vito Corleone, Brando created one of the most memorable—and most imitated—film characters of all time. His performance earned him another best-actor Oscar, but he refused the award in protest against the stereotypical portrayals of Native Americans throughout motion picture history. Brando was further vindicated as an actor by his leading role in Bernardo Bertolucci's sexually explicit *L'ultimo tango a Parigi* (1972; *Last Tango in Paris*). He appeared in only five more films during the remainder of the decade—including noted supporting roles in *Superman* (1978) and *Apocalypse Now* (1979)—whereupon he retreated to his private Polynesian atoll.

Brando reemerged nine years later to play a crusading antiapartheid attorney in *A Dry White Season* (1989) and received his eighth Oscar nomination—his first for best supporting actor—for the role. He appeared in six films during the 1990s, highlighted by a send-up of his *Godfather* character in *The Freshman* (1990) and by his sensitive portrayal of an aging psychiatrist in *Don Juan DeMarco* (1995). He also received good notices for his role as a corrupt prison warden in the comedy *Free Money* (1998), though the film was not widely distributed. In 2001 he appeared in the heist thriller *The Score* (2001). Brando's extensive collection of personal audio diaries—recorded over many years—were the basis of the documentary *Listen to Me Marlon* (2015).

Brando was something of a paradox: he is regarded as the most influential actor of his generation, yet his open disdain for the acting profession—as detailed in his autobiography, *Songs My Mother Taught Me* (1994)—often manifested itself in the form of questionable choices and uninspired performances. Nevertheless, he remains a riveting screen presence with a vast emotional range and an endless array of compulsively watchable idiosyncrasies.

PAUL NEWMAN

(b. Jan. 26, 1925, Cleveland, Ohio, U.S.–d. Sept. 26, 2008, Westport, Conn., U.S.)

Paul Leonard Newman was an American actor and director whose striking good looks, intelligence, and charisma became hallmarks in a film career that spanned more than 50 years, during which time he became known for his compelling performances of iconic antiheroes. He was also active in a number of philanthropic endeavours.

EARLY LIFE

Newman grew up in Shaker Heights, Ohio. He attended Ohio University—from which he was reportedly expelled—before serving as a navy radio operator during World War II. Upon his discharge, he enrolled at Ohio's Kenyon College (B.A., 1949), where he acted in a number of plays. After graduation he appeared in stock productions, but he returned home following the death of his father in 1950. Newman ran the family's sporting-goods store for one year before enrolling in Yale University's drama department. He left the program in 1952 and moved to New York City, where he studied at The Actors Studio, which he credited for his later acting success.

FIRST FILMS

In 1953 Newman made his Broadway debut in William Inge's *Picnic*. While working on the production, he met Joanne Woodward, an understudy; the two married in 1958

PAUL NEWMAN

and became one of Hollywood's most-enduring couples. Newman's performance in *Picnic* led to a film contract with Warner Brothers, and in 1954 he made his first feature, the widely panned *The Silver Chalice*, which the actor claimed was the worst movie made in the 1950s. Despite his inauspicious film debut, Newman was earning positive reviews for his work in live television dramas, notably *Our Town* (1955) and *Bang the Drum Slowly* (1956), which aired on *Producers' Showcase* and *The United States Steel Hour*, respectively. In addition, he continued to act on the stage.

Classically handsome—with piercing blue eyes—and possessing a natural magnetism, Newman was soon offered another screen role. In 1956 he starred in Robert Wise's *Somebody Up There Likes Me*, and his impressive portrayal of boxer Rocky Graziano secured his future in films. A string of acclaimed performances in notable dramas soon followed. *Cat on a Hot Tin Roof* (1958) was a highly praised adaptation of the Tennessee Williams play that also starred Elizabeth Taylor and Burl Ives; for his performance as a self-destructive former football player who is at odds with his father, Newman earned his first Academy Award nomination. *The Long, Hot Summer* (1958), which was based on short stories by William Faulkner, was the first of 10 feature films in which he would costar with Woodward. The drama centres on a drifter who becomes entangled with a wealthy family. In the biopic *The Left Handed Gun* (1958), Newman appeared as Billy the Kid. He closed out the decade with the melodrama *The Young Philadelphians* (1959), in which he played a manipulative attorney.

THE ANTIHEROES: "FAST" EDDIE FELSON TO BUTCH CASSIDY

In 1960 Newman led an international cast in Otto Preminger's epic film *Exodus*, based on the novel by Leon

Uris about the founding of Israel. In 1961 he essayed the role that perhaps best defined his screen persona, that of pool shark "Fast" Eddie Felson in *The Hustler*. Earning him another Oscar nomination, *The Hustler* was the first in a series of 1960s films in which Newman eschewed more-traditional leading-man roles to portray antiheroic protagonists. In *Hud* (1963)—which was based on the Larry McMurtry novel *Horseman, Pass By*—he played a womanizing self-centred manipulator who is anxious to control his aging father's cattle empire. In a testament to Newman's likability, moviegoers embraced the character, much to the surprise of the actor, who received his third Oscar nomination. The mystery *Harper* (1966) featured the actor as a hard-drinking private detective. He reprised the role for the 1975 sequel, *The Drowning Pool*. After Alfred Hitchcock's *Torn Curtain* (1966), Newman starred in the revisionist western *Hombre* (1967), which was based on an Elmore Leonard novel. In *Cool Hand Luke* (1967) Newman gave another Oscar-nominated performance, creating one of the screen's most-memorable characters, a wisecracking convict who stands up to his sadistic jailers. The series of performances solidified Newman's image as an ingratiating iconoclast.

Two enormously popular films teamed Newman with costar Robert Redford and director George Roy Hill. The comic western *Butch Cassidy and the Sundance Kid* (1969) received seven Oscar nominations and was among the top-grossing films of the year. In 1973 the pair portrayed Depression-era con men in *The Sting*, a widely seen work that won the Academy Award for best picture.

LATER ROLES

Newman worked for a number of noted directors on pictures that were box-office failures at the time of their release but went on to become cult favourites. He played alongside Lee Marvin and Strother Martin in the antiheroic western *Pocket Money* (1972), directed by Stuart Rosenberg. John Huston directed Newman in the title role of the darkly comic *The Life and Times of Judge Roy Bean* (1972) and again in the British private-eye thriller *The Mackintosh Man* (1973). Director Robert Altman used Newman effectively in his spoof on American western folklore, *Buffalo Bill and the Indians* (1976), and again in the controversial *Quintet* (1979), a futuristic saga. Newman also maintained his star status by appearing in such popular films as *The Towering Inferno* (1974), an action thriller that starred Steve McQueen and William Holden; *Slap Shot* (1977), a comedy about a hapless minor-league hockey team that is often ranked among the best sports films; and *Fort Apache, the Bronx* (1981), in which he starred as a policeman who refuses to cover up a murder. In Sydney Pollack's *Absence of Malice* (1981), Newman gave an Oscar-nominated performance as a businessman whom a reporter (played by Sally Field) wrongly implicates in a murder. He also received an Academy Award nomination for his work in *The Verdict* (1982), a courtroom drama about an alcoholic lawyer in a malpractice case.

Having received six Academy Award nominations for best actor and one career-achievement Oscar (1985), Newman finally won an Academy Award for director Martin Scorsese's *The Color of Money* (1986), the sequel to *The Hustler*. In 1989 he portrayed Louisiana Gov. Earl K. Long in *Blaze*. At age 70 he was nominated yet again, for his depiction of Sully, an irresponsible yet humorous construction worker in *Nobody's Fool* (1994), directed by Robert Benton and based on the novel by Richard Russo; Newman once claimed that the character was the closest to himself that he had ever played. That same year the actor gave a broadly satirical performance as an unscrupulous tycoon in Joel and Ethan Coen's *The Hudsucker Proxy*. Benton also directed him in the detective thriller *Twilight* (1998).

Subsequent roles for Newman included a mob boss in Sam Mendes's *Road to Perdition* (2002), which earned him another Oscar nomination. In 2005 he starred with Woodward in the television miniseries *Empire Falls* (2005), which was based on a Russo novel; Newman won an Emmy, a Golden Globe, and a Screen Actors Guild Award for his portrayal of the cantankerous father of protagonist Miles Roby (Ed Harris). After he voiced a character in the animated film *Cars* (2006), Newman retired in 2007, saying, "I'm not able to work anymore as an actor at the level I would want to...so that's pretty much a closed book to me." That year he was diagnosed with cancer, which would prove fatal.

DIRECTING

Newman occasionally directed films. He frequently cast Woodward in the lead—beginning with *Rachel, Rachel* (1968), a subtle but powerful drama about a repressed schoolteacher; it earned an Oscar nomination for best picture. Newman next directed and starred in an adaptation of Ken Kesey's sprawling novel about Oregon loggers, *Sometimes a Great Notion* (1971). Although a disappointment at the box office, the film received generally positive reviews. In 1972 Newman helmed *The Effect of Gamma Rays on Man-in-the-Moon Marigolds*, which was based on Paul Zindel's Pulitzer Prize-winning play. Woodward starred as an overbearing mother whose daughters long to escape from her domineering presence. The potent *The Shadow Box* (1980) was a made-for-TV movie about the interaction among three terminally ill patients and their visiting families; it starred Woodward, Valerie Harper, and Christopher Plummer.

Harry & Son (1984) featured Newman and Robby Benson as a widowed father and his unsympathetic son, respectively. However, the dynamics were less than convincing, despite a screenplay cowritten by Newman. In 1987 Newman directed his last film, *The Glass Menagerie*, which was a tasteful adaptation of Tennessee Williams's classic play; Woodward, John Malkovich, Karen Allen, and James Naughton starred.

PHILANTHROPY

A noted political liberal, Newman was outspoken in support of causes such as same-sex marriage and global disarmament, and he occasionally wrote articles for *The Nation*. He was also a businessman and a philanthropist. He launched the successful Newman's Own line of food products in 1982, with its profits going to a number of charitable causes. Some 25 years after its founding, the food line comprised about 80 products and was sold worldwide, generating a reported $250 million of profits donated to charity. Newman joked, "The embarrassing thing is that the salad dressing is outgrossing my films." In 2008 he turned over his ownership of the firm to the Newman's Own Foundation.

Newman's other philanthropic works included the Scott Newman Foundation (later Scott Newman Center), an organization he established in 1980 to educate the public about substance abuse; it was created in honour of his son (from his first marriage), who had died of an accidental overdose of drugs and alcohol in 1978. In 1988 he founded the Hole in the Wall Gang Camp in northeastern Connecticut for children with serious medical conditions; at the beginning of the 21st century, Hole in the Wall had expanded to 14 camps located around the world. Newman

THE 100 MOST INFLUENTIAL ENTERTAINERS OF STAGE AND SCREEN

later helped establish (2006) a gourmet restaurant to support the Westport Country Playhouse, a theatre group in which he and Woodward were long active.

A passionate race-car driver since the early 1970s, Newman became co-owner of Newman/Haas Racing in 1982. In 2003 he cowrote the memoir *Shameless Exploitation in Pursuit of the Common Good* with Newman's Own business partner A.E. Hotchner. Newman was the recipient of numerous honours, including the Cecil B. DeMille Award (1984) from the Golden Globes and the Jean Hersholt Humanitarian Award (1993) from the Academy of Motion Picture Arts and Sciences.

JOHNNY CARSON

(b. Oct. 23, 1925, Corning, Iowa, U.S.–d. January 23, 2005, Los Angeles, Calif., U.S.)

Johnny Carson (the byname of John William Carson) was an American comedian who, as host of *The Tonight Show* (1962–92), established the standard format for television chat shows—including the guest couch and the studio band—and came to be considered the king of late-night television.

Following high school graduation and service in the navy during World War II, Carson enrolled at the University of Nebraska. While there he participated in student theatrical activities and worked for a radio station in Lincoln. After graduating in 1949, Carson took another radio job, in Omaha, and in 1951 he began working as an announcer at a television station in Los Angeles. He was also given a Sunday afternoon comedy show, which led to his being hired as a writer for Red Skelton's show. After Carson substituted successfully for Skelton at the last minute on one occasion, he was given his own short-lived variety show, *The Johnny Carson Show*. He then moved to

New York City and in 1957 became host of the game show *Who Do You Trust?* In 1962 Carson replaced Jack Paar as host of *The Tonight Show.*

As the host of that nightly program for nearly three decades, Carson had an unprecedented influence on a generation of television viewers, and his decision in 1972 to move his show from New York to California was instrumental in shifting the power of the TV industry to Los Angeles. He created such memorable characters as Aunt Blabby and Carnac the Magnificent, as well as a large number of classic skits, and became one of the most beloved performers in the country. Carson won four Emmy Awards, was inducted into the Hall of Fame of the Academy of Television Arts and Sciences (1987), and was given the Presidential Medal of Freedom (1992) and a Kennedy Center Honor (1993). On May 22, 1992, Carson's final appearance as the host of *The Tonight Show* attracted an estimated 50 million viewers, the largest audience in the program's history. Comedian Jay Leno replaced Carson as the late-night staple's host.

SAMMY DAVIS, JR.

(b. Dec. 8, 1925, New York, N.Y., U.S.—d. May 16, 1990, Los Angeles, Calif., U.S.)

Sammy Davis, Jr. was an American singer, dancer, and entertainer.

At age three Davis began performing in vaudeville with his father and uncle, Will Mastin, in the Will Mastin Trio. Davis studied tap dancing under Bill ("Bojangles") Robinson but never received a formal education. After serving in the U.S. Army he became the central figure of the Mastin Trio, not only singing and dancing but also playing trumpet, drums, piano, and vibraphone; moreover, he was an accomplished mime and comedian. He

Sammy Davis Jr. in the film Porgy and Bess *(1959).*

encountered virulent racial prejudice early in his career, but he endured to become one of the first African American stars to achieve wide popularity.

Along with his extremely successful nightclub career, Davis was a popular recording artist, and he was success-ful on Broadway in *Mr. Wonderful* (1956) and in a 1964 revival of Clifford Odets's *Golden Boy* and in films, including *Porgy and Bess* (1959) and *Sweet Charity* (1969). He also appeared in a series of motion pictures with friends such as Frank Sinatra and Dean Martin, including *Ocean's Eleven* (1960), *Sergeants 3* (1962), and *Robin and the 7 Hoods* (1964). Davis wrote two autobiographical books, *Yes I Can* (1965) and *Why Me?* (1989).

MARILYN MONROE

(b. June 1, 1926, Los Angeles, Calif., U.S.–d. Aug. 5, 1962, Los Angeles, Calif., U.S.)

Born Norma Jeane Mortenson and later called Norma Jeane Baker, Marilyn Monroe was an American actress who became a major sex symbol, starring in a number of commercially successful motion pictures during the 1950s.

Norma Jeane Mortenson later took her mother's name, Baker. Her mother was frequently confined in an asylum, and Norma Jeane was reared by 12 successive sets of foster parents and, for a time, in an orphanage. In 1942 she married a fellow worker in an aircraft factory, but they divorced soon after World War II. She became a popular photographer's model and in 1946 signed a short-term contract with Twentieth Century-Fox, taking as her screen name Marilyn Monroe. After a few brief appearances in movies made by the Fox and Columbia studios, she was again unemployed, and she returned to modeling for photographers. Her nude photograph on a calendar brought her a role in the film *Scudda-Hoo! Scudda-Hay!* (1948), which was followed by other minor roles.

In 1950 Monroe played a small uncredited role in *The Asphalt Jungle* that reaped a mountain of fan mail. An appearance in *All About Eve* (1950) won her another contract from Fox and much recognition. In a succession of movies, including *Let's Make It Legal* (1951), *Love Nest* (1951), *Clash by Night* (1952), and *Niagara* (1953), she advanced to star billing on the strength of her studio-fostered image as a "love goddess." With performances in *Gentlemen Prefer Blondes* (1953), *How to Marry a Millionaire* (1953), and *There's No Business Like Show Business* (1954), her fame grew steadily and spread throughout the world, and she became the object of unprecedented popular adulation. In 1954 she married baseball star Joe DiMaggio, and the attendant publicity was enormous. With the end of their marriage less than a year later she began to grow discontented with her career.

Monroe studied with Lee Strasberg at the Actors' Studio in New York City, and in *The Seven Year Itch* (1955) and *Bus Stop* (1956) she began to emerge as a talented comedian. In 1956 she married playwright Arthur Miller and briefly retired from moviemaking, although she costarred with Sir Laurence Olivier in *The Prince and the Showgirl* (1957). She won critical acclaim for the first time as a serious actress for *Some Like It Hot* (1959). Her last role, in *The Misfits* (1961), was written by Miller, whom she had divorced the year before.

In 1962 Monroe began filming the comedy *Something's Got to Give*. However, she was frequently absent from the set because of illnesses, and in May she traveled to New York City to attend a gala where she famously sang "Happy Birthday" to Pres. John F. Kennedy, with whom she was allegedly having an affair. In June Monroe was fired from the film. Although she was later rehired, work never resumed. After several months as a virtual recluse, Monroe died from an overdose of sleeping pills in her Los Angeles home. Her death was ruled a "probable suicide," though conspiracy theories persisted.

In their first runs, Monroe's 23 movies grossed a total of more than $200 million, and her fame surpassed that of any other entertainer of her time. Her early image as a dumb and seductive blonde gave way in later years to the tragic figure of a sensitive and insecure woman unable to escape the pressures of Hollywood. Her vulnerability and sensuousness combined with her needless death eventually raised her to the status of an American cultural icon.

MEL BROOKS

(b. June 28, 1926, Brooklyn, New York, N.Y., U.S.)

Melvin Kaminsky, better known by his byname of Mel Brooks, is an American film and television director, producer, writer, and actor whose motion pictures elevated outrageousness and vulgarity to high comic art.

EARLY LIFE AND WORK

Brooks was an accomplished mimic, pianist, and drummer by the time he graduated from high school and enlisted in the U.S. Army in 1944. As part of his assignment to the Army Specialized Training Program, he received instruction at the Virginia Military Institute. After serving as a combat engineer in Europe during World War II, he became a professional entertainer, working as a stand-up comic, an emcee, and a social director at resorts in the Catskill Mountains (the so-called Borscht Belt). In 1949 he joined the writing staff for *The Admiral Broadway Revue*, a weekly television series starring Sid Caesar. Brooks remained with Caesar until 1958, contributing material to the comedian's subsequent TV efforts, most memorably to the landmark comedy series *Your Show of Shows* (1950–54) as part of a writing staff that included Carl Reiner, Neil Simon, and Larry Gelbart. Additionally, Brooks collaborated on the librettos for the musicals *Shinbone Alley* (1957) and *All American* (1962).

As a performer, Brooks came to prominence in 1960 when he teamed with Reiner (who acted as an interviewer) to bring to life "The 2,000 Year Old Man," a mostly improvised bit that the duo performed in television appearances and on best-selling comedy record albums. Brooks entered the motion picture industry as the writer and narrator of the Academy Award-winning animated short *The Critic* (1963), a devastating lampoon of avant-garde films. He and Buck Henry then created *Get Smart* (1965–70), a television situation comedy spoofing the espionage genre popularized by the James Bond films.

FIRST FILMS

All this was but a prelude to his auspicious feature-film directorial debut, *The Producers* (1968), which was not a major success at the box office, even though Brooks's screenplay won an Academy Award. In *The Producers*, Zero Mostel starred as a financially troubled stage producer who teams with his accountant (played by Gene Wilder) to purposefully oversell shares in their upcoming production to investors. With the pro-Nazi musical *Springtime for Hitler*, they hope to create a production so obviously bad and offensive that it will quickly bomb and close, allowing them to abscond with the investors' money. To their horror, they end up with a hit. Despite its initial poor showing at the box office and a mixed response from critics, the film had some ardent champions, including actor Peter Sellers, and Brooks won an Academy Award for his screenplay.

Moreover, with the passage of time, *The Producers* became a cult favourite and was eventually widely lauded as one of the greatest comedies ever made. Its celebrated centrepiece, an absurdly upbeat Busby Berkeley–like musical number ("Springtime for Hitler"), and Dick Shawn's bohemian portrayal of the play-within-the-movie's protagonist, Adolf Hitler, both typified Brooks's comedic approach as they shockingly defied audience expectations. Brooks, whose artistic sensibility had largely been shaped by his sense of being an outsider as a Jew in mainstream American society, boldly put the ultimate villain of Jewish history, Hitler, at the heart of his comedy and transformed him into a clown. In so doing, he embodied the approach to comedy (and, more specifically, to parody) that film historian Gerald Mast called the "anomalous surprise"—the interjection of a character, a situation, or an event that makes no sense given the context. Brooks would return to this approach again and again throughout his career as a filmmaker.

Brooks followed *The Producers* with another broad comedy, *The Twelve Chairs* (1970), that was set in newly communist Russia and concerned a trove of jewels hidden inside a dining-chair leg. A priest, an aristocrat, and a confidence man vie to be the first to discover them, to great comic effect, though the film was little seen.

FILMS OF THE 1970S

It was with his third directorial effort, *Blazing Saddles* (1974), that Brooks cemented his reputation as Hollywood's foremost purveyor of hilarious tastelessness. He collaborated with writer-director Andrew Bergman and stand-up comedian-actor Richard Pryor, among others, on the script for this uninhibited burlesque of the western genre, the comic targets of which ranged from racial prejudice to flatulence. Its stellar cast included Wilder, Cleavon Little, Harvey Korman, Slim Pickens, and Madeline Kahn, who earned an Academy Award nomination for best supporting actress for her parody of Marlene Dietrich's saloon singer in the classic western *Destry Rides Again* (1939). The film reaped a fortune at the box office and earned Brooks another Academy Award nomination, this one for best original song ("I'm Tired").

Equally popular was his next film, a broad but affectionate parody of the Universal horror films of the 1930s titled *Young Frankenstein* (1974), which earned Brooks and the film's star and cowriter, Wilder, an Academy Award nomination for best screenplay. *Young Frankenstein* was more carefully structured than *Blazing Saddles*, and its elegant black-and-white cinematography replicated the look of the 1935 *Bride of Frankenstein*. Brooks reined in his more anarchic impulses (though his trademark lewd jokes are abundant), and many critics found the result more sophisticated than *Blazing Saddles*, which had been released less than a year previously.

Less successful was *Silent Movie* (1976), in which Brooks himself starred as a washed-up director who persuades the head of a motion-picture studio (played by Caesar) to make a silent picture. Without dialogue and loaded with sight gags, *Silent Movie* was less a spoof than an affectionate homage to the Mack Sennett-directed comedies of the silent era. *High Anxiety* (1977) was a more centred parody, with the films of Alfred Hitchcock as its target. Brooks again starred, this time as a psychiatrist whose life is put in jeopardy when he goes to work at the Psycho-Neurotic Institute for the Very, Very Nervous (the staff of which includes a sinister pair played by Cloris Leachman and Korman).

(Left to right) Mel Brooks, Peter Boyle, Marty Feldman, Gene Wilder, and Teri Garr in a promotional photograph for Young Frankenstein *(1974), directed by Brooks.*

Films of the 1980s and 1990s

Despite the presence of Korman, Leachman, and several other fine actors who were members of the loose ensemble that appeared in Brooks's films, including Kahn and Caesar, *History of the World—Part I* (1981) was poorly received by most critics and at the box office. Similarly disappointing were *Spaceballs* (1987), a takeoff on the *Star Wars* series, and *Life Stinks* (1991). Brooks then directed *Robin Hood: Men in Tights* (1993), a send-up of *Robin Hood: Prince of Thieves* (1991), in which Kevin Costner had starred (and was generally maligned) as the legendary outlaw hero. Brooks's final motion picture as a director was the unremarkable *Dracula: Dead and Loving It* (1995).

Work as Producer and Actor

As founder of Brooksfilms, an independent moviemaking concern, Brooks also engaged in a parallel career as an executive producer of serious "quality" films, including *The Elephant Man* (1980), *Frances* (1982, uncredited), and *84 Charing Cross Road* (1987), the last of which starred his second wife, Anne Bancroft, whom he married in 1964. Brooks costarred with Bancroft in *To Be or Not to Be* (1983), a remake of the Ernst Lubitsch-directed film of the same name. His work as an actor also included regular appearances on the popular TV sitcom *Mad About You* in the late 1990s and a guest stint on the HBO series *Curb Your Enthusiasm*. In his later career, Brooks also contributed his voice to several animated features, including *Robots* (2005), *Mr. Peabody & Sherman* (2014), and *Hotel Transylvania 2* (2015).

Brooks made a spectacular comeback in 2001 as producer, composer, and librettist of the hugely popular Tony Award-winning Broadway stage musical based on *The*

Producers. He followed this in 2007 with a Broadway musical based on *Young Frankenstein*. Brooks was named a Kennedy Center honoree in 2009 for his contributions to American comedy.

SIDNEY POITIER
(b. Feb. 20, 1927, Miami, Fla., U.S.)

Sidney Poitier is a Bahamian American actor, director, and producer known for having broken the colour barrier in the U.S. motion-picture industry and made the careers of other black actors possible. He was the first African American to win an Academy Award for best actor (for *Lilies of the Field* [1963]).

EARLY LIFE AND WORK

Poitier was born prematurely in the United States while his parents were visiting from The Bahamas. He grew up on Cat Island, Bahamas, and returned as a teenager to the United States, where he enlisted in the U.S. Army during World War II and served a brief stint in a medical unit. Upon his discharge, he applied to the American Negro Theatre (ANT) in New York City. Refused a place because of his accent, he practiced American enunciation while listening to the accents of radio voices and reapplied to ANT six months later. This time he was accepted, and he began studying acting while appearing in a series of ANT productions. In 1946 he made his Broadway debut in *Lysistrata*.

HOLLYWOOD TRAILBLAZER

Poitier's first credited film role was Dr. Luther Brooks, a black doctor who treats a bigoted white criminal, in *No*

Way Out (1950). The movie established a significant pattern both for Poitier himself and for the black actors who followed him: by refusing roles that played to racial stereotypes, Poitier pushed the restrictive boundaries set by Hollywood and made inroads into the American mainstream. He next appeared in *Cry, the Beloved Country* (1951), an adaptation of Alan Paton's novel about a murder in apartheid South Africa; Poitier portrayed a reverend. Another of his notable early roles was Gregory Miller, an alienated high school student in the 1955 film adaptation of Evan Hunter's novel *The Blackboard Jungle* (1954). Although he had a budding film career, Poitier continued to perform in live theatre and won critical acclaim on Broadway in 1959 with his starring role in Lorraine Hansberry's *A Raisin in the Sun*. He also starred in the 1961 film adaptation of the drama.

In the gripping drama *Edge of the City* (1957), Poitier starred as a dockworker whose friendship with a white coworker (John Cassavetes) raises the ire of a racist union boss. *Band of Angels* (1957) also examined racial tensions. Set at the time of the American Civil War, the melodrama featured Poitier as a rebellious overseer whose boss (Clark Gable) buys the daughter (Yvonne De Carlo) of a once-wealthy family, who, after her father's death, discovers she is part black and is sold into slavery. In *The Defiant Ones* (1958), Poitier was cast as a prisoner who escapes with a white inmate (Tony Curtis); the two must overcome their racial prejudices in order to elude the police. The film, which was considered provocative at the time because of its call for racial harmony, earned Poitier an Oscar nomination for best actor; he became the first African American male performer to earn a nod in the lead category. He also earned acclaim for his work in *Porgy and Bess* (1959); he portrayed the disabled Porgy, who loves Bess (Dorothy Dandridge), a drug addict being pursued by a number of suitors.

Poitier made history as Homer Smith, an ex-GI who helps nuns build a chapel in *Lilies of the Field* (1963). His Academy Award win marked the first time a competitive Oscar had been awarded to an African American male. (James Baskett had received an honorary Oscar in 1948 for his role as Uncle Remus in *Song of the South* [1946].) Poitier was also just the second black actor to win an Academy Award (Hattie McDaniel had won a best supporting actress Oscar for *Gone with the Wind* [1939]). After appearing in the biblical epic *The Greatest Story Ever Told* (1965), Poitier portrayed a man who befriends a blind girl (Elizabeth Hartman) in *A Patch of Blue* (1965); the moving drama also starred Shelley Winters as her abusive mother.

After the western *Duel at Diablo* (1966), Poitier starred in a series of acclaimed films. In *To Sir, with Love* (1967), he portrayed a charismatic schoolteacher who earns the respect of his students at an inner-city school. Next was *In the Heat of the Night* (1967), a crime drama that focused on the uneasy partnership that develops between a bigoted white Southern police chief (played by Rod Steiger) and Virgil Tibbs, an intellectual black Philadelphia detective (Poitier). The film received the Oscar for best picture, and Poitier later reprised the role in *They Call Me Mister Tibbs!* (1970) and *The Organization* (1971). Poitier's other movie from 1967 was *Guess Who's Coming to Dinner*, in which he portrayed the fiancé of a white woman (Katharine Houghton) who takes him home to meet her liberal parents (Spencer Tracy, in his last film, and Katharine Hepburn). The success of the movies made Poitier the top box-office draw of the year.

POITIER AS A DIRECTOR

In 1972 Poitier made his directorial debut with *Buck and the Preacher*, an amiable western in which he played a con-man preacher; his costars were Harry Belafonte and Ruby

Dee. He next helmed *A Warm December* (1973), a melo-drama that featured Poitier as a widowed doctor who falls in love with a woman (Esther Anderson) who has sickle cell anemia. Both films were disappointments at the box office, but the comedy *Uptown Saturday Night* (1974) was an enormous hit, thanks to the chemistry between Poitier and costars Bill Cosby and Belafonte. Poitier then reteamed with Cosby on *Let's Do It Again* (1975) and *A Piece of the Action* (1977).

Poitier did not act in *Stir Crazy* (1980), which featured Gene Wilder and Richard Pryor as a pair of losers who mistakenly are sent to prison; the film was an enormous box-office hit. Poitier had less success with *Hanky Panky* (1982), which teamed Wilder and his real-life wife, Gilda Radner, and *Fast Forward* (1985), a musical about break dancers. Cosby returned for Poitier's last directorial effort, *Ghost Dad* (1990), but the film failed to match their earlier successes.

RETURN TO ACTING

After more than a decade-long break from acting, in 1988 Poitier appeared in the action thrillers *Shoot to Kill* and *Little Nikita*. His other films include *Sneakers* (1992) and *The Jackal* (1997), but most of his later credits were made-for-television movies, notably *Separate but Equal* (1991) and *Mandela and de Klerk* (1997), in which he played Thurgood Marshall and Nelson Mandela, respectively. His final role was in *The Last Brickmaker in America* (2001), a TV movie about a grieving widower whose job is becoming obsolete.

In 2001 Poitier, the recipient of many prestigious act-ing awards, was presented with an honorary Academy Award for "his remarkable accomplishments as an artist and as a human being." A dual citizen of the United States and The Bahamas, he was appointed ambassador to Japan for The Bahamas in 1997. In 2009 he was awarded the U.S. Presidential Medal of Freedom. Poitier chronicled his experiences in *This Life* (1980) and *The Measure of a Man: A Spiritual Autobiography* (2000). *Life Beyond Measure: Letters to My Great-Granddaughter* (2008) was a volume of advice and insights in epistolary form. He also released a suspense novel, *Montaro Caine*, in 2013.

STANLEY KUBRICK

(b. July 26, 1928, Bronx, New York, N.Y., U.S.—d. March 7, 1999, Childwickbury Manor, near St. Albans, Hertfordshire, Eng.)

Stanley Kubrick was an American motion-picture director and writer whose films are characterized by his dramatic visual style, meticulous attention to detail, and a detached, often ironic or pessimistic perspective. An expatriate, Kubrick was nearly as well known for his reclusive lifestyle in the English countryside as for his painstaking approach to researching, writing, photographing, and editing his infrequent but always much-debated films.

EARLY LIFE AND FILMS

Kubrick grew up in the Bronx, the son of a physician whose interest in chess and photography he began to share at an early age. Bright but bored, Kubrick was a poor student; however, he immersed himself in the role of his high school's photographer. At age 16 he sold an expressive photo (showing a dejected newspaper vendor surrounded by headlines announcing U.S. Pres. Franklin D. Roosevelt's death) to *Look* magazine. Kubrick aborted his studies at the City College of New York shortly after he had started them so that he could join the staff of *Look* at age 17, and he then traveled the county as a photojournalist for more than four years. He also became a habitué of the retrospective film screenings at the Museum of Modern Art in New York and was especially influenced by the work of Orson Welles and Sergey Eisenstein. In 1950 he shot a short documentary about the run-up to a boxing match, which was released by RKO as *Day of the Fight* (1951). Kubrick left *Look*, began auditing classes at Columbia University, became a voracious reader, and turned to full-time filmmaking.

After directing a pair of documentaries, he persuaded his father and uncle to help finance the production of his first fiction feature, an ultralow-budget war film, *Fear and Desire* (1953). Kubrick then scraped together the financing for another low-budget effort, a boxing-related film noir romance, *Killer's Kiss* (1955). At this point he joined forces with producer James B. Harris to form Harris-Kubrick Productions. Encouraged by the respectable reviews for *Killer's Kiss*, United Artists provided Kubrick with enough money to hire a cast of quality B-film supporting actors — including Sterling Hayden, Marie Windsor, Vince Edwards, and Elisha Cook, Jr. — for his next film. The result was *The Killing* (1956), a taut caper film about the robbing of a racetrack. It is regarded as an important late-period film noir, largely because of its creative use of flashbacks and its nonlinear narrative.

Continuing his progression up the Hollywood ladder, Kubrick was given a healthy budget ($850,000) by United Artists to shoot the antiwar drama *Paths of Glory* (1957) in West Germany. Set during World War I, it focused on the suicidal attack by French troops on a German position and the repercussions in its aftermath. Because of its damning portrayal of the French officer corps, the film was not shown in France until 1975. Kirk Douglas, Adolphe Menjou, and Ralph Meeker gave commanding performances. *Paths of Glory* also featured a fine screenplay by Calder Willingham, cult novelist Jim Thompson, and Kubrick, who nearly always did the lion's share of the writing on his films' scripts regardless of his collaborators. Throughout his career, Kubrick took a hands-on approach to the details of all aspects of his films, not least production design, editing, and cinematography. Indeed, he was personally responsible for the bravura handheld tracking shots in *Paths of Glory*. Unfortunately, Kubrick had waived his salary for profit participation in the film, which, despite its excellence, did not fare well at the box office.

Kubrick worked on developing *One-Eyed Jacks* (1961) for several months with Marlon Brando, but the creative differences between the two finally became too great, and Kubrick left the project, which was ultimately directed by Brando himself. Kubrick then accepted Douglas's offer to take over the direction of *Spartacus* (1960) from Anthony Mann, who had just been fired. *Spartacus*, the epic recounting of a slave rebellion in the Roman Empire, was more than three hours long—considered overlong by some critics—but most agreed that it was significantly better than the standard "sword-and-sandal" adventure film. It benefited from Dalton Trumbo's adaptation of a novel by Howard Fast and a distinguished cast that included Douglas, Laurence Olivier, Peter Ustinov, and Charles Laughton. *Spartacus* was arguably Kubrick's most-accessible film, but it was also his most-anonymous film and the one over which he had the least control.

Breakthrough to Success

Kubrick then moved his family to England, where he took advantage of the so-called Eady plan, which provided considerable tax incentives for foreign film producers who used at least 80 percent British labour. His first project there was *Lolita* (1962), a film version of Vladimir Nabokov's controversial examination of love and lechery. Nabokov was credited as a coscenarist, but Kubrick wrote the bulk of the screenplay for that darkest of dark comedies, which most critics believed never fully solved the problem of transposing Nabokov's difficult novel to the screen. Many agreed, however, that James Mason was superb as Humbert Humbert, the professor who becomes obsessed with a 13-year-old girl (Sue Lyon), and Peter Sellers and Shelley Winters also submitted striking performances. Despite stirring up plenty of controversy of its own with its subject matter (particularly with the Catholic League of Decency), *Lolita* was a box-office hit.

Notwithstanding the success of *Lolita*, Kubrick's big breakthrough came with the inimitable *Dr. Strangelove; or, How I Learned to Stop Worrying and Love the Bomb* (1964). This wickedly nihilistic comedy about the Cold War arms race was written by Kubrick, Terry Southern, and Peter George (on whose novel *Red Alert* it was based). In the planning stages, Kubrick sought to treat the material seriously, but he kept finding himself gravitating toward farce and eventually gave in to that impulse while still managing to powerfully convey the horrible prospect of nuclear annihilation. He made the most of wonderfully inventive performances by George C. Scott, Sterling Hayden, and especially Sellers, who plays three very different but equally memorable characters. *Dr. Strangelove* earned Kubrick his first Academy Award nomination for best direction and also garnered nominations for best picture, best actor (Sellers), and best screenplay.

Kubrick spent the next four years making *2001: A Space Odyssey* (1968), a metaphysical science-fiction epic based on a haunting short story by Arthur C. Clarke, who worked with him on the screenplay. The film is divided into three parts, with only the middle section resembling a traditional narrative. In that section two astronauts on a spaceship bound for Jupiter (Gary Lockwood and Keir Dullea) are forced to match wits with HAL 9000, the ship's all-seeing, conscious onboard computer, when it malfunctions. Prehistoric apes are the focus of the first section, and the last section contains a sequence of wildly impressionistic images as the spaceship is sucked into a dimension in which time and space are disrupted. Beyond its meditation on humanity's relationship with machines and artificial intelligence, the themes and meaning of *2001: A Space Odyssey* are elusive. Kubrick himself said that he hoped that the film's significance would transcend language and reason. Few critics failed to note his stunning use of classical music, most notably Richard Strauss's *Thus Spoke Zarathustra*. Kubick's powerful application of music to amplify atmosphere, character, and story was a signature of his filmmaking. *2001: A Space Odyssey* also set a new standard for movie special effects.

Audiences and critics were polarized by *2001: A Space Odyssey*. Noted critic Pauline Kael famously derided it, but many other critics hailed the film as a masterpiece, and it has consistently appeared on lists of the greatest films of all time. In its day the film was a countercultural phenomenon and a box-office smash that gave Kubrick the latitude to make any movie he desired with a degree of creative freedom and control experienced by few filmmakers.

FILMS OF THE 1970S

Kubrick's next film was *A Clockwork Orange* (1971), which he adapted himself from the 1963 novel of the same name by Anthony Burgess, set in England's not too distant future. Kubrick's rendering of this world was visually stunning, and he cast Malcolm McDowell as the violence-addicted teenage hoodlum who is caught and reprogrammed in horrifying fashion by the government. Brutal and cynical, this deliberately provocative, nihilistic view of society and its discontented earned an X rating for excessive violence when it was released in the United States. *A Clockwork Orange* divided critics even more dramatically than *2001: A Space Odyssey* did, yet it was nominated for Academy Awards for best picture, best director, and best screenplay. Kubrick became the focus of much criticism in Britain in the wake of a rash of violent crimes that appeared to have been inspired by the film, and he used his considerable clout to see that *A Clockwork Orange* was pulled from British distribution.

Another four years passed in the preparation of *Barry Lyndon* (1975), which Kubrick adapted himself from William Makepeace Thackeray's novel of the same name. Ryan O'Neal starred as the title character, an 18th-century Irish rogue who narrates his story in voiceover. Kubrick's obsessive insistence on filming with natural lighting of the period (including scenes illuminated only by candles) necessitated the construction of a special camera. He was equally meticulous in his demands regarding the production design and in the costumes, and the result was arguably one of the handsomest period films ever made and one which evocatively mirrors the 18th-century paintings that he had used as his models. Many critics in Britain and the United States dismissed *Barry Lyndon* as tedious or boring, and it was a major disappointment commercially. In continental Europe, however, it was effusively praised. Moreover, Kubrick received his fourth consecutive nomination for an Academy Award for best director, and the film was nominated for best picture. Perhaps not surprisingly, John Alcott won the award for best cinematography.

For his next project, Kubrick—seemingly mindful of *Barry Lyndon*'s failure at the box office—acquired the rights to a bestseller, Stephen King's updated gothic horror novel *The Shining*. Jack Nicholson played a writer who becomes increasingly deranged and eventually turns upon his wife and young son while acting as the winter caretaker of an isolated hotel. *The Shining* (1980) earned what had come to be the usual mixed critical reception for a Kubrick film, with some reviewers arguing that it was among his finest work. Similarly, opinions varied widely regarding the effectiveness of Nicholson's intense (in the eyes of many critics, over-the-top) performance. Ultimately, the film was a commercial success and became a cult favourite.

LAST FILMS

It took seven years for Kubrick's next film to appear. Having made an antiwar film with *Paths of Glory*, he undertook an examination of war as a phenomenon in *Full Metal Jacket* (1987). Set during the Vietnam War, the film begins as a cerebral critique of the way U.S. Marines are dehumanized during basic training to operate efficiently as killing machines when sent into combat. The action then shifts to Vietnam; as Kubrick shot the whole film in England, an abandoned gasworks in East London stood in for the besieged city of Hue. *Full Metal Jacket* boasted a solid cast that included Matthew Modine, Adam Baldwin, and Vincent D'Onofrio. Its screenplay, which was nominated for an Academy Award, was written by Kubrick; Michael Herr, whose reporting on the Vietnam War became the acclaimed book *Dispatches* (1977); and Gustav Hasford, the author of *The Short-Timers* (1979), the novel on which the script was based. Despite its visceral power, the film did not succeed commercially.

In the mid-1990s Kubrick began working on a script that Steven Spielberg would eventually direct as *A.I.:*

Artificial Intelligence (2001). Deciding that Spielberg's sensibility was better suited to the material than was his own, Kubrick had turned over the directorial reins to Spielberg and decided to act as producer. However, ever the perfectionist, Kubrick delayed filming because the special-effects technology that he required was not yet available. Instead, he turned his attention to another project, *Eyes Wide Shut* (1999), which would be his final film, released only a few months after his death. Based on Arthur Schnitzler's 1926 novella *Traumnovelle* ("Dream Story"), it became yet another controversial entry in Kubrick's oeuvre. Tom Cruise and Nicole Kidman, then married to each other offscreen, played a modern-day New York City couple whose marriage is tested by a sequence of intense, erotically charged encounters with others. The film's highly sexualized content became a subject of debate when Warner Brothers elected to digitally alter several of the more sexually explicit images in postproduction, following Kubrick's death, in order to avoid an NC-17 rating, which the studio believed would have harmed the film's commercial prospects. Notwithstanding those changes, the film performed poorly at the box office.

Although his career extended over nearly half a century, Kubrick made only 13 feature films. Nevertheless, he is remembered as a master filmmaker and supreme visual stylist. Arguably, he is even more admired by other filmmakers than he is by critics and cineastes. The releases of his films were events. Kubrick was a perfectionist whose passionate involvement with his art meant that he could often be very difficult to work with (occasionally harsh or cruel to his collaborators, though also very warm). For all of the planning that went into his projects, he often discovered the structure of his films as he made them, and he was extremely open to experimentation and the ideas of others. Kubrick's meticulous involvement with seemingly

every detail that went into his films earned him a reputation as a control freak, but it also guaranteed that his
signature was indelibly imprinted on every film that he
made.

ALEJANDRO JODOROWSKY
(b. Feb. 7, 1929, Tocopilla, Chile)

Alejandro Jodorowsky is a Chilean-born French filmmaker and author known for his surrealistic films,
especially *El Topo* (1970) and *The Holy Mountain* (1973).

EARLY WORK

Jodorowsky's parents were Ukrainian Jewish immigrants.
When he was eight years old, the family moved from
Tocopilla to Santiago. He enrolled in the University of
Chile in 1947 but dropped out two years later. He began
writing plays in 1948 and founded an experimental theatre
group in 1950.

In 1953 Jodorowsky moved to Paris, where he worked
with French mime Marcel Marceau. He made his first film,
the short *La Cravate* (1957; *The Severed Heads*), about a
young man (played by Jodorowsky) who falls in love with
the proprietor of a shop where one can swap out one's
head. In the early 1960s Jodorowsky, Spanish-born French
author Fernando Arrabal, and French artist and author
Roland Topor formed a loose avant-garde movement,
Panique, named after the Greek god Pan and dedicated to
the shocking and the surreal. Jodorowsky's most-noted
work in that period was the four-hour-long performance
Mélodrame sacrementel (1965; "Sacramental Melodrama"),
in which he slit the throats of two geese, was whipped, and
nailed a cow's heart to a cross, among other bizarre
happenings.

Jodorowsky divided his time between Paris and Mexico, where he wrote a series of comic books, *Anibal 5* (1966), and wrote and drew a weekly comic strip, *Fábulas pánicas* (1967–73; "Panic Fables"). In 1968 he directed his first feature film, *Fando y Lis* (*Fando and Lis*), which was based on a play by Arrabal. Fando and his paralyzed lover, Lis, journey across a desert and encounter a gang of transvestites, blood drinkers, and a man playing a burning piano. The film caused a public outcry at its premiere at the Acapulco Film Festival and was banned in Mexico.

EL TOPO AND THE HOLY MOUNTAIN

Jodorowsky's next film, *El Topo* (1970; "The Mole"), brought him worldwide notoriety. In a western setting saturated with sex, violence, and religious symbolism, the gunfighter *El Topo* (Jodorowsky) crosses the desert with his naked son (played by Jodorowsky's son Brontis) but leaves him behind to go on a quest to kill the four master gunfighters. At the quest's end, *El Topo* is left for dead, but he awakes 20 years later in a cave where he is worshipped as a god by dwarves and the physically deformed. *El Topo* and a dwarf woman, seeking to raise money to build a tunnel out of the cave, climb out to a nearby town, an evil place where slavery is legal and a church service includes Russian roulette.

Because of *Fando and Lis*'s reception in Mexico, Jodorowsky took *El Topo* to the United States. American movie-theatre owner Ben Barenholtz saw *El Topo* at a private screening and booked it to play at midnight at the Elgin Theater in New York City. The film became a word-of-mouth success and was the first "midnight movie." *El Topo* divided critics, with some praising it as a masterpiece and others deriding it as a repulsive freak show. John Lennon's manager, Allen Klein, bought the rights to *El*

Topo on Lennon's recommendation, distributed it through-out the United States, and immediately engaged Jodorowsky to produce another film.

In *The Holy Mountain* (1973) a Thief climbs down from a cross and enters a town where tourists film public execu-tions and a circus of toads and chameleons reenacts the Spanish conquest of Mexico. The Thief then encounters the Alchemist (Jodorowsky), who transmutes the Thief's excrement into gold. The Alchemist, the Thief, and seven wealthy people (thieves in their own way) journey to the Holy Mountain, where they must kill the Nine Masters of the Summit to gain eternal life.

LATER FILMS, COMIC BOOKS, AND PSYCHOMAGIC

The Holy Mountain was not a hit like *El Topo*. Klein then wanted Jodorowsky to do a more commercial film, an adaptation of Pauline Réage's pornographic novel *Story of O*. Jodorowsky instead decided to adapt Frank Herbert's science-fiction novel *Dune*. (In retaliation, Klein withdrew *El Topo* and *The Holy Mountain* from circulation until 2006.) For *Dune* he assembled a cast that included Salvador Dalí, Orson Welles, Gloria Swanson, Mick Jagger, and David Carradine. Jodorowsky engaged designs from Swiss artist H.R. Giger and French comic-book artist Moebius. Pink Floyd would have composed some of the score. The project was never filmed, but some film historians con-tend that, through its extensive amount of preproduction design, it influenced later science-fiction movies, most notably Ridley Scott's *Alien* (1979), for which Giger designed the creature.

Jodorowsky and Moebius collaborated on comic books, beginning with *Les Yuex du chat* (1978; *The Eyes of the Cat*) and including most notably *L'Incal* (1981–88; *The Incal*), a science-fiction story in which a bumbling private

detective comes into possession of the powerful title arti-
fact. Jodorowsky became a prolific and acclaimed author
of comic books, many set in the same universe as *The Incal*.

Tusk (1980) was a children's film, set in British colonial
India, about the attachment between a young English girl
and an elephant, both born on the same day. Jodorowsky
was dissatisfied with the film's technical deficiencies and
later disowned it.

During his long hiatus from filmmaking in the 1980s,
Jodorowsky developed a form of personal therapy that he
called "psychomagic," which combined insights from
Jungian psychology and the tarot. (He was an avid tarot
reader and for years performed weekly mass readings.) A
key aspect of psychomagic is "acts" that one must perform
that enact a metaphorical solution to one's emotional
problems.

In *Santa Sangre* (1989; *Holy Blood*), insane-asylum
inmate Fenix (Jodorowsky's son Axel) remembers his
childhood growing up in the circus and the horrific event
of his father's cutting off his mother's arms and then killing himself. Fenix escapes from the institution and
reunites with his mother. However, under her influence,
Fenix becomes her arms and kills any woman he loves.

Jodorowsky was a director-for-hire on *The Rainbow
Thief* (1990), a gentle fantasy in which a petty thief (Omar
Sharif) befriends a prince (Peter O'Toole), and the two live
underground in the sewers while waiting for the prince to
assume his inheritance. Jodorowsky subsequently disowned the film.

Jodorowsky appeared in *Jodorowsky's Dune* (2013), a
documentary about his ill-fated project. He returned to
filmmaking with *La danza de la realidad* (2013; *The Dance of
Reality*), an account of his childhood in Tocopilla under
the harsh influence of his domineering father (Brontis
Jodorowsky). In 2015 Jodorowsky resorted to

crowdfunding to raise the funds for his next feature film, *Poesía sin fin* (*Endless Poetry*). The film was announced as a sequel to *La danza de la realidad*, intending to follow Jorowsky's years as a young poet in Santiago, Chile. Jodorowsky's own son, Adan, and grandson, Dante, were cast to play the director as a young adult and teenager, respectively.

AUDREY HEPBURN
(b. May 4, 1929, Brussels, Belg.–d. Jan. 20, 1993, Tolochenaz, Switz.)

Edda Kathleen van Heemstra Hepburn-Ruston, better known by her screen name Audrey Hepburn, was a slender, stylish motion picture actress known for her radiant beauty, her ability to project an air of sophistication tempered by a charming innocence, and her tireless efforts to aid needy children.

Although born in Belgium, Hepburn had British citizenship and attended school in England as a child. In 1939, however, at the onset of World War II, her mother (Hepburn's father left the family when she was six years old) moved the child to the Netherlands, thinking that neutral country safer than England. Throughout World War II, Hepburn endured hardships in Nazi-occupied Holland. She still managed, however, to attend school and take ballet lessons. After the war, she continued to study ballet in Amsterdam and in London. During her early 20s, she studied acting and worked as a model and dancer. She also began to get some small film roles.

While making a film in Monte-Carlo, Hepburn caught the eye of the French novelist Colette, who felt that Hepburn would be ideal for the title role in the stage adaptation of her novel *Gigi*. Despite her inexperience, Hepburn was cast, earning rave reviews when the play opened on Broadway in 1951. Her next project took her to

Rome, where she starred in her first major American film, *Roman Holiday* (1953). As a young princess who exchanges the burden of royalty for a day of adventure and romance, Hepburn demonstrated her ability to combine a regal bearing with a tomboyish winsomeness that utterly charmed audiences, and she won an Academy Award for best actress.

Hepburn returned to the stage early in 1954 as a water nymph in *Ondine*, costarring Mel Ferrer, whom she married later that year. She won a Tony Award for her performance, which turned out to be her last on Broadway. She continued to enchant movie audiences, however, in such light romantic comedies as *Sabrina* (1954; this role provided her first occasion to appear in designs by Hubert de Givenchy, with whose fashions she became identified) and *Funny Face* (1957), as well as in major dramatic pictures such as *War and Peace* (1956) and *The Nun's Story* (1959).

By the 1960s, Hepburn had outgrown her ingenue image and began playing more sophisticated and worldly, albeit often still vulnerable characters, including the effervescent and mysterious Holly Golightly in *Breakfast at Tiffany's* (1961), a chic young widow caught up in a suspenseful *Charade* (1963), and a free-spirited woman involved in a difficult marriage in *Two for the Road* (1967). Her most controversial role was perhaps that of Eliza Doolittle in the motion picture musical *My Fair Lady* (1964). Although Hepburn gave an admirable performance as the Cockney flower girl who is transformed into an elegant lady, many viewers had trouble accepting Hepburn in a role they felt belonged to Julie Andrews, who had created the part on stage.

After appearing in the thriller *Wait Until Dark* (1967), Hepburn went into semiretirement. Having divorced Ferrer in 1968, she married a prominent Italian psychiatrist and chose to focus on her family rather than her career. She did not return to acting until 1976, when she costarred in the nostalgic love story *Robin and Marian*. She appeared in a few more films, and in 1988 she began a new career as a special goodwill ambassador for United Nations Children's Fund (UNICEF). She devoted herself to her humanitarian work, visiting famine-stricken villages in Latin America, Africa, and Asia, until shortly before her death of cancer in 1993.

JOHN CASSAVETES

(b. Dec. 9, 1929, New York, N.Y., U.S.—d. Feb. 3, 1989, Los Angeles, Calif., U.S.)

John Cassavetes was an American film director and actor regarded as a pioneer of American cinema verité and as the father of the independent film movement in the United States. Most of his films were painstakingly made over many months or years and were financed by Cassavetes's acting, which was much sought after by the same studios that were reluctant to back his filmmaking projects. As a result, Cassavetes essentially carved out his own one-man domain in independent filmmaking, which, while not truly part of Hollywood, eventually earned the industry's respect and admiration. He was one of the few filmmakers in the history of the Academy Awards to be nominated for directing, acting, and writing awards.

EARLY WORK

Cassavetes was the son of Greek immigrants. He grew up on Long Island, New York. He studied English at Mohawk College and Colgate University before becoming an acting student at the American Academy of Dramatic Arts, from which he graduated in 1950. He began his acting career in earnest with a small role in the motion picture *Taxi* (1953) and an appearance on television the next year in an episode of *Omnibus*. By the end of 1955, he had acted in many live television shows. In 1956 Cassavetes appeared in *Crime in the Streets*, Don Siegel's drama about juvenile delinquency. That year he also began teaching a Method acting class. In 1957 Cassavetes starred alongside Sidney Poitier in Martin Ritt's *Edge of the City*, a high-profile role that helped him land the lead as the eponymous private eye in the television series *Johnny Staccato* (1959–60).

Cassavetes' low-budget directorial debut, *Shadows* (1959), was financed partly by some $20,000 sent to the fledgling filmmaker after he made an appeal for donations during an appearance on a radio program. Made over a period of about two and a half years and shot on 16-mm film stock, this semi-improvised downbeat slice of cinema verité focused on three African American siblings. The older brother, a jazz musician (played by Hugh Hurd), encounters greater racial discrimination than his lighter-complected younger sister (who dates white men) and brother. *Shadows*'s jazz score was composed by Charles Mingus. The film was first shown to a few audiences in November 1958 and was exhibited again about a year later after the addition of some new scenes and reediting. When Cassavetes could not find an American distributor for the film, he entered it in the 1960 Venice Film Festival, where it won the Critics Award. After it finally received distribution in the United States in 1961, critics were effusive in their praise of *Shadows*, which is generally acknowledged to have inaugurated the American independent filmmaking movement.

Fresh from the success of *Shadows*, Casssavetes signed with Paramount to produce and direct *Too Late Blues* (1961), another downbeat film about a jazz musician, this time with teen singing idol Bobby Darin as the leader of a jazz combo waiting for its big break. Although critics liked

Stella Stevens in her role as the love interest, they generally found the rest of the performances wanting. Nevertheless, Paramount gave Cassavetes a multifilm contract, which he subsequently broke in the interest of gaining greater creative autonomy.

Independent Filmmaker: 1960s and '70s

Independent producer Stanley Kramer then signed Cassavetes to direct *A Child Is Waiting* (1963), an earnest drama written by Abby Mann. Burt Lancaster played a psychologist and Judy Garland a new teacher who disagree in their approaches to working with developmentally challenged children. After Kramer took the film out of Cassavetes' hands and reedited it as a sentimental "social problem" film, Cassavetes broke with Hollywood to pursue filmmaking his own way. He was determined to make motion pictures grounded in character development that would depict real-life situations with real-world consequences. He also was committed to involving the cast and crew in an organic improvisatory process. No matter how dark his subject matter, he was also not beyond punctuating the proceedings with humour.

Faces, which Cassavetes wrote in 1965 and shot in black and white in 1966, starred John Marley and Lynn Carlin as a husband and wife facing a split after 14 years of marriage. Both have one-night stands, the husband with a prostitute (played by Cassavetes' wife, Gena Rowlands) and the wife with a hippie (Seymour Cassel). Originally six hours long, the film was painstakingly edited down over the next two years to slightly more than two hours and released in 1968 to rave reviews. Cassavetes received an Academy Award nomination for his screenplay, and Carlin and Cassel were nominated as best supporting actors. Cassavetes had helped finance

Faces by acting in films such as Robert Aldrich's World War II drama *The Dirty Dozen* (1967), for which he was nominated for an Academy Award as best supporting actor, and Roman Polanski's *Rosemary's Baby* (1968).

As a director, Cassavetes was a master at dramatizing marital problems. For *Husbands* (1970), his first colour 35-mm effort, he assembled his first high-profile cast. Peter Falk, Ben Gazzara, and Cassavetes himself portrayed a triumvirate of suburban husbands who, shocked by the sudden death of a friend, treat themselves to a spree of boozing, basketball, and sex that includes a quick trip to London. *Husbands* was dismissed by influential critic Pauline Kael as "agonizingly banal," but other critics likened it to the work of Ingmar Bergman and found moments of uncommon power in the mostly improvised interaction between the principals.

The modest commercial success of *Husbands* helped Cassavetes secure a deal with Universal to make *Minnie and Moskowitz* (1971). More hopeful and romantic than any of his other films, *Minnie and Moskowitz* was Cassavetes' version of a screwball comedy. Cassel played a slightly demented parking-lot attendant with a crush on a museum curator (Rowlands), who is trying to pull herself together after being dumped by her married lover (Cassavetes).

After this lighter fare, Cassavetes returned to psychodrama with *A Woman Under the Influence* (1974), a harrowing, unrelievedly raw portrait of a Los Angeles housewife's nervous breakdown. Although the story was originally intended as a stage vehicle for Rowlands, it was brought to the screen instead by Cassavetes' newly formed Faces International production company. Falk was appropriately detestable as the brutish husband, and Rowlands's majestic portrayal of the tortured woman at the centre of the film earned an Academy Award nomination for best actress. Despite some critics' judgment that Cassavetes had dissipated the power of the performances by letting some scenes go on too long, *A Woman Under the Influence* was still his biggest hit up to that point. Moreover, it earned Cassavetes his only Academy Award nomination for best director. It seemed as if Cassavetes had beaten the system: he was making deeply personal movies entirely on his own terms and still winning the admiration of the industry on which he had turned his back.

Cassavetes was less sure-footed when he ventured into genre filmmaking with the crime drama *The Killing of a Chinese Bookie* (1976), in which Gazzara played the debt-ridden owner of a strip joint forced by the mob to commit a murder. The ambitious *Opening Night* (1977) also had its problems, including one that often plagued Cassavetes' films, the perception of excessive length. Nevertheless, Rowlands again excelled as a stage actress suffering an existential crisis after a fan dies on the opening night of her new play. Cassavetes the actor (every bit the equal of Cassavetes the director) also gave a notably strong performance, as did veteran character actress Joan Blondell.

1980s

Gloria (1980), made for Columbia rather than Faces International, featured yet another superb effort by Rowlands as a former prostitute who goes on the lam with an eight-year-old boy after his family is killed by the mobsters who employed his dad as an accountant. In between killings the film offers plenty of Cassavetes' distinctive humour. Though the narrative was more loosely structured than that of the standard crime drama, *Gloria* remained one of Cassavetes' most accessible films.

Cassavetes' most significant turns as an actor in the late 1970s came in Elaine May's *Mikey and Nicky* (1976) and

Brian De Palma's *The Fury* (1978). In 1982 he and Rowlands played the leads in Paul Mazursky's 1982 *Tempest*, the first time they had acted together in a picture not directed by Cassavetes. They then starred together in Cassavetes' moving and unusual love story *Love Streams* (1984) as a brother and sister who lead wildly differing lifestyles but who care deeply about each other.

Cassavetes' final project was the little-seen mainstream comedy *Big Trouble* (1985), in which Alan Arkin starred as an insurance salesman who becomes involved in a scheme to fake the death of another man (Falk). It provided an unfortunate and premature end to Cassavetes' adventurous filmmaking career. He died of cirrhosis of the liver at age 59.

CLINT EASTWOOD

(b. May 31, 1930, San Francisco, Calif., U.S.)

Clinton Eastwood, Jr. is an American motion-picture actor who emerged as one of the most popular Hollywood stars in the 1970s and went on to become a prolific and respected director-producer.

EARLY LIFE AND CAREER

Growing up during the Great Depression, Eastwood moved from town to town with his family, spending little more than a few months in each of the many schools he attended. After graduating from high school in California and briefly attending Los Angeles City College, Eastwood held various jobs and served in the U.S. Army before moving to Hollywood. A screen test with Universal in 1954 netted him a 40-week contract, but after one renewal and a series of bit parts in such movies as *Tarantula* (1955) and

Revenge of the Creature (1955), his option was dropped. He appeared in several TV series before he got his big break in 1959 by being cast as Rowdy Yates in the popular TV western *Rawhide* (1959–65).

Eastwood achieved international stardom during this same period when he played The Man with No Name—a laconic, fearless gunfighter whose stoicism masks his brutality—in three Italian westerns (popularly known as "spaghetti westerns") directed by Sergio Leone: *Per un pugno di dollari* (1964; *A Fistful of Dollars*), *Per qualche dollari in più* (1965; *For a Few Dollars More*), and *Il buono, il brutto, il cattivo* (1966; *The Good, the Bad, and the Ugly*). In 1967 the three films played in the United States and were immediate commercial successes, establishing Eastwood as a box-office star.

For Eastwood's first American western, *Hang 'Em High* (1968)—Ted Post's expert imitation of the Leone formula, enlivened by a superior group of character actors—he formed his own production company, Malpaso. He also worked with Don Siegel on the popular police story *Coogan's Bluff* (1968); it was Siegel who taught him most of what he needed to know about directing, a debt Eastwood often acknowledged. He also worked with Siegel on the western *Two Mules for Sister Sara* (1970), the psychological Civil War drama *The Beguiled* (1971), and the prison-break film *Escape from Alcatraz* (1979). Their best-known collaboration was *Dirty Harry* (1971), in which Eastwood first portrayed the ruthlessly effective police inspector Harry Callahan. The film proved to be one of Eastwood's most successful, spawning four sequels and establishing the no-nonsense character Dirty Harry—known for such catchphrases as "Go ahead, make my day"—as a cinema icon.

FIRST DIRECTORIAL EFFORTS

Eastwood turned to directing in such films as the thriller *Play Misty for Me* (1971), the westerns *High Plains Drifter* (1972) and *The Outlaw Josey Wales* (1976), and the espionage thriller *The Eiger Sanction* (1975), all films in which he also played leading roles. Eastwood took over the western *The Outlaw Josey Wales* (1976) from Philip Kaufman, who cowrote the story of a Missouri farmer driven to violence after his family has been slaughtered by renegade Union soldiers. Stylishly photographed by Bruce Surtees, with a fine performance by Chief Dan George as a Cherokee elder, this work humanized Eastwood's mythic avenger archetype for the first time.

Eastwood went on to make *The Gauntlet* (1977), a kinetic but formulaic action film in which he played a police detective trying to transport a witness (Sondra Locke) to an Arizona courthouse where she can testify. The gentle good humour pervading *Bronco Billy* (1980) was far removed from the mayhem of his westerns and cop movies; Eastwood was deft as the proprietor of a two-bit Wild West show who gives shelter to, then falls in love with, a runaway heiress (Locke). *Firefox* (1982) was a high-tech Cold War story that had Eastwood as a pilot stealing a supersonic jet from the Soviets. The whimsical and sentimental *Honkytonk Man* (1982), set during the Great Depression, featured Eastwood as a country singer dying of tuberculosis whose dream is to make it to the Grand Ole Opry before he passes on.

Having wandered rather far afield from his star action persona, Eastwood directed the fourth *Dirty Harry* film, *Sudden Impact* (1983), with Locke portraying a rape victim on a vengeful murder spree. He then returned to his screen roots with the neo-mythic *Pale Rider* (1985), a quasi-religious western. It showcased Eastwood's iconic presence and Surtees's gorgeous photography and was one of the few hit westerns of the 1980s.

Heartbreak Ridge (1986) was an enjoyable drama about an old-school marine sergeant (Eastwood) on the verge of retirement whose tough approach whips a group of raw recruits into shape for the invasion of Grenada. *White Hunter, Black Heart* (1990) was Eastwood's most audacious project of this period of his career, an adaptation of Peter Viertel's roman à clef about his on-location collaboration with director John Huston on *The African Queen* (1951). Bravely tackling the part of Huston, Eastwood embodied the great director's rugged physical presence.

A lifelong devotee of jazz and an accomplished pianist, Eastwood also directed the well-regarded *Bird* (1988), a film biography of saxophonist Charlie Parker (Forest Whitaker), and produced the documentary *Thelonious Monk: Straight, No Chaser* (1988). Offscreen, Eastwood made national headlines in 1986 when he was elected mayor of Carmel, California; he served for two years.

FILMS OF THE 1990S

Because Eastwood's style of acting was minimally expressive, his films initially drew little praise from critics. Yet his strong resonant screen presence earned him success at the box office. His standard role was that of a tough loner whose violent behaviour conformed to his own understated moral principles. However, Eastwood's willingness to demythologize such stock characters as western heroes and cops eventually brought him critical acclaim, as did his lean, crisp directorial style. He became known as a director equally adept at presenting deep character studies and fluid action sequences. After the unsuccessful police drama *The Rookie* (1990), his revisionist western

Unforgiven (1992) featured a towering performance by Eastwood as an erstwhile "regulator" who lays down his plowshare to execute a thug who has disfigured a prostitute. Both the picture and Eastwood (for best director) won Academy Awards. The film was critically lauded for Eastwood's unsentimental look at frontier violence.

In the quiet drama *A Perfect World* (1993), an escaped convict (Kevin Costner) takes a boy (T.J. Lowther) hostage, and an unlikely bond forms between them. Eastwood played a Texas Ranger tracking them down. He made a rare appearance in another director's film when he played a Secret Service agent trying to thwart a presidential assassination in Wolfgang Petersen's popular action thriller *In the Line of Fire* (1993).

The Bridges of Madison County (1995) was Eastwood's effective mounting of the enormously popular novel by Robert James Waller. Eastwood was excellent as a photographer traveling through Iowa for a magazine piece on its historic covered bridges, and Meryl Streep played a farmer's wife who, against her better judgment, enters into an affair with him.

Midnight in the Garden of Good and Evil (1997) was also based on a book that became a publishing phenomenon, the nonfiction best seller by John Berendt about a murder that rocks the community of Savannah, Georgia, which is populated almost entirely by eccentrics. In the thriller *Absolute Power* (1997) Eastwood played a thief who, in the midst of a robbery, witnesses the Secret Service murder a woman whom the president of the United States (Gene Hackman) has just attacked sexually. In *True Crime* (1999) Eastwood starred as a veteran reporter whose investigative skills revive when he learns that a prisoner (Isaiah Washington) scheduled for execution that night is probably innocent.

2000 AND BEYOND

Space Cowboys (2000) had Eastwood as the head of a team of elderly test pilots (Tommy Lee Jones, James Garner, and Donald Sutherland) who have been summoned out of retirement to rescue NASA when an obsolete Russian satellite requires disarming. *Blood Work* (2002) was a serviceable thriller about a retired Federal Bureau of Investigation (FBI) profiler who is convinced that only he can locate a murderer.

Mystic River (2003) set a new standard for Eastwood as a director. Sean Penn, Kevin Bacon, and Tim Robbins starred as childhood pals who have grown up to live widely disparate lives while still bound to the working-class neighbourhood they were born into. Eastwood took another best director Oscar nomination, and the film was also a best picture nominee.

Million Dollar Baby (2004) was another success for Eastwood. A crusty fight trainer (Eastwood) is haunted by his failed relationship with his daughter and a female aspiring boxer (Hilary Swank) who wants to train under him. But tragedy strikes in the midst of her big match, and the rest of the movie is concerned with what makes life worth living. Probably the biggest dark-horse success of Eastwood's career, *Million Dollar Baby* won Oscars for best picture, best actress (Swank), and best supporting actor (Morgan Freeman). It also brought Eastwood his second Oscar for best director. The film broke the $100 million mark at the American box office. Eastwood next directed the World War II films *Flags of Our Fathers* (2006) and *Letters from Iwo Jima* (2006), both of which focus on the Battle of Iwo Jima. The latter, told from the Japanese perspective, was nominated for several Oscars, including best director and best film.

Changeling (2008) was a period piece set in Los Angeles in 1928. It was based on a grim true story of a missing boy whose mother, Christine Collins (Angelina Jolie), is horrified when, several months later, the police "return" him to her in the person of an entirely different child. Eastwood won a special award for *Changeling* at that year's Cannes film festival. In *Gran Torino* (2008), Eastwood played Walt Kowalski, an irascible retired autoworker living in a blue-collar suburb of Detroit who is forced to shake off a lifetime of suspicion toward minorities so as to don the role of protector to a family of Hmong immigrants. The film was a major box-office hit.

Shot in Capetown, South Africa, *Invictus* (2009) took as its subject Pres. Nelson Mandela (Freeman) and his plan to unite his racially divided country by using the 1995 Rugby World Cup, in which South Africa's almost all-white Springboks team, typically reviled by the majority black populace, faced heavily favoured New Zealand in the finals. Their inspirational victory was presented in thrilling fashion by Eastwood, but the film's real strength was its painstaking attention to the political and cultural issues negotiated by the players and Mandela.

Hereafter (2010) was an oddity in the Eastwood canon—a measured, quiet drama about three characters whose widely divergent life experiences have left them convinced of the reality of an afterlife. The anguish experienced by each is etched expertly by Eastwood, but the story is told at a languid pace. *J. Edgar* (2011) was a weighty biopic of J. Edgar Hoover (Leonardo DiCaprio), the longtime head of the FBI. Armie Hammer had the film's other key role, Clyde Tolson, Hoover's right-hand man and the love of Hoover's life. Thus, *J. Edgar* was as much a romance as an account of a power-hungry bureaucrat who became one of the most feared—and loathed—figures in American life. Eastwood then helmed a film adaptation (2014) of the

Tony Award-winning (2006) musical *Jersey Boys*, about the rise of the American rock-and-roll group the Four Seasons. Eastwood's adaptation of a Navy SEAL sniper's memoir, *American Sniper* (2014), was lauded for the finesse with which it depicted both the violence of the Iraq War and the difficulty of a soldier's adjustment to civilian existence. The film received an Academy Award nomination for best picture.

Besides his Academy Awards, Eastwood received the Irving G. Thalberg Award for lifetime achievement in 1995 and the American Film Institute's Life Achievement Award in 1996. In 2007 he was made a chevalier of the French Legion of Honour; he was elevated to commander two years later.

SIR SEAN CONNERY

(b. Aug. 25, 1930, Edinburgh, Scot.)

Born Thomas Connery, Sir Sean Connery is a Scottish-born actor whose popularity in James Bond spy thrillers led to a successful, decades-long film career.

After a three-year stint in the navy and a series of odd jobs, Connery became a model for student artists and men's fashion catalogs. He represented Scotland in the 1953 Mr. Universe contest (he finished third in the tall-man's division), which in turn led to work as an extra in stage productions. In 1954 he landed a small part in a touring production of the Rodgers and Hammerstein musical *South Pacific* and eventually took the leading role. More stage and television work followed, including a much-praised performance as washed-up boxer Mountain Rivera in the BBC television production of Rod Serling's *Requiem for a Heavyweight*. Connery made his film debut in *Lilacs in the Spring* (1954; U.S. title *Let's Make Up*) and received top billing for the first time in *On the Fiddle* (1961; also released as *Operation Snafu*). His other notable films of the period include the Disney fantasy *Darby O'Gill and the Little People* (1959) and the World War II epic *The Longest Day* (1962).

In 1962 Connery was cast in the role of James Bond, Agent 007 of the British Secret Intelligence Service, in the screen adaptation of Ian Fleming's spy thriller *Dr. No*. The immense success of the film and its immediate sequels, *From Russia with Love* (1963) and *Goldfinger* (1964), established the James Bond films as a worldwide phenomenon and Connery as an international celebrity. Not wanting to be typecast as the superspy, Connery continued to take other acting roles, notably in Alfred Hitchcock's psychological thriller *Marnie* (1964). After completing the next two James Bond films, *Thunderball* (1965) and *You Only Live Twice* (1967), Connery renounced the role of Bond. Four years later, however, he was persuaded to return to the role for *Diamonds Are Forever* (1971), which he declared was his last movie as Bond.

He spent the 1970s playing mostly in period dramas and science-fiction films, the best among them being *The Molly Maguires* (1970), *Zardoz* (1973), *Murder on the Orient Express* (1974), *The Man Who Would Be King* (1975), *The Wind and the Lion* (1975), *Robin and Marian* (1976), and *The First Great Train Robbery* (1979; also released as *The Great Train Robbery*). In 1981 he made a

Sean Connery in You Only Live Twice *(1967).*

memorable appearance as King Agamemnon in Terry Gilliam's time-travel fantasy *Time Bandits*, and two years later he delighted Bond fans by returning to the role of 007 in the slyly titled *Never Say Never Again* (1983).

Two films in the mid-1980s reestablished him as a major star. He won a British Academy Film Award for his portrayal of a monk turned detective in the film adaptation of Umberto Eco's *The Name of the Rose* (1986) and followed this with a best supporting actor Oscar for his role as a veteran Chicago cop in pursuit of Al Capone in *The Untouchables* (1987). In Steven Spielberg's *Indiana Jones and the Last Crusade* (1989) Connery played the title figure's father, and in *The Hunt for Red October* (1990) he played a defecting Soviet submarine captain. Connery's memorable films of the 1990s include *Robin Hood: Prince of Thieves* (1991), *First Knight* (1995), *The Rock* (1996), *Dragonheart* (1996), and *Entrapment* (1999). Connery officially retired from acting following his appearance in the film adaptation (2003) of the comic-book series *The League of Extraordinary Gentlemen*, though he went on to perform various voice roles.

Connery received a Kennedy Center Honor for lifetime achievement in 1999 and was knighted by Queen Elizabeth II in 2000. In addition to his film work, Connery was an outspoken advocate of Scottish independence, strongly supporting the Scottish National Party.

JEAN-LUC GODARD
(b. Dec. 3, 1930, Paris, France)

Jean-Luc Godard is a French film director who came to prominence with the New Wave group in France during the late 1950s and the '60s.

Godard spent his formative years on the Swiss side of Lake Geneva, where his father directed a clinic. His higher education consisted of study for a degree in ethnology at the University of Paris, interminable student café conversations, and a labouring job on a dam, which inspired his first short film, *Opération Béton* (1954; *Operation Concrete*). His ethnological interests link with the influence on his work of Jean Rouch, an anthropologist who became the first practitioner and theoretician of the documentary-like film style *cinéma vérité* ("cinema truth"). Filmmakers of this school employ lightweight television equipment to observe their subject with the utmost informality and so completely without preconceived bias that the theme and motifs of the film emerge only while shooting or even later, at the editing stage.

Godard's first feature film, *À bout de souffle* (1959; *Breathless*), which was produced by François Truffaut, his colleague on the journal *Cahiers du cinéma*, won the Jean Vigo Prize. It inaugurated a long series of features, all celebrated for the often drastic nonchalance of Godard's improvisatory filmmaking procedures. *Breathless* was shot without a script; Godard sketched the dialogue overnight and revised it between and during rehearsals. In subsequent films he even resorted to speaking the characters' replies to the actors from behind the camera during takes. Thus, he used improvisatory techniques sometimes to observe reality, sometimes to impose his own vision, and often to interrelate the two so as to create a strangely abstract effect. *Breathless* recounts the misadventures of a petty crook (played by Jean-Paul Belmondo, often Godard's alter ego on-screen) who admires Humphrey Bogart and is betrayed to the police by an American girl. Being uncertain whether she loves him, she informs on him simply to see if she can.

For some years, Godard's work showed an increasingly desperate obsession with themes of fickleness (both male and female), indignity, caprice, and the impossibility of distinguishing a meaningful reality from the imposture perpetrated by others, by one's own mind, by ideology, and by art. Godard used the face of the actress who was then his wife, Anna Karina, as a sphinxlike icon representing this existential duplicity in several films, notably *Le Petit Soldat* (1960; *The Little Soldier*), an ironically flippant tragedy, banned for many years, about torture and countertorture. *Vivre sa vie* (1962; *My Life to Live*), a study of a young Parisian prostitute, used, with ironical solipsism, pastiches of documentary form and clinical jargon. Godard's 1963 film *Le Mépris* (*Contempt*), based on a story by the Italian novelist Alberto Moravia, marked his only venture into orthodox and comparatively expensive filmmaking. Afterward he maintained an almost unique position as an absolute, independent creator, using extraordinarily cheap alfresco production methods and enjoying repeated success on the international "art cinema" circuit. On the strength of *Pierrot le fou* (1965; "Pierrot the Madman"), he was asked to direct what was to be an immensely successful American film, *Bonnie and Clyde* (he refused it because of his distrust of the Hollywood system).

Godard offered his visual and verbal images as delusive counterfeits for a life whose meaning has become irretrievably lost or perhaps was always intrinsically absurd. These images are endowed with additional depth by his extensive culture. Increasingly, his films came to include shots of books brandished or read from and suggestive street signs or posters and dialogue that is delivered as if the performers were alienated from their roles, merely reading texts. Historically impossible or subtly fantastic settings are juxtaposed, and his films compel a disrupting awareness of the medium itself. His allusions to other films in themselves constitute an intricate maze. The heroine of *The Little Soldier*, for instance, is surnamed "Dreyer" after Carl Dreyer, a director whom Godard admires; an extract from one of Dreyer's films is watched by the heroine of *My Life to Live*. *Alphaville* (1965) features scenes from *Metropolis* (1926), whose director, Fritz Lang, plays a film director in *Contempt*. In these ways, Godard's films become intellectual essays: in them, the acted, experienced fictions of earlier motion pictures are transformed into the illustrative ideological cinema of the late 1960s. In 1966 two features — *Made in U.S.A.*, devoted to America, and *Deux ou trois choses que je sais d'elle* (*Two or Three Things I Know About Her*), devoted to Paris — marked a nadir of Godard's generalized despair, which by then was aimed at society as well as at interpersonal relationships. An increasing interest in left-wing thought was implicit in *La Chinoise* (1967; its title is slang for Parisian Maoists) and was confirmed by Godard's active participation in the Paris student riots of 1968 and other demonstrations. *Weekend*, also made in 1967, was a hard-hitting denunciation of modern French society.

By then married to the actress Anne Wiazemsky, he moved from fiction and aesthetic preoccupation to the Marxism of Herbert Marcuse, Che Guevara, Frantz Fanon, and others. *Le Gai savoir* (1968; *The Joy of Knowledge*) is a flatly illustrated text spoken by two students named Émile Rousseau and Patricia Lumumba. His texts for the next decade exhibited a complete indifference to their appeal to the public and were intended as intellectual agitprop (i.e., agitation-propaganda): in Godard's own words, they are "not a show, a struggle." With this ideological twist, Godard disconcerted those who had admired him, whether their particular enthusiasm was for the dexterity of his film form, for his skill in posing complex cultural riddles, or for his cool but sad recording of Western man's crises of identity. His evolution also posed a problem for his detractors, whether they criticized him for solipsism, for nihilism, or for his suspiciously complacent celebration of the ignominies of the bourgeois life under the shadow of revolution. Even the minority that declared his earlier films to be honourable failures, or exercises in intellectual tedium, had to agree that, of all directors, he remained the most recklessly volatile and his development the most fascinatingly unpredictable. During the 1970s he became involved with politically militant programs for television. *Numéro deux* (1975; "Number Two") was a video experiment about family life in contemporary France and the power of ideology and the media—and was commercially unsuccessful.

Godard began making successful narrative feature films again in 1979 with *Sauve qui peut (la vie)* (*Every Man for Himself*), a story of three young Swiss people and their problems of work and love. In the 1980s he was involved in film projects at home as well as in California and Mozambique. His most notable work of the decade was his "trilogy of the sublime," which consisted of three films—*Passion* (1982), *Prénom Carmen* (1983; *First Name: Carmen*), and the highly controversial *Je vous salue, Marie* (1985; *Hail Mary*)—that served as personal statements on femininity, nature, and Christianity. Godard directed few feature films in the 1990s, concentrating instead on the multipart television documentary *Histoire(s) du cinéma*, which offered his iconoclastic views on the first 100 years of motion-picture history. *Éloge de l'amour* (2001; *In Praise of Love*), a narrative film that examined the nature of love and a life in film, stirred controversy over its harsh criticism of Hollywood filmmaking. Later movies include *Notre musique* (2004; "Our Music"), a meditation on war, the experimental collage *Film socialisme* (2010; *Socialism*), and *Adieu au langage* (2014; *Goodbye to Language*), a fragmented narrative about a man, a woman, and a dog, filmed in 3D.

Godard was the recipient of numerous awards, including honorary Césars (1987 and 1998), the Japan Art Association's Praemium Imperiale for theatre/film (2002), and an honorary Academy Award (2010).

JAMES DEAN

(b. Feb. 8 1931, Marion, Ind., U.S.–d. Sept. 30, 1955, Cholame, Calif., U.S.)

Although U.S. method actor James Dean starred in just three motion pictures before his sudden death at age 24, he became a hero for many young Americans. In *East of Eden*, *Rebel Without a Cause*, and *Giant*, all filmed in 1954–55, he created a romantic image of the rebellious, idealistic, and misunderstood teenager that made him the embodiment of his generation.

James Byron Dean was born in Marion, Ind., on Feb. 8, 1931. His mother died when he was young, and he was brought up on a farm by an aunt and uncle. After high school graduation he went to live with his father in California, where he studied drama for two years at the University of California at Los Angeles. He was introduced to the Stanislavsky Method at James Whitmore's drama workshop in Los Angeles and through Lee Strasberg at the Actors Studio in New York City.

Before becoming a film star, Dean played bit parts in a few Hollywood movies and on television and appeared in two Broadway plays. In 1954 director Elia Kazan cast him as the brooding Cal Trask in *East of Eden*, a film adaptation of the novel by John Steinbeck. The following year Dean played two more troubled misfits, Jim Stark in *Rebel Without a Cause* and Jett Rink in *Giant*.

On Sept. 30, 1955, six months after the release of Dean's first major film, he died on the way to a sports car rally. Relatively unknown at the time, he attracted a cult following after the release a month later of *Rebel*, which remains the definitive film of teenage alienation. Decades afterward fans still made pilgrimages to his grave in Fairmount, Ind., and to the intersection on California Highway 46 near Paso Robles where he was killed at the wheel of his Porsche Spyder.

DAME ELIZABETH TAYLOR

(b. Feb. 27, 1932, London, Eng.–d. March 23, 2011, Los Angeles, Calif., U.S.)

Elizabeth Rosemond Taylor was an American motion picture actress noted for her unique beauty and her portrayals of volatile and strong-willed characters.

Taylor's American parents were residing in England at the time of her birth. Shortly before the outbreak of World War II, the family returned to the United States, settling in Los Angeles. Her father was an art dealer, and his business brought him into contact with members of the Hollywood elite. Though her mother, a former stage actress, initially balked at allowing the young Taylor to enter the film industry, an introduction to the chairman of Universal Pictures through one of her father's clients led to a screen test. In 1942 Taylor made her first film, *There's One Born Every Minute*. Though she was soon dropped by Universal, MGM Studios signed her to a contract and cast her in *Lassie Come Home* (1943). That was followed by a star-making performance in *National Velvet* (1944) as a young woman who rescues a horse and trains it to race.

Taylor made a smooth transition from juvenile to adult roles in the films *Life with Father* (1947), *Father of the Bride* (1950), and *An American Tragedy* (1951). She appeared as the frivolous wife of a writer in *The Last Time I Saw Paris* (1954) and as an East Coast woman who marries the patriarch of a disintegrating Texas ranching family (played by Rock

Hudson) in *Giant* (1956). In *Raintree County* (1957), Taylor channeled a deracinated Southern belle who marries an abolitionist (Montgomery Clift). Her mature screen persona—that of a glamorous, passionate woman unafraid of expressing love and anger—reached its peak in film adaptations of Tennessee Williams's *Cat on a Hot Tin Roof* (1958) and *Suddenly, Last Summer* (1959).

Taylor won an Academy Award for her performance as a conflicted New York call girl in *Butterfield 8* (1960), though she publicly expressed her dislike of the film. She met and fell in love with the British actor Richard Burton while they were filming *Cleopatra* (1963). Both were still married at the time, and their affair became a scandal. The couple was hounded by photographers and denounced as immoral in forums as diverse as the Vatican newspaper and the floor of the U.S. House of Representatives. The two ultimately divorced their respective spouses and were themselves married twice (1964–74, 1975–76).

Taylor won a second Academy Award for her performance opposite Burton as the vituperative but vulnerable Martha in *Who's Afraid of Virginia Woolf?* (1966), directed by Mike Nichols from the play by Edward Albee. She costarred with him again in an adaptation of Shakespeare's *The Taming of the Shrew* (1967); the couple made five further films together. After the mid-1970s, however, Taylor appeared only intermittently in films, Broadway plays, and television films.

Taylor's closely scrutinized personal life presaged the advent of the tabloid frenzy of the latter decades of the 20th century. Her eight marriages provided no shortage of fodder: among her husbands were film producer Michael Todd, singer Eddie Fisher, and U.S. Sen. John Warner. An active philanthropist, Taylor helped to establish the American Foundation for AIDS Research (1985), partly motivated by the death of her friend Rock Hudson from the disease. She traveled the world as spokeswoman for the organization and in 1991 established the Elizabeth Taylor AIDS Foundation to provide direct services to those suffering from the disease. Taylor also used the allure of her public image to market lucrative perfume and costume jewelry lines. In 1993 she received the American Film Institute's Life Achievement Award. She received the French Legion of Honour in 1987 and was made Dame Commander of the Order of the British Empire (DBE) in 2000.

CAROL BURNETT
(b. April 26, 1933, San Antonio, Tex., U.S.)

Carol Burnett (full name Carol Creighton Burnett) is an American comedian and actress who starred in a long-running eponymous television variety show in the 1960s and '70s.

As a young girl growing up during the Great Depression, Burnett spent many hours in movie theatres, developing a love for motion pictures and a desire to act. She studied acting at the University of California, Los Angeles (UCLA), in the 1950s, discovering in herself a natural ability to make audiences laugh. In 1955 a mysterious benefactor who enjoyed her work loaned her the money to move to New York City, where she eventually found work in television on the *Winchell-Mahoney Show* and, a year later, on the short-lived comedy *Stanley*, in which she portrayed the girlfriend of the character played by Buddy Hackett. A guest appearance with Garry Moore on the Columbia Broadcasting System (CBS) *Morning Show* in 1956 led to increased exposure for the young comedian, and in 1959 Moore added Burnett to the cast of *The Garry Moore Show*. That same year, she received excellent reviews for her stage work in the Broadway musical comedy *Once Upon a Mattress*.

Burnett had developed a loud sloppy slapstick style of comedy and projected an immense likability on the small screen. In 1961 she won an Emmy Award for her work on *The Garry Moore Show*. Although her 1964 variety series *The Entertainers* lasted only one season, her next program, also a variety show, was a tremendous success. *The Carol Burnett Show* debuted on CBS in 1967 and, at a time when most variety shows had lost their popularity on American television, the show ran until 1979.

With a talented cast that included comedic actor Harvey Korman, handsome straight man Lyle Waggoner, singer Vicki Lawrence, and, later, comedian Tim Conway, *The Carol Burnett Show* featured comedy sketches, musical numbers, weekly guest stars, and an opening segment in which Burnett answered questions from the audience. By the end of 1971, *The Carol Burnett Show* was capping a memorable Saturday night lineup of television comedy that included *All in the Family*, *M*A*S*H*, and *The Mary Tyler Moore Show*. Burnett ended each show by singing her theme song, "It's Time to Say Goodbye," and tugging on her left ear, a special signal to her grandmother.

Over the years Burnett and company developed some popular characters in recurring sketches. Notably, Burnett played the overly proportioned lackadaisical secretary Mrs. Wiggins to Conway's slow-burning Mr. Tudball in a series of slapstick vignettes. A more realistic approach was employed in sketches involving a working-class married couple, Eunice and Ed (played by Burnett and Korman), and the domineering Mama (Lawrence); the characters were later featured in the TV series *Mama's Family* (1983–84 and 1986–90).

Burnett, a six-time Emmy winner, also appeared in a number of motion pictures, including *Who's Been Sleeping in My Bed?* (1963), *Pete 'n' Tillie* (1972), *The Four Seasons* (1981), and *Annie* (1982). She displayed her dramatic skill in the television movie *Friendly Fire* (1979), for which she received an Emmy nomination. Aside from her work on *The Carol Burnett Show*, Burnett was best known for a series of television specials with her friend Julie Andrews, including *Julie and Carol at Carnegie Hall* (1962) and *Julie and Carol at Lincoln Center* (1971).

Burnett's later credits include roles in numerous TV movies and shows; among the latter were *Magnum P.I.*, *Mad About You*, *Desperate Housewives*, and *Glee*. She appeared on Broadway opposite Brian Dennehy in a limited-engagement run of A.R. Gurney's *Love Letters* in 2014.

In 2013 Burnett received the Kennedy Center's Mark Twain Prize for American Humor. Her books include the memoirs *One More Time* (1986), *This Time Together* (2010), and *Carrie and Me* (2013).

JOAN RIVERS

(b. June 8, 1933, Brooklyn, New York, N.Y., U.S.–d. Sept. 4, 2014, New York, N.Y., U.S.)

Born Joan Alexandra Molinsky, Joan Rivers was an American entertainer who launched her career in show business in the 1960s as a raspy-voiced no-holds-barred nightclub and television comic and who was especially known for skewering both herself and celebrities.

After graduating from Barnard College, Rivers joined (1961) the Chicago comedy troupe Second City and performed in nightclubs. Her big break came in 1965, when she was a guest on Johnny Carson's *The Tonight Show*. Her popular performance led to numerous return visits, and from 1983 to 1986 she was a frequent guest host on the show. During that time Rivers—whose acerbic jokes were often preceded by the catchphrase "Can we talk?"—was also a headliner in Las Vegas and a sought-after guest on other TV shows. Though expected to succeed Carson, Rivers was lured by Rupert Murdoch, who had purchased the Fox TV channel, to host the short-lived *The Late Show Starring Joan Rivers* (1986–87); the move ignited a feud with Carson, who never spoke to her again. Three months after she was fired by Fox, Rivers's husband, TV producer Edgar Rosenberg, committed suicide.

Rivers subsequently reinvented herself as a writer, producer, and entrepreneur and launched a TV talk show, *The Joan Rivers Show* (1989–93; also the name of her radio program [1997–2002]). In the mid-1990s Rivers and her daughter, Melissa, became fixtures on the E! Entertainment cable network, interviewing celebrities and commenting (often disparagingly) on their appearance and ensembles worn during their red-carpet entrances to such events as the Grammys, Golden Globes, and Academy Award ceremonies. In 2010 she became the star of the E! show *Fashion Police*, a program that critiqued the stars' wardrobes, and the following year she and her daughter appeared on another reality program, *Joan and Melissa: Joan Knows Best?*

Rivers's acting credits included television movies and series, and she provided voices for characters in such films as *Spaceballs* (1987) and the animated *Shrek 2* (2004). Her life and career are chronicled in the documentary *Joan Rivers: A Piece of Work* (2010), the title of which was partly a reference to her numerous cosmetic surgeries. Rivers also authored a number of books, including the autobiographies *Enter Talking* (1986) and *Still Talking* (1991), both cowritten with Richard Meryman, and the comedic work *I Hate Everyone...Starting with Me* (2012).

On Aug. 28, 2014, Rivers experienced complications and stopped breathing during a medical procedure on her vocal cords. She remained in a medically induced coma for several days before passing on September 4. An estimated 1,500 guests including many celebrities and fans attended a memorial service held on September 7 at which Rivers was eulogized by fellow comedian Howard Stern.

JACK NICHOLSON

(b. April 22, 1937, Neptune, N.J., U.S.)

John Joseph Nicholson, better known as Jack Nicholson, is one of the most prominent American motion-picture actors of his generation, especially noted for his versatile portrayals of unconventional, alienated outsiders.

EARLY LIFE AND CAREER

Nicholson, whose father abandoned his family, grew up believing that his grandmother was his mother and that his mother was his older sister; it was not until he had attained fame that Nicholson himself learned the truth. After graduating from high school, he moved to California, where he took an office job in Metro-Goldwyn-Mayer's animation department. During the years 1957–58 he performed on stage with the Players Ring Theater in Los Angeles and landed some small roles on television. About this time he met B-film king Roger Corman, who offered him the leading role in his low-budget film *The Cry Baby Killer* (1958). Nicholson spent the next decade playing major roles in B-films (including several more for Corman), occasional supporting roles in A-films (such as *Ensign Pulver*, 1964), and guest roles on such television series as *The Andy Griffith Show*. He also dabbled in screenwriting, with his best-known credits being Corman's LSD-hallucination film *The Trip* (1967) and the surrealistic romp

Head (1968), a box-office failure starring the Monkees that has since attracted a cult following.

STARDOM: *EASY RIDER*, *FIVE EASY PIECES*, AND *ONE FLEW OVER THE CUCKOO'S NEST*

Nicholson's big break finally came with *Easy Rider* (1969), a seminal counterculture film starring Peter Fonda and Dennis Hopper as drifting, drug-dealing bikers and Nicholson in a scene-stealing, Oscar-nominated support-ing performance as an alcoholic lawyer. Nicholson's newfound stardom was secured with his leading role in *Five Easy Pieces* (1970), an episodic, existentialist drama and a major entry in Hollywood's "art film" movement of the early 1970s. Nicholson's portrayal of a man alienated from his family, friends, career, and lovers garnered him an Oscar nomination for best actor. His next successful film, director Mike Nichols's *Carnal Knowledge* (1971), was a darkly humorous condemnation of male sexual mores; it was perhaps mainstream Hollywood's most sexually explicit film to date. Nicholson's performance as an emo-tionally empty, predatory chauvinist showcased his talent for interjecting humour into serious situations as a means to underscore inherent irony—typically, his darkest char-acters are wickedly funny.

Nicholson earned another Oscar nomination for *The Last Detail* (1973), in which he portrayed a rowdy military police officer who reluctantly escorts a young sailor to military prison. He next starred in Roman Polanski's *Chinatown* (1974), an homage to the film noir detective films of the 1940s and a widely acknowledged cinematic masterpiece. Nicholson's brilliant performance as stylish private eye Jake Gittes, who realizes too late his impo-tence in the face of wealth and corruption, earned him a fourth Oscar nomination. The actor capped this highly successful period with his first Oscar win, for *One Flew over the Cuckoo's Nest* (1975), in which his iconoclastic, free-spirited characterization of mental institution inmate R.P. McMurphy serves as a metaphor for the hopelessness of rebellion against established authority. Other notable Nicholson films from this period include Michelangelo Antonioni's *Professione: reporter* (1975; *The Passenger*), in which Nicholson portrays a depressed reporter who assumes a dead man's identity, and *Tommy* (1975), director Ken Russell's garish production of the Who's rock opera, featuring Nicholson in a supporting singing role as the title character's doctor.

THE SHINING, TERMS OF ENDEARMENT, AND AS GOOD AS IT GETS

His stardom assured, Nicholson worked sporadically during the next few years. He costarred with Marlon Brando in the Arthur Penn western *The Missouri Breaks* (1976), an uneven yet compellingly quirky film; and he directed and starred in another revisionist western, *Goin' South* (1978). His next notable role was in director Stanley Kubrick's *The Shining* (1980); an adaptation of the Stephen King novel, it is a film over which critical opinion remains divided but the one with Nicholson's ax-wielding rampage—culminating in his demonic cry of "Heeeere's Johnny!"—that became one of the indelible cinematic images of the era. Nicholson appeared in several quality films during the 1980s, garnering further Academy Award nominations for *Reds* (1981), *Prizzi's Honor* (1985), and *Ironweed* (1987) and winning a best supporting actor Oscar for his role as a drunken-but-decent ex-astronaut in *Terms of Endearment* (1983). Two of his most popular performances of the decade came in *The Witches of Eastwick*

(1987) and *Batman* (1989), which featured Nicholson's over-the-top comic turns as the Devil and the Joker, respectively.

By the 1990s Nicholson was regarded as a screen icon. He began the decade by directing and starring in *The Two Jakes* (1990), a sequel to *Chinatown* that generated luke-warm reviews. Better-received were *Hoffa* (1992), in which he portrayed the controversial Teamsters boss Jimmy Hoffa, and *A Few Good Men* (1992), in which his supporting performance as a dyspeptic marine colonel earned him his 10th Oscar nomination, an all-time record for a male actor. His 11th nomination, for his portrayal of a misanthropic writer in *As Good as It Gets* (1997), resulted in Nicholson's third Oscar (his second for best actor).

LATER WORK

At the beginning of the 21st century, Nicholson continued to star in dramatic roles. After playing a world-weary former cop in Sean Penn's *The Pledge* (2001), he scored another personal triumph with his much-lauded performance as the title character in *About Schmidt* (2002), a movie about a retired widower seeking to mend his relationship with his daughter. Nicholson's understated acting in the melancholic comedy earned him a 12th Academy Award nomination. In 2006 he appeared as Irish mobster Frank Costello in Martin Scorsese's *The Departed*. Nicholson continued his success in comedic roles when he starred as an over-the-top psychiatrist in *Anger Management* (2003) and as an aging playboy who falls in love with a playwright (played by Diane Keaton) in *Something's Gotta Give* (2004). In *The Bucket List* (2007) Nicholson and Morgan Freeman portray two terminally ill men who escape a hospital ward so they can accomplish everything they want to do before dying. He later appeared as an irascible father in the romantic comedy *How Do You Know* (2010), his fourth collaboration with director James L. Brooks.

Although Nicholson's widely imitated trademarks of a devilish smile and a slow, detached speaking style remained constant throughout the years, his screen persona mellowed in its metamorphosis from iconoclastic leading man to mainstream character actor, and his characters of later years reflect in many ways the maturation of his generation. As he entered his 60s, he often played men with a youthful rebellious streak but who have also learned the value of sensitivity. Nicholson was awarded the American Film Institute's Life Achievement Award in 1994.

GEORGE CARLIN

(b. May 12, 1937, New York, N.Y., U.S.–d. June 22, 2008, Santa Monica, Calif., U.S.)

George Denis Patrick Carlin, commonly known as George Carlin, was an American comedian whose "Seven Words You Can Never Say on Television" routine led to a U.S. Supreme Court ruling that gave the Federal Communications Commission (FCC) the right to determine when to censor radio and TV broadcasts.

Carlin began working in the late 1950s as a wisecracking radio disc jockey and low-key stand-up comedian known for such whimsical routines as "Wonderful WINO" and the "Hippy Dippy Weatherman." Beginning in the 1970s, however, he transformed himself into a provocative and incisive antiestablishment comic icon. Carlin was most closely identified with the monologue "Seven Words You Can Never Say on Television," in which he satirically analyzed the use and misuse of seven of the raunchiest obscenities in the English language. Carlin was arrested in 1972 for performing the monologue onstage, but a judge dismissed the case. In 1973 New York City radio station

George Carlin performs a comedy show on February 28, 2007.

WBAI-FM triggered a lawsuit by the FCC after it aired a recorded version of the routine called "Filthy Words." The landmark "Carlin case" was finally settled in 1978 by the U.S. Supreme Court: in a 5–4 ruling, it gave the FCC the ability to censor offensive content in radio and TV broadcasts.

Carlin released more than 20 comedy albums and starred in 14 HBO television specials. As an actor, he usually played a character inspired by his own comic persona (as in the short-lived situation comedy *The George Carlin Show* [1994]), with the notable exception of his stint in the 1990s as the amiable narrator (and onscreen host, Mr. Conductor) of the children's programs *Thomas the Tank Engine and Friends* and *Shining Time Station*. Carlin was honoured with the American Comedy Awards' Lifetime Achievement Award (2001) and the Mark Twain Prize for American Humor (2008). In 2004 the cable television network Comedy Central ranked Carlin second on its list of the "100 Greatest Stand-Ups of All Time," behind African American actor-comedian Richard Pryor and just ahead of the legendary Lenny Bruce. His final HBO special, *It's Bad for Ya*, aired just months before his death, and it won the Grammy Award for best comedy album in 2009. His memoir, *Last Words*, was published later that year.

MORGAN FREEMAN

(b. June 1, 1937, Memphis, Tenn., U.S.)

Morgan Freeman is an American actor whose emotional depth and versatility made him one of the most-respected performers of his generation. Over a career that included numerous memorable performances on stage, screen, and television, Freeman was one of the few African American actors who consistently received roles that were not specifically written for black actors.

As a young man, Freeman had aspirations of being a fighter pilot; however, a stint in the air force (1955–59) proved disappointing, and he turned his attention to acting. He made his Broadway debut in an all-black production of *Hello Dolly!* in 1967. In the 1970s he continued to work on stage and also appeared on the educational children's television show *The Electric Company* as the character Easy Reader. Freeman's performance in the film *Brubaker* (1980) and on the soap opera *Another World* (1982–84), along with

Morgan Freeman.

several enthusiastic reviews for his theatrical work in the early 1980s, led to more challenging film roles. His portrayal of a dangerous hustler in *Street Smart* (1987) earned Freeman his first Academy Award nomination, for best supporting actor. He was later nominated for a best-actor Oscar for his work in *Driving Miss Daisy* (1989), in which he re-created the role of Hoke after first performing it on stage. He evinced a disciplinarian principal in *Lean on Me* (1989), a hard-hearted Civil War soldier in *Glory* (1989), and an aging gunslinger in *Unforgiven* (1992). He made his directorial debut with the antiapartheid film *Bopha!* (1993). A third Oscar nomination came for his soulful turn as a convict in *The Shawshank Redemption* (1994).

Freeman later appeared in several crime dramas, including *Se7en* (1995), *Kiss the Girls* (1997), and *Along Came a Spider* (2001)—the latter two based on James Patterson novels—as well as *The Sum of All Fears* (2002). He won an Academy Award for best supporting actor for his performance as a former boxer in Clint Eastwood's *Million Dollar Baby* (2004) before appearing as Lucius Fox, a research and development guru, in Christopher Nolan's *Batman Begins* (2005). Freeman reprised the latter role in the sequels *The Dark Knight* (2008) and *The Dark Knight Rises* (2012). In *The Bucket List* (2007) he and Jack Nicholson played terminally ill cancer patients who make the most of their remaining time.

In 2008 Freeman returned to Broadway after nearly 20 years away from the stage, taking the role of Frank Elgin, a talented yet dispirited actor who has lost the will to perform, in *The Country Girl*. The following year he reteamed with Eastwood on *Invictus*, a drama in which he played Nelson Mandela, who sought to unite divided South Africa by supporting the national rugby team's quest to win the 1995 World Cup. Freeman later appeared as a former CIA agent in the action comedy *Red* (2010), as a high-ranking

U.S. politician in the thriller *Olympus Has Fallen* (2013), and as a postapocalyptic survivalist in the science-fiction adventure *Oblivion* (2013). He also pursued less-suspenseful fare with roles in the sentimental dramas *Dolphin Tale* (2011) and its sequel, *Dolphin Tale 2* (2014), and in *The Magic of Belle Isle* (2012). He went for laughs in the buddy comedy *Last Vegas* (2013), in which he starred opposite Robert De Niro, Michael Douglas, and Kevin Kline. And he voiced a wizard in *The LEGO Movie* (2014), a computer-animated adventure that featured renderings of LEGO toys as the characters and settings. In *Transcendence* (2014) he played an anti-artificial-intelligence activist, and in *Lucy* (2014) he portrayed a psychology professor.

Freeman was the recipient of numerous awards, including a Kennedy Center Honor in 2008 and the Cecil B. DeMille Award (a Golden Globe for lifetime achievement) in 2012.

DUSTIN HOFFMAN

(b. Aug. 8, 1937, Los Angeles, Calif., U.S.)

Dustin Hoffman is an acclaimed American actor known for his versatile portrayals of antiheroes and vulnerable types. Short in stature and not typically handsome, he helped to usher in a new Hollywood tradition of average-looking but emotionally explosive leading men.

Hoffman began acting at age 19 after dropping out of music studies at California's Santa Monica City College. He then moved to New York City, where he struggled for several years in odd jobs and eventually landed small parts on television and leading roles Off-Broadway, where he won an Obie Award.

After appearing in one forgettable Spanish-Italian coproduction, Hoffman was cast in his second film, Mike Nichols's *The Graduate* (1967), beating out contemporaries

Robert Redford and Charles Grodin. Hoffman was 30 years old when he played the 21-year-old Benjamin Braddock, an upper-middle-class college graduate who, in a search for a meaningful future, aimlessly drifts into an affair with a married woman who is the age of his parents. A tremendously successful social comedy, the film struck a nerve with youthful audiences disenchanted with the American establishment, and Hoffman was launched as a star.

In John Schlesinger's *Midnight Cowboy*, which won an Academy Award for best picture of 1969, Hoffman played "Ratso" Rizzo, a homeless man with tuberculosis who develops a friendship with an unsuccessful male prostitute (played by Jon Voight). Grim and downbeat in its depiction of a heartless New York City, the film was another unlikely success for Hoffman.

The actor moved smoothly into the 1970s playing numerous antiheroes such as the powerless witness to Native American genocide in *Little Big Man* (1970), the cowardly mathematician who violently defends his home in *Straw Dogs* (1971), the self-destructive comic Lenny Bruce in *Lenny* (1974), and an ex-convict who cannot resist the lure of crime in *Straight Time* (1978).

Thrice previously nominated for the Oscar, Hoffman finally won a best actor award for his sympathetic portrayal of a divorced single father in *Kramer vs. Kramer* (1979) and earned another nomination for *Tootsie* (1982), in which he played an out-of-work actor who, while masquerading as a woman, finds steady employment on a daytime soap opera.

Two returns to the stage proved great triumphs for Hoffman in the 1980s. First was his much-lauded performance as Willy Loman in the 1984 Broadway revival of Arthur Miller's *Death of a Salesman*, which was adapted for television the following year by CBS and earned Hoffman an Emmy Award and a Golden Globe Award. Always determined to select a challenging variety of roles, he next appeared on stage in London as Shylock in Sir Peter Hall's production of *The Merchant of Venice* (1989). For his film work, Hoffman closed out the decade with another best actor Oscar for his convincing depiction of a middle-aged autistic savant in *Rain Man* (1988). Not unlike Hoffman's earlier roles, *Rain Man*'s Raymond Babbitt is a difficult character to embrace because of his emotionless nature, but the actor elicits just the right amount of sympathy from an audience.

After a disappointing series of big-budget Hollywood projects such as *Hook* (1991), *Billy Bathgate* (1991), *Hero* (1992), *Outbreak* (1995), and *Sphere* (1998), the actor returned to form as a sleazy, fame-hungry Hollywood producer who coconspires to fool the entire world into believing that the United States is at war with Albania in *Wag the Dog* (1997), a biting political satire that gave Hoffman his seventh Academy Award nomination. He later portrayed the grand inquisitor in the French production of *Messenger: The Story of Joan of Arc* (1999), and in 2003 he appeared in the courtroom thriller *Runaway Jury*. In 2004 he starred opposite Lily Tomlin in *I Heart Huckabees*, a comedy about a husband-and-wife detective team that helps clients solve their existential problems, and with Robert De Niro in the broad comedy *Meet the Fockers*.

Hoffman's subsequent films include *Stranger Than Fiction* (2006) and the children's fantasy *Mr. Magorium's Wonder Emporium* (2007). Hoffman and *Stranger Than Fiction* costar Emma Thompson played lonely strangers who fall in love in *Last Chance Harvey* (2008). He reprised his *Meet the Fockers* role in its sequel, *Little Fockers* (2010), and later appeared as the title character's father in the dark comedy *Barney's Version* (2010). In addition, Hoffman lent his voice to the computer-animated films *The Tale of Despereaux* (2008), *Kung Fu Panda* (2008), *Kung Fu Panda 2* (2011), and *Kung Fu Panda 3* (2016). Shifting his focus to television, Hoffman starred as an ex-con gambler on the HBO series *Luck* (2011–12), a drama set in the world of professional horse racing, and as Mr. Henry Hoppy in a BBC adaptation of the Roald Dahl's novel *Esio Trot* (2015). On the big screen, he starred as a restaurant owner in *Chef* (2014), as a choirmaster at a music academy in *Boychoir* (2014), as the father of a cobbler whose sewing machine has magical powers in *The Cobbler* (2015). Also in 2015 Hoffman had a role in *The Program*, a biographical drama about disgraced cyclist Lance Armstrong based on David Walsh's book *Seven Deadly Sins*.

In 2012, at the age of 75, Hoffman made his debut as a film director with *Quartet*, an ensemble comedy about former opera singers residing in an English retirement home. That same year he was named a Kennedy Center honoree.

SIR ANTHONY HOPKINS
(b. Dec. 31, 1937, Port Talbot, West Glamorgan, Wales)

S ir Philip Anthony Hopkins, better known as simply Anthony Hopkins, is a Welsh stage and film actor of burning intensity, often seen at his best when playing pathetic misfits or characters on the fringes of insanity.

Hopkins had early ambitions to be a concert pianist. He began acting at age 18 when he joined a YMCA dramatic club. He received a scholarship to the Cardiff College of Music and Drama, and he toured with the Arts Council as a stage manager and actor after his graduation. He then spent two years with the Royal Artillery. Upon his demobilization he resumed his acting career, making his professional debut in 1960. A self-described "actor of instinct," he gained needed training by enrolling at the Royal Academy of Dramatic Art in 1961 and graduated as a silver medalist two years later. He first appeared on the London stage in Lindsay Anderson's production of *Julius Caesar* (1964). It was during this period that he appeared in his first film, the Anderson-directed short subject *The White Bus* (released in 1967).

Hopkins was accepted into Laurence Olivier's National Theatre company in 1965, and he understudied Olivier in several productions before attracting critical attention with his performances as Edgar in August Strindberg's *The Dance of Death* and as Andrey Prozorov in Anton Chekhov's *Three Sisters* (both 1967). At last attracting the attention of the critics, he soon found himself being promoted as the "new Olivier," and it was during this initial burst of adulation that he landed the juicy role of Prince Richard the Lion-heart in the 1968 film version of James Goldman's play *The Lion in Winter*. In 1974 he enjoyed a double professional triumph when he starred in the American television miniseries *QB VII* and also played the role of Dr. Martin Dysart in the original Broadway production of *Equus*.

Despite years of promise and glowing reviews, Hopkins found his career impeded by his recalcitrant attitude and battles with alcoholism. After waking up in a Phoenix hotel room in 1975 and not being able to remember how he got there, Hopkins resolved to reform: "I led a pretty self-destructive life for a few decades. It was only after I put my demons behind me that I was able to fully enjoy acting." His career gained momentum, and his subsequent screen credits include acclaimed performances as a mentally unhinged ventriloquist in *Magic* (1978) and as Joseph Merrick's doctor in *The Elephant*

Man (1980), as well as sharply etched portrayals of two roles previously associated with Charles Laughton: Quasimodo in *The Hunchback of Notre Dame* (1982) and *Captain Bligh in The Bounty* (1984). During this period Hopkins won Emmy Awards for his performances as Bruno Richard Hauptmann in *The Lindbergh Kidnapping Case* (1976) and as Adolf Hitler in *The Bunker* (1981). In 1989 he made his West End stage debut in the musical drama *M. Butterfly*.

While critical acclaim has been lavished upon Hopkins's rich, full-blooded characterizations of such real-life personalities as Yitzhak Rabin, John Quincy Adams, Richard M. Nixon, C.S. Lewis, and Pablo Picasso, the film role with which he is most identified, and for which he received an Academy Award, was that of the horrifyingly brilliant serial killer Hannibal ("the Cannibal") Lecter in *The Silence of the Lambs* (1991). He received subsequent Oscar nominations for his roles as a duty-bound butler in *Remains of the Day* (1993), as the 37th U.S. president in *Nixon* (1995), and as Adams in *Amistad* (1997). Other notable roles in the 1990s include early 20th-century patriarchs in *Howards End* (1992) and *Legends of the Fall* (1994), as well as storied adventurers in Bram Stoker's *Dracula* (1992) and *The Mask of Zorro* (1998).

Hopkins revived his celebrated portrayal of Hannibal Lecter in *Hannibal* (2001) and *Red Dragon* (2002) before leading the cast of a 2003 adaptation of Philip Roth's novel *The Human Stain*. In 2005 he starred as a brilliant mathematician afflicted with mental illness in *Proof* and as a New Zealand motorcycle racer in *The World's Fastest Indian*. After enlivening the legal thriller *Fracture* (2007), Hopkins appeared in several big-budget movies rooted in mythology, including *Beowulf* (2007; as King Hrothgar) and *The Wolfman* (2010). He played the Norse god Odin in *Thor* (2011) and its sequel, *Thor: The Dark World* (2013). He also starred in the kaleidoscopic drama *360* (2011) and as film director Alfred Hitchcock in *Hitchcock* (2012), which centred on the making of the classic suspense movie *Psycho* (1960). In the ensemble action comedy *Red 2* (2013) Hopkins stole scenes as an eccentric nuclear scientist, and in the biblical drama *Noah* (2014) he dispensed wisdom to the title character as Methuselah.

For lifetime achievement, Hopkins received a Golden Globe Award (2006) and a British Academy of Film and Television Arts (BAFTA) Award (2008). After being made Commander of the Order of the British Empire (CBE) in 1987, he was knighted in 1993.

FRANCIS FORD COPPOLA
(b. April 7, 1939, Detroit, Mich., U.S.)

Francis Ford Coppola is an American motion-picture director, writer, and producer whose films range from sweeping epics to small-scale character studies. As the director of films such as *The Godfather* (1972), *The Conversation* (1974), and *Apocalypse Now* (19379), he enjoyed his greatest success and influence in the 1970s, when he attempted to create an alternative to the Hollywood system of film production and distribution.

EARLY YEARS

Coppola's father, Carmine, a frustrated composer who played flute in several orchestras, including Arturo Toscanini's NBC Symphony orchestra, settled his family in the New York City area. Coppola grew up in and around Queens and in Great Neck, on Long Island.

Confined to bed with polio at age nine, he devised puppet shows for his own entertainment and soon began making 8-mm films. After earning a B.A. in drama from Hofstra University, he pursued a Master of Fine Arts degree at the University of California at Los Angeles, studying filmmaking. During that period Coppola began working for noted low-budget exploitation-film producer-director Roger Corman, for whose American International Pictures he performed second-unit photography and direction, among other tasks. One of Coppola's first projects was writing dialogue to be dubbed into his reedited versions of a pair of Russian-made films that became *The Magic Voyage of Sinbad* and *Battle Beyond the Sun* (both 1963). While on location in Ireland, Coppola persuaded Corman to put up $20,000 to bankroll his first directorial effort, *Dementia 13* (1963), a gory horror film based on a script that Coppola had hastily written.

After contributing to the scripts of *This Property Is Condemned* and *Is Paris Burning?* (both 1966) as a contract writer for Seven Arts, Coppola wrote and directed the charming coming-of-age tale *You're a Big Boy Now* (also 1966), which served as his master's thesis film. Short on plot but rich with incident, it was the story of a virginal young man (played by Peter Kasner) looking for love while in the employ of the New York Public Library. It featured a remarkable cast (including Elizabeth Hartman, Karen Black, Rip Torn, Tony Bill, Julie Harris, and Geraldine Page) and a soundtrack by the Lovin' Spoonful. Impressed by the film, Warner Brothers signed Coppola to direct the big-budget musical *Finian's Rainbow* (1968). Based on a Broadway play from the 1940s that subversively satirized racism, it starred masterful dancer Fred Astaire but stumbled partly as a result of the mid-production departure of choreographer Hermes Pan.

Warner Brothers provided the financing ($750,000) for Coppola's next project, *The Rain People* (1969). Scripted and directed by Coppola, it followed a pregnant Long Island housewife (Shirley Knight) who leaves her husband and takes to the road. Her path crosses most significantly with those of a brain-damaged former football player (James Caan) and a Nebraska policeman (Robert Duvall). Warner Brothers had tied its financing of *The Rain People* to another project from Coppola's fledgling Zoetrope Productions, *THX-1138*, directed by his friend George Lucas. Disappointed by the box-office results of Coppola's film and unimpressed by the first cut of Lucas's, the studio ended the partnership. In the meantime, Coppola won an Academy Award for his collaboration with Franklin Schaffner on the screenplay for *Patton* (1970).

THE 1970S

Coppola's breakthrough came with *The Godfather* (1972), a brilliant, enormously successful, muscular adaptation of Mario Puzo's blockbuster novel of the same name. A huge box-office hit (the fifth highest-grossing film of the 1970s), *The Godfather* was also lauded by critics and was ranked third on the American Film Institute's 1998 list of the top 100 American films of all time. A violent, emotionally charged exploration of a Mafia family, *The Godfather* is a mythic gangster film, but it is also the story of a father and his sons. Marlon Brando won the Academy Award for best actor for his portrayal of the title capo, Vito Corleone. John Cazale, Caan, and Al Pacino played his sons and Duvall his trusted adviser (the last three

Francis Ford Coppola (right) directing Marlon Brando (left) in The Godfather *(1972).*

were nominated for best supporting actor awards). Coppola was nominated as best director, and he and Puzo won the award for best adapted screenplay.

Financially empowered to make a less commercial, more personal film, Coppola wrote, directed, and produced *The Conversation* (1974), a meditation on technology's dehumanizing power. Gene Hackman starred as a surveillance expert who suspects that a couple upon whom he has electronically eavesdropped are about to be murdered. Too bleak for some tastes, the film nonetheless boasted an Academy Award-nominated screenplay as well as strong performances, and it was nominated for the Academy Award for best picture.

Coppola, however, ended up competing against himself, as his masterful sequel *The Godfather: Part II* (1974) won that year's Academy Award for best picture. Moving both forward in time through the 1950s and back to the early years of the 20th century, *Godfather II* bookended the events in *The Godfather* with contrapuntal stories that enriched each other (and, in the process, the original film). Robert De Niro played the young Vito Corleone, who, having immigrated from Italy, takes over New York's Little Italy bit by bit, ruthlessly ascending to the rank of "godfather." In the parallel 1950s story, Vito's son Michael (Pacino) endeavours (just as ruthlessly) to make the Corleone family legitimate. *The Godfather: Part II* made explicit the immigrant struggle for survival in America that was at the root of the first "Godfather." Michael Gazzo and Actors Studio guru Lee Strasberg were nominated for the Academy Award for best supporting actor, which was won by De Niro. Moreover, Coppola won the award for best director and shared the best screenplay award with Puzo while Carmine Coppola and Nino Rota won the award for their musical score.

At the peak of his influence—no other writer-director had ever had two best picture nominations and two best screenplay nominations in the same year—Coppola set about the arduous task of filming *Apocalypse Now* (1979), which transposed Joseph Conrad's novella *Heart of Darkness* to the Vietnam War with a script by Coppola, John Milius, and Michael Herr. The troubled production was plagued by natural disasters (shot on location in the Philippines, it was struck by a typhoon and an earthquake), personal tragedy (star Martin Sheen suffered a heart attack and nearly died), and simple hubris. Coppola's original $12 million budget finally exceeded $30 million, much of it due to his own profligacy, and a considerable portion of the overrun was paid for by Coppola himself.

Moreover, the excessive cost of production and the rumours from the troubled set besmirched the reputation Coppola had earned as the crown prince of Hollywood directors. The quixotic making of the film was chronicled by Coppola's wife, Eleanor, in her journal *Notes* (1979) and later in the documentary *Hearts of Darkness* (1991).

Despite its well-documented problems and setbacks, *Apocalypse Now* is an assault on the senses that is generally regarded as a flawed masterpiece. It is especially compelling when Duvall and Frederic Forrest are front and centre. Brando's darkly complex depiction of the monomaniacal colonel Kurtz was celebrated by some critics and dismissed by others, but it remains hard to forget. In the end, *Apocalypse Now* earned eight Academy Award nominations, including best picture, and was anything but a failure at the box office, finishing as the year's sixth highest-grossing motion picture.

THE 1980S

In 1980, with the money he had made from his films — especially the *Godfather* movies — Coppola set about trying to realize his dream of establishing a creator-friendly antiestablishment studio to compete with the major Hollywood studios. Purchasing the lot of the former Hollywood General Studios, he established Zoetrope Studios, determined to employ the latest filmmaking technology and distribution techniques (including his vision of satellite-enabled distribution). His dream proved to be short-lived, however, as the studio's first film — the Coppola-written and -directed *One from the Heart* (1982), an ultra-stylized romantic comedy — cost some $27 million to make and crashed at the box office. Coppola was forced to sell many of his assets and to close the studio in Los Angeles, though he continued to operate his production company in San Francisco, his home.

Returning to work for hire, Coppola retrenched by directing a pair of film adaptations of young-adult novels by S.E. Hinton, both of which were released in 1983. Made first, *The Outsiders*—a *Rebel Without a Cause*-style story of teenage alienation starring Matt Dillon and a raft of soon-to-be stars including Patrick Swayze, Tom Cruise, Rob Lowe, Emilio Estevez, and Diane Lane—was the more popular of the two films. However, the expressionistic black-and-white *Rumble Fish*, which also featured Dillon, was arguably the better film.

The Cotton Club (1984) marked Coppola's much-antici-pated return to big-budget gangster films, but, although his re-creation of 1930s Harlem was stylish, well cast, and opulently produced, most critics felt that his reach had exceeded his grasp this time. An atypical effort for Coppola, the quirky *Peggy Sue Got Married* (1986) followed. In it an unhappily married woman (Kathleen Turner) is transported in time back to her senior year of high school, where she gets a second chance to evaluate her awful hus-band (Nicolas Cage, Coppola's nephew). Coppola's next project, the sombre *Gardens of Stone* (1987), was a portrait of the soldiers assigned to guard duty at Arlington National Cemetery during the Vietnam War, with Caan as the ser-geant in charge, Anjelica Huston as his girlfriend, and D.B. Sweeney as the gung ho kid whose wish to fight overseas is tragically granted. The film fared badly with critics and audiences, but Coppola's life at that time was much more disturbed by the loss of his son Giancarlo in a boating accident.

Tucker: The Man and His Dream (1988) did no better commercially, but this handsome biographical film was arguably Coppola's best film in years. Jeff Bridges played visionary car designer Preston Tucker, whose superior product (the "Tucker Torpedo") is squelched through the collusion of Detroit's giant manufacturers and their Washington lobbyists. The parallel between Tucker's ambitions as an automaker and Coppola's as a filmmaker was not lost on many critics. Coppola also contributed the "Life Without Zoe" segment to *New York Stories* (1989), a trilogy that also included segments by Martin Scorsese and Woody Allen.

THE 1990s

Coppola and Puzo were invited by Paramount to submit another installment of the *Godfather* saga, and the result was *The Godfather: Part III* (1990). While not in the same league as the first two films in the series, it did possess some merit. The cast included Pacino, Keaton, Andy Garcia, Talia Shire, Joe Mantegna, and Eli Wallach, but Coppola was taken to task by critics for replacing Winona Ryder with his daughter Sofia Coppola, who failed to rise to the challenge of her key part. (Notwithstanding this disappointment, she would go on become a successful film director in her own right.)

The moderate commercial success of *The Godfather: Part III* helped Coppola produce another big-budget film, *Dracula* (1992). A florid, bloody, occasionally silly, violently erotic version of the oft-filmed tale, with eccentric Gary Oldham as the count and Ryder as his (possibly) reincarnated love, it was easily the most faithful and horrific version of Bram Stoker's famous novel. It also returned Coppola, at long last, to bankability.

In *Jack* (1996), Robin Williams starred as a 10-year-old boy whose cells age him four times as fast as a normal person's, making his interactions with other children extremely difficult. Based on a best-selling novel by John Grisham, *The Rainmaker* (1997) starred Matt Damon as a young attorney in Memphis whose idealism clashes with the greed of his ambulance-chasing boss. Although it was only a modest commercial success, *The Rainmaker* received positive reviews. Coppola then entered into a long fallow period, primary as a result of his embroilment in a legal dispute with Warner Brothers involving a three-picture deal for an adaptation of *Pinocchio*, the children's classic *The Secret Garden*, and a biography of J. Edgar Hoover. In the end Coppola won a 1998 court judgment against the studio that awarded him $20 million for the studio's abandonment of the project along with another $60 million in punitive damages.

LATER WORK

In the wake of that protracted legal struggle, Coppola released *Apocalypse Now Redux* (2001), which contained more than 40 minutes of restored footage not seen in the original 1979 version. For much of the early 21st century, Coppola acted as an executive producer for others' films, ran a winery, published a literary magazine, and continued to oversee his company American Zoetrope, which produced films and provided postproduction services. Throughout his career Coppola had produced many of the films he directed and, even when not directing, had many successes as a producer, including *American Graffiti* (1973), directed by George Lucas; *The Black Stallion* (1979), directed by Carroll Ballard; and *Lost in Translation* (2003), the film with which his daughter Sofia established herself as a director.

In 2007 he returned to directing with the self-financed *Youth Without Youth*, a fantastical drama about a septuagenarian Romanian professor (Tim Roth) who becomes decades younger when he is struck by lightning on the eve of World War II. After that film's commercial failure,

Coppola was on surer footing with *Tetro* (2009), about a teenager who travels to Argentina and reunites with his expatriate older half-brother. Although not a box-office success, the film (shot primarily in black and white) earned Coppola some of his best reviews in years. *Twixt* (2011), a thriller starring Val Kilmer, fared much less well critically and commercially.

For his achievements in film, Coppola was given the Irving Thalberg award by the Academy of Motion Picture Arts and Sciences in 2010.

AL PACINO
(b. April 25, 1940, New York, N.Y., U.S.)

Born Alfredo James Pacino, American actor Al Pacino is best known for his intense, explosive acting style.

After growing up in East Harlem and the Bronx, Pacino moved at age 19 to Greenwich Village, where he studied acting at the Herbert Berghof Studio and appeared in many Off-Broadway and out-of-town pro- ductions, including *Hello, Out There* (1963) and *Why Is a Crooked Letter* (1966). He took further acting lessons from Lee Strasberg and played a small part in the film *Me, Natalie* in 1969. The same year, he made his Broadway debut and won a Tony Award for his performance in the play *Does the Tiger Wear a Necktie?* Pacino's first leading role in a film came with *The Panic in Needle Park* (1971), a grim tale of heroin addiction that became something of a cult classic.

Director Francis Ford Coppola cast Pacino in the film that would make him a star, *The Godfather* (1972). The saga of a family of gangsters and their fight to main- tain power in changing times, *The Godfather* was a wildly popular film that won the Academy Award for best pic- ture and earned Pacino numerous accolades for his intense performance as Michael Corleone, a gangster's son who reluctantly takes over the "family business." Pacino solidified his standing as one of Hollywood's most dynamic stars in his next few films. In *Scarecrow* (1973), he teamed with Gene Hackman in a bittersweet story about two transients, and his roles in *Serpico* (1973) and *Dog Day Afternoon* (1975) displayed Pacino's characteristic screen qualities of brooding seriousness and explosive rage. He also repeated the role of Michael Corleone for Coppola's *The Godfather: Part II* (1974), a film that, like its predecessor, won the best picture Oscar.

Pacino's next few films did not fare as well. *Bobby Deerfield* (1977) was notable as his first box-office failure since he had become a star. The dark comedy ...*And Justice for All* (1979) featured some of Pacino's most memorable scenes, but *Cruising* (1980) and the light comedy *Author! Author!* (1982) were critical and popular disasters.

In Brian De Palma's *Scarface* (1983), Pacino returned to the kind of combustible, high-intensity role that had made him famous. As gangster Tony Montana, Pacino gave a highly charged, unrestrained performance that, although loved by some and deplored by others, ranks among his most unforgettable. His next film, *Revolution* (1985), was an expensive flop, and Pacino did not appear in another film for four years.

Sea of Love (1989), his biggest hit in years, reestablished Pacino as a major film star. He reprised the role of Michael Corleone in *The Godfather: Part III* (1990), but it was his hilarious portrayal of grotesque gangster Big Boy Caprice in *Dick Tracy* (1990) that won him a supporting actor Oscar nomination. *Frankie and Johnny* (1991) and *Glengarry Glen Ross* (1992), both adaptations of plays, continued his string of well-received films, and he won a best actor Oscar for his portrayal of a bitter blind man in *Scent of a Woman* (1992). Pacino's other notable films of the 1990s include *Carlito's Way* (1993); *Heat* (1995), a crime drama in which he played a detective hunting a thief (Robert De Niro); *Donnie Brasco* (1997), in which he starred as a low-level mobster who unknowingly befriends an FBI agent (Johnny Depp); and Oliver Stone's *Any Given Sunday* (1999). Also in 1999 Pacino appeared opposite Russell Crowe in *The Insider*; based on real-life events, it examines tobacco companies and their efforts to conceal the dangerous side effects of cigarettes.

Pacino's prolific acting career continued into the 21st century. In 2002 he starred with Robin Williams in the thriller *Insomnia*, and he later appeared in *Ocean's Thirteen* (2007), the final installment of a popular

Al Pacino dances with actress Gabrielle Anwar in the movie Scent of a Woman *(1992).*

comedy trilogy that featured George Clooney and Brad Pitt. After skewering his public persona with a role as himself in the Adam Sandler comedy *Jack and Jill* (2011), Pacino played an aging gangster in *Stand Up Guys* (2012). He evinced the isolation of a small-town locksmith in *Manglehorn* (2014) and the late-life epiphany of a rock star in *Danny Collins* (2015).

In between his big-screen work, Pacino appeared in several television productions for HBO. For his role as homophobic lawyer Roy Cohn in *Angels in America* (2003), an adaptation of Tony Kushner's two-part play about AIDS in the 1980s, he won an Emmy Award and a Golden Globe Award. His performance as Jack Kevorkian, a doctor who assisted in the suicide of terminally ill patients, in the movie *You Don't Know Jack* (2010) earned him the same awards. He later starred as another controversial figure in David Mamet's *Phil Spector* (2013), which was set during the embattled record producer's first trial for murder.

Pacino frequently returned to the stage throughout his career, notably winning a Tony Award for his leading role in *The Basic Training of Pavlo Hummel* (1977). He also starred in such plays as Shakespeare's *Richard III* (1973, 1979), *Julius Caesar* (1988), and *The Merchant of Venice* (2010); Mamet's *American Buffalo* (1980, 1981, 1983) and *Glengarry Glen Ross* (2012); and Oscar Wilde's *Salomé* (1992, 2003, 2006). In 1992 Pacino originated the role of Harry Levine, a washed-up writer who is depressed about his lack of success, in the Broadway drama *Chinese Coffee*; he later directed and starred in a 2000 film adaptation. He also directed the documentary films *Looking for Richard* (1996) and *Wilde Salomé* (2011), which offered behind-the-scenes looks at two of his stage productions.

BRUCE LEE

(b. Nov. 27, 1940, San Francisco, Calif., U.S.–d. July 20, 1973, Hong Kong)

Bruce Lee (Chinese name: Li Jun Fan) was an American-born film actor who was renowned for his martial arts prowess and who helped popularize martial arts movies in the 1970s.

Lee was born in San Francisco, but he grew up in Hong Kong. He was introduced to the entertainment industry at an early age, as his father was an opera singer and part-time actor. The younger Lee began appearing in films as a child and was frequently cast as a juvenile delinquent or street urchin. As a teenager, he took up with local gangs and began learning kung fu to better defend himself. At that time he also started dance lessons, which further refined his footwork and balance; in 1958 Lee won the Hong Kong cha-cha championship.

Lee's parents were increasingly disturbed by his street fighting and run-ins with the police, and they sent him to live in the United States shortly after he turned 18. He lived with family friends in Seattle, where he finished high school and studied philosophy and drama at the University of Washington. While in Seattle he opened his first martial arts school, and in 1964 he relocated to Oakland, California, to found a second school. It was about that time that he developed his own technique—*jeet kune do*, a blend of ancient kung fu, fencing, boxing, and philosophy—which he began teaching instead of traditional martial arts. He drew the attention of a television producer after giving a kung fu demonstration at a Los Angeles-area karate tournament, and he was cast as the sidekick Kato in the television series *The Green Hornet* (1966–67).

Lee had difficulty finding acting jobs after the cancellation of *The Green Hornet*, and he began supplementing his income by giving private *jeet kune do* lessons to Hollywood stars, including Steve McQueen. In the 1969 film *Marlowe*, Lee received notice for a scene in which he destroyed an entire office through kickboxing and karate moves. Troubled by his inability to find other suitable roles, however, he moved back to Hong Kong in 1971. There Lee starred in two films that broke box-office records throughout Asia, and he later found success in the United States with *Jeet kune do* (1971; *Fists of Fury* [U.S.], or *The Big Boss* [Hong Kong English title]) and *Jing wu men* (1972; *The Chinese Connection* [U.S.], or *Fist of Fury* [Hong Kong English title]).

Lee used his sudden box-office clout to form his own production company, and he coproduced, directed, wrote, and starred in his next film, *Meng long guo jiang* (1972; *Return of the Dragon* [U.S.], or *The Way of the Dragon* [Hong Kong English title]). Lee's following film, *Enter the Dragon* (1973), was the first joint venture between Hong Kong- and U.S.-based production companies, and it became a worldwide hit, thrusting Lee into international movie stardom. Tragically, he died six days before the film's Hong Kong release. The mysterious circumstances of his death were a source of speculation for fans and historians, but the cause of death was officially listed as swelling of the brain caused by an allergic reaction to a headache medication. At the time, Lee had been working on a film called *Game of Death*, which was pieced together with stand-ins and cardboard cutouts of Lee's face and was released in 1978.

After Lee's death, his films gained a large cult following. Lee himself became one of the biggest pop culture icons of the 20th century, and he is often credited with changing the way Asians were presented in American films. A slightly fictionalized biopic, *Dragon: The Bruce Lee Story*, appeared in 1993. His son, Brandon, followed Lee into acting, and he died after being shot with a misloaded prop gun while filming *The Crow* (1994).

RICHARD PRYOR

(b. Dec. 1, 1940, Peoria, Ill., U.S.–d. Dec. 10, 2005, Los Angeles, Calif., U.S.)

R ichard Franklin Lennox Thomas Pryor III, or simply Richard Pryor, was an American comedian and actor, who was one of the leading comics of the 1970s and '80s. His comedy routines drew on a variety of downtrodden urban characters, rendered with brutal emotional honesty.

Pryor, an African American, began working in clubs in the early 1960s, developing his brand of controversial, race-based humour. His success influenced many later comics. He appeared in motion pictures such as *Lady Sings the Blues* (1972) and *Silver Streak* (1976), becoming a major box-office attraction. He also had success with his own concert films, including *Richard Pryor: Live on the Sunset Strip* (1982). In 1986 he starred in the autobiographical *Jo Jo Dancer, Your Life Is Calling*. His stand-up performances also were documented in comedy albums, for which he won five Grammy Awards. As a comedy writer, Pryor received an Emmy for the Lily Tomlin television special *Lily* (1973) and a Writers Guild Award as cowriter of the screenplay for *Blazing Saddles* (1974).

Pryor struggled with drug problems, and in 1980 he was seriously burned in what was reported as a cocaine-related incident. Diagnosed with multiple sclerosis in 1986, he made few appearances after the early 1990s. Pryor was presented with the Kennedy Center's Mark Twain Prize in 1998. His autobiography, *Pryor Convictions and Other Life Sentences* (cowritten with Todd Gold), was published in 1995.

NORA EPHRON

(b. May 19, 1941, New York, N.Y., U.S.–d. June 26, 2012, New York, N.Y., U.S.)

Nora Louise Ephron was an American author, playwright, screenwriter, and film director known for romantic comedies featuring biting wit and strong female characters.

Ephron was the eldest daughter of Hollywood screenwriters Henry and Phoebe Ephron, who based two of their Broadway plays, *Three's a Family* and *Take Her, She's Mine*, on their family life with young Nora. After graduating from Wellesley College in Massachusetts in 1962, she returned to New York City, where she made her living as a reporter with the *New York Post* and wrote humorous essays for publications such as *Esquire*. Her collected essays became popular books, and she began branching out into script writing.

After authoring several television episodes, Ephron made the jump to feature films, cowriting, with Alice Arlen, the screenplay for *Silkwood* (1983), based on the true story of Karen Silkwood (portrayed in the movie by Meryl Streep), a union activist who died while investigating safety violations at a nuclear fuel production plant. *Silkwood* won Ephron her first Academy Award nomination for best original screenplay. She then turned to her own life for movie fodder, transforming her 1983 novelization of the breakup of her marriage to journalist Carl Bernstein into her first solo screenplay, *Heartburn* (1986). The comedy-drama starred Streep in the Ephron role and Jack Nicholson as her philandering husband.

Ephron earned her second and third Academy Award nominations for best original screenplay for the wildly popular romantic comedy classics *When Harry Met Sally...* (1989) and *Sleepless in Seattle* (1993). She also directed the latter film, which starred Tom Hanks and Meg Ryan. After several critical and commercial failures, Ephron returned to *Sleepless in Seattle*'s winning formula in the late 1990s, once again pairing Hanks and Ryan in the romantic comedy *You've Got Mail* (1998), which updates the anonymous epistolary romance of the 1940 film *The Shop Around the Corner* for the age of online communication. Meanwhile, her first script for the stage—*Imaginary Friends*, about the longtime enmity between writers Lillian Hellman and Mary McCarthy—was produced on Broadway in 2002.

I Feel Bad About My Neck, Ephron's first essay collection in nearly 30 years, reached the top of *The New York Times*'s best-seller list for nonfiction in 2006. In 2009 she reunited with Streep for the box-office hit *Julie & Julia*. Ephron adapted the screenplay and directed the film, a dual biography of renowned chef Julia Child and writer Julie Powell, who blogged about cooking every recipe in Julia Child's famous cookbook *Mastering the Art of French Cooking* (1961). Ephron continued her playwriting career with *Love, Loss, and What I Wore* (2009), which she and her sister Delia adapted from Ilene Beckerman's 1995 book. *Lucky Guy*, which centres on the gritty life of *New York Daily News* columnist Mike McAlary, premiered on Broadway a year after Ephron's death. That play, along with many of her newspaper columns, blog posts, speeches, and other works, was published in the collection *The Most of Nora Ephron* (2013).

BARBRA STREISAND

(b. April 24, 1942, Brooklyn, New York, N.Y., U.S.)

Barbra Streisand (born Barbara Joan Streisand) is an American singer, composer, actress, director, and producer. She is considered by many to be the greatest popular singer of her generation. The first major female star to command roles as a Jewish actress, Streisand redefined female stardom in the 1960s and '70s with her sensitive portrayal of ethnic urban characters. Her immense popularity matched only by her outspokenness, she became one of the most powerful women in show business, noted for her liberal politics and her philanthropy.

Initially aspiring to be a dramatic actress, Streisand joined a summer theatre group in Malden Bridge, New York, and began studying acting while still in high school. After graduation she moved to Manhattan, where her first break came in 1960 when she sang at a small local nightclub and won an amateur talent contest (and dropped the second a from her first name). Following singing engagements in Greenwich Village cabarets, she landed a small comic role as Miss Marmelstein in the Broadway musical *I Can Get It for You Wholesale* (1962) and stole the show. An immediate sensation, she made frequent television appearances, notably on *The Judy Garland Show*, and, beginning in 1963, released a series of best-selling record albums that featured vibrant and original interpretations of popular songs. Her first solo album, *The Barbra Streisand Album*, won Grammy Awards for album of the year and best female vocal performance—the first two of many.

Streisand established herself as a major Broadway star in the career-making role of Fanny Brice in the musical *Funny Girl* (1964). In 1965 she won two Emmy Awards for *My Name Is Barbra*, the first of a series of tremendously successful television specials. She made her movie debut in 1968 in an Academy Award-winning reprise of her role as Fanny Brice. Although *Funny Girl* portrays Brice's life, not Streisand's, it established many enduring elements of Streisand's screen image, including her transition from an awkward ugly duckling to a stylish, sophisticated star, her Jewish origins, and her persistence and determination. Her self-deprecating opening line ("Hello, gorgeous," said into a mirror) and her first solo number ("I'm the Greatest Star") underscored the fact that Streisand had succeeded despite widespread early opinion that her unconventional looks would keep her from becoming a major movie star.

Streisand starred in several film musicals in the 1960s and '70s, including *Funny Lady* (1975), the sequel to *Funny Girl*, as well as *Hello, Dolly!* (1969), *On a Clear Day You Can See Forever* (1970), and *A Star Is Born* (1976). She played screwball heroines in such comedies as *The Owl and the Pussycat* (1970) and *What's Up, Doc?* (1972) and the romantic lead in the enormously popular *The Way We Were* (1973). She made her directorial debut in 1983 with *Yentl*, based on a story by Isaac Bashevis Singer about a young woman who pretends to be a man in order to continue her studies. Streisand starred in the title role — which she had wanted to play since 1968 — as well as cowriting and coproducing the movie. She concentrated on straight dramatic roles in *Nuts* (1987), *The Prince of Tides* (1991), and *The Mirror Has Two Faces* (1996); the last two she also directed. However, she subsequently appeared in the broad comedies *Meet the Fockers* (2004), *Little Fockers* (2010), and *The Guilt Trip* (2012). Despite the seeming variety, most of Streisand's characters share the qualities of strength and fierce independence combined with vulnerability.

Although admired as a filmmaker, Streisand has perhaps inspired even greater devotion from her fans as a singer. In addition to the albums featuring the soundtracks from her films and television specials, her most popular recordings include *The Barbra Streisand Album* (1963), *The Second Barbra Streisand Album* (1963), *The Third Album* (1964), *People* (1964), *Je m'appelle Barbra* (1966), *Stoney End* (1971), *Streisand Superman* (1977), *Guilty* (1980), *The Broadway Album* (1985), *Higher Ground* (1997), *Love Is the Answer* (2009), and *Partners* (2014). The number one chart position of *Partners* on the *Billboard* 200 album chart made

Streisand the only artist in history to have achieved a number one album on that chart in each of six decades. She avoided performing live for several years, but in the 1990s she appeared in a series of live concerts that broke box office sales records. Her numerous accolades include an award from the Recording Academy for lifetime achievement (1995) and a medal from the French Legion of Honour (2007).

MARTIN SCORSESE

(b. Nov. 17, 1942, Queens, New York, N.Y., U.S.)

Martin Marcantonio Luciano Scorsese, best known as simply Martin Scorsese, is an American

Martin Scorsese.

filmmaker known for his harsh, often violent depictions of American culture. From the 1970s Scorsese created a body of work that was ambitious, bold, and brilliant. But even his most acclaimed films are demanding, sometimes unpleasantly intense dramas that have enjoyed relatively little commercial success. Thus, Scorsese bears the not totally undeserved reputation as a cult director who works with big budgets and Hollywood's most desirable stars. In terms of artistry, he was perhaps the most significant American director of the late 20th and early 21st centuries.

EARLY LIFE AND WORK

Scorsese was a frail, asthmatic child who grew up in the Italian American neighbourhood of Little Italy on the Lower East Side of Manhattan. His early interest in film returned after he tried unsuccessfully to enter the Roman Catholic priesthood, and he went on to earn undergraduate (1964) and graduate (1966) degrees in film from New York University, where he subsequently taught. His student films showed a wide range of influences, from foreign classics to Hollywood musicals. Among them were shorts such as *What's a Nice Girl like You Doing in a Place like This?* (1963) and *It's Not Just You, Murray!* (1964).

Scorsese's first theatrical film, *Who's That Knocking at My Door* (1967), was an intimate portrayal of life in the streets of Little Italy. Harvey Keitel (who went on to do five more films with Scorsese in the 1970s and '80s) starred as Scorsese's alter ego, a streetwise but sensitive Italian American Catholic plagued by the knowledge that his girlfriend (Zina Bethune) had been raped. The film earned Scorsese encouraging reviews, and he was offered the position of assistant director and supervising editor on *Woodstock* (1970), which translated into converting the more than 100 hours of raw footage of the 1969 rock concert into a 3-hour movie that won an Academy Award for best documentary.

FILMS OF THE 1970S: *MEAN STREETS, TAXI DRIVER,* AND *NEW YORK, NEW YORK*

Scorsese directed a less widely seen documentary about protests against the Vietnam War, *Street Scenes* (1970), and he then worked as an editor on the concert films *Medicine Ball Caravan* (1971) and *Elvis on Tour* (1972). Producer Roger Corman invited him to direct *Boxcar Bertha* (1972). Scorsese made the most of the opportunity with an exciting if ultimately empty yarn about train robbers (Barbara Hershey, David Carradine, and Bernie Casey) wreaking havoc in the Depression-era South.

Far more significant was the boundary-breaking *Mean Streets* (1973), Scorsese's reworking of the themes introduced in *Who's That Knocking at My Door.* Filled with violent sequences, rapid-fire dialogue, and blaring rock music, the film was typical of his early work in its realistic detail and its naturalistic performances. Keitel starred as a small-time collector for the mob in Little Italy, stricken with guilt over his affair with his epileptic girlfriend Teresa (Amy Robinson) and frustrated by his inability to control his dangerously unhinged friend (and Teresa's brother) Johnny Boy (Robert De Niro, who did eight films with Scorsese between 1973 and 1995). The moving, often hilarious performances of Keitel and De Niro were as much responsible for igniting this low-budget masterpiece as Scorsese's atmospheric locations, shockingly frank language, explosive violence, and showy camera technique.

After making the documentary *Italianamerican* (1974) about his parents, Scorsese went to work on his first mainstream studio picture, the tamer *Alice Doesn't Live Here*

Anymore (1974), which had little of the pyrotechnic invention of *Mean Streets*. But in its own subdued way, *Alice Doesn't Live Here Anymore* was an effective drama about a widow, Alice (Ellen Burstyn), who strikes out from New Mexico to California after the death of her abusive husband to make a new life for herself and her adolescent son (Alfred Lutter). Burstyn's Oscar for best actress helped convince the Hollywood establishment that Scorsese could discipline his maverick talent.

Having proved that he could make a fairly conventional movie, Scorsese then shocked filmgoers with *Taxi Driver* (1976), a hellish tour of a disturbed Vietnam veteran's peculiar madness. Brilliantly written by Paul Schrader, photographed by Michael Chapman, and scored by Bernard Herrmann (his final film), this unsettling work is as fascinating as it is horrifying. De Niro gave what is regarded as his definitive performance as the pathetically alienated but dangerously unhinged Travis Bickle, and Keitel exuded menace in the small but key role of the seductive pimp Sport, who keeps the 12-year-old Iris (Jodie Foster) in thrall. Perhaps the most controversial, and the most disturbing, Oscar nominee for best picture to date, *Taxi Driver* also earned Oscar nominations for De Niro, Foster, and Herrmann. Scorsese cast himself in a small but telling cameo as a murderously jealous husband, and the film was awarded the Palme d'Or at the Cannes film festival. Many rank it as Scorsese's best work.

Scorsese's artistic risk taking had been vindicated, but his status as Hollywood's newest enfant terrible lasted only until the release of *New York, New York* (1977), a rethinking of the 1950s Hollywood musical, marked by nonnaturalistic lighting and elaborate sets. Deliberately stylized to evoke past screen triumphs by Vincente Minnelli and George Cukor, it featured De Niro as the cocky Jimmy Doyle, a novice saxophone player who works in a big band behind talented singer Francine Evans (Liza Minnelli). Their torrid love affair proves impossible to sustain, and the vain, self-destructive Jimmy drifts away from domestic bliss with the pregnant Francine. De Niro was compelling in an unsympathetic part, and Minnelli evoked her mother (Judy Garland) with frightening authority. While critical opinion was mixed, it was a commercial flop. However, the film later developed a cult following largely because of its obvious affection for old Hollywood.

Stung by this rejection, Scorsese edited his footage of The Band's November 1976 farewell concert into the well-received rockumentary *The Last Waltz* (1978), with unparalleled performance footage of Bob Dylan, Joni Mitchell, Van Morrison, Muddy Waters, Eric Clapton, and other musical luminaries. Next came *American Boy: A Profile of Steven Prince* (1978), in which Prince, a friend of Scorsese, recounted stories from his life as a road manager for singer Neil Diamond and as a heroin addict.

FILMS OF THE 1980S: *RAGING BULL*, *THE KING OF COMEDY*, AND *THE COLOR OF MONEY*

Scorsese then made the brutal but beautiful *Raging Bull* (1980). Loosely adapted by Schrader and Mardik Martin from the memoir of former middleweight boxing champ Jake La Motta, this vitriolic essay on the pleasurable pain of violence is immediately impressive for its stunning black-and-white cinematography by Michael Chapman and for its meticulous re-creation of 1940s New York City. The acting was also first-rate, particularly that of Joe Pesci as Joey, Jake's loyal brother, and Cathy Moriarty as Vickie, Jake's abused wife. But it is De Niro's towering, Oscar-winning performance as the self-destructive La Motta, a proud but foolish man undone by forces he can neither understand nor control, that unified this pitiless psycho-drama. *Raging Bull* has come to be regarded as one of Scorsese's greatest films.

In *The King of Comedy* (1982), De Niro gave yet another wholly original performance — this time, as Rupert Pupkin, a self-styled stand-up TV comedian. Blissfully unaware of his profound lack of talent, Rupert practices his pathetic comedy routines to no avail. Finally he kidnaps reigning late-night TV star Jerry Langford (Jerry Lewis) in exchange for a 10-minute stint on his program. The film failed at the box office but later climbed in critical regard. *After Hours* (1985) was a minor but amusing diversion, with Griffin Dunne as a mild-mannered office worker who finds himself imperiled by a colourful variety of lunatics on one long, strange night. Shot on location by cinematographer Michael Ballhaus, this is an exhilarating, unusual illustration of what a Scorsese movie can be like when his only mission is fun.

The Color of Money (1986) was an adaptation of Walter Tevis's sequel to his earlier novel *The Hustler* (1959, film 1961). "Fast Eddie" Felson (Paul Newman, reprising his Oscar-nominated role) is now retired from competition. He smells raw talent in callow pool shark Vincent Lauria (Tom Cruise) and takes him under his wing, sharing all his hard-earned knowledge about the game. But they part ways and end up facing each other at an Atlantic City tournament. This was Scorsese's most commercial and conventional film. However, it reminded Hollywood that Scorsese could deliver a hit of at least modest proportions.

The Last Temptation of Christ (1988) was, but for some protests from conservative Christians prior to its release, a well-received version of Nikos Kazantzákis's epic novel (adapted by Schrader) about the self-doubts of Jesus as he carries out his mission. Willem Dafoe was well cast as

Jesus, but some critics had problems with the more unusual casting of Keitel as Judas, Hershey as Mary Magdalene, and Harry Dean Stanton as Paul. The evocative cinematography by Ballhaus and the neotraditional score by Peter Gabriel enlivened this variation on the Gospels, which earned Scorsese his second Oscar nomination.

Scorsese's vivid "Life Lessons," loosely based on Fyodor Dostoyevsky's *Igrok* (*The Gambler*), was a segment of the *New York Stories* (1989) triptych (which also contained segments by Woody Allen and Francis Ford Coppola). Nick Nolte played a middle-aged bearish slob of a painter desperate to keep his restless paramour-disciple (Rosanna Arquette) from moving out.

FILMS OF THE 1990S: *GOODFELLAS*, *CAPE FEAR*, AND *CASINO*

Another kind of New York story—the kind that helped fashion Scorsese's reputation—was the basis of the acclaimed *GoodFellas* (1990). Adapted from Nicholas Pileggi's nonfiction *Wiseguy*, this knowing portrait of small-time Brooklyn mobster Henry Hill's life and crimes (scripted by Pileggi and Scorsese) was as authentic as any Scorsese film since *Raging Bull*. Ray Liotta played Hill, and Paul Sorvino, Joe Pesci, Lorraine Bracco, and De Niro excelled in their supporting roles. Scorsese displayed his mastery of the medium in new and unexpected ways, especially in a much-studied tracking shot that followed Hill through a crowded restaurant. Scorsese was again Oscar nominated, both for directing and, with Pileggi, for best adapted screenplay.

The commercially successful *Cape Fear* (1991) was an ultraviolent remake of a suspenseful 1962 film. Nolte starred as Sam Bowden, a Southern lawyer whose family is terrorized by ex-con Max Cady (De Niro), who blames the lawyer for his prison conviction and seeks revenge. Screenwriter Wesley Strick's script complicated the premise of the original by making Bowden culpable on several levels, from his framing of Cady 14 years earlier to his current infidelity to his wife (Jessica Lange).

Cape Fear's success enabled Scorsese to attract the big budget he desired for his 1993 version of Edith Wharton's novel *The Age of Innocence*. A lovingly rendered, subtly acerbic portrait of New York City's upper crust in the late 19th century, the film revolves around the unconsummated love affair between sensitive lawyer Newland Archer (Daniel Day-Lewis) and Countess Ellen Olenska (Michelle Pfeiffer), whose separation from her brutish husband and general flouting of convention are a scandal proper society cannot tolerate. In a more subtle role, Winona Ryder excelled as Archer's deceptively vapid fiancée, May, who understands far more than she lets on. With his most fluid camera work yet, Scorsese demonstrated that his sensibility—thought by some to be too coarse for such refined period themes and nuances—had an extremely wide range. Scorsese and screenwriter Jay Cocks were Oscar nominated for best adapted screenplay.

The 1970s Las Vegas morality tale *Casino* (1995) marked the return of the *GoodFellas* talent pool, reuniting Scorsese with screenwriter Pileggi and actors De Niro and Pesci, but it did not receive the critical acclaim or commercial success of the earlier film. *Casino* had an epic running time of just short of three hours, and the De Niro–Pesci pairing had little of the chemistry seen in *GoodFellas*. However, the film had excellent supporting performances (especially by Sharon Stone, Alan King, James Woods, Don Rickles, and Dickie Smothers). *Kundun* (1997) followed; it was a respectful, handsomely mounted biography of the 14th Dalai Lama that proceeded at a stately pace, unspooling through the remarkable events of his life, commencing with the Dalai Lama's discovery as a two-year-old who had become the vessel for the previous Dalai Lama's spirit and ending with his escape from Tibet in 1959.

Bringing Out the Dead (1999) starred Nicolas Cage as a New York paramedic who is beginning to crack under the stress of his job and offered some of the same surreal nighttime ambience as *Taxi Driver*. The film had one of Cage's more effective performances and costarred Patricia Arquette, John Goodman, and Ving Rhames.

FILMS OF THE 2000S: *GANGS OF NEW YORK*, *THE AVIATOR*, AND *THE DEPARTED*

Gangs of New York (2002) was a project Scorsese had sought to film since the late 1970s. It had an epic canvas: the chaotic peril of 1860s New York City, culminating in the Draft Riot of 1863. Leonardo DiCaprio (in the first of a number of films he did with Scorsese) starred as Amsterdam Vallon, a young man seeking to avenge the death of his father at the hands of Bill the Butcher (Day-Lewis at his most mordant), a kind of godfather to the unruly Five Points mobs. *Gangs of New York* was nominated for 10 Oscars, including nods for best picture and director.

The Aviator (2004) was a biopic of aviator and movie producer Howard Hughes, and Scorsese lavishly re-created 1930s and 1940s Hollywood. As Hughes, DiCaprio gave an appropriately intense interpretation of a man driven by both his own genius and an acute case of obsessive-compulsive disorder. The film was a box-office success and garnered 11 Oscar nominations, including best picture and director. Scorsese and cinematographer Robert Richardson did impressive work in replicating the various stages of colour-film technology that evolved over the years in which the film was set.

Scorsese then made *The Departed* (2006), which was based on the Hong Kong action film *Mou gaan dou* (*Infernal Affairs*, 2002). DiCaprio and Matt Damon starred as doppelgängers who live on opposite sides of the law—Billy (DiCaprio) as an undercover cop assigned the highly perilous task of penetrating the organization of crime lord Frank Costello (Jack Nicholson, submitting one of his showiest performances as a psychopathic mastermind based on Boston mobster Whitey Bulger) and Colin (Damon) as a Boston detective raised since childhood by Frank to become his mole. The film became one of Scorsese's biggest box-office hits, and it enabled him to finally win an Oscar for best director. The film itself also won for best picture.

In the 2000s Scorsese also directed a pair of musical documentaries. *No Direction Home: Bob Dylan* (2005) was a wide-ranging exploration of the iconic singer-songwriter, and the concert film *Shine a Light* (2008) starred the Rolling Stones.

FILMS OF THE 2010S: *SHUTTER ISLAND*, *HUGO*, AND *THE WOLF OF WALL STREET*

Shutter Island (2010) starred DiCaprio as a U.S. marshal who in 1954 travels to a psychiatric facility isolated in Boston Harbor to search for a missing patient. However, it soon becomes clear that what began as a noirish detective story has become something much closer to a horror movie. DiCaprio's hard-boiled mien played well against Ben Kingsley's Dr. Cawley, the crafty, evasive director of the gothic facility. Michelle Williams, Max von Sydow, and Jackie Earle Haley also provided top-notch support. The film was as much a box-office smash as *The Departed*, but reviews were not as universally enthusiastic.

Hugo (2011) was a radical departure for Scorsese. Based on Brian Selznick's young-adult novel *The Invention of Hugo Cabret*, the film was Scorsese's first shot in 3D and was easily the most expensive production he had ever undertaken, with costs estimated as high as $170 million. In 1931 Paris 12-year-old orphan Hugo (Asa Butterfield) lives inside the recesses of the Gare Montparnasse train station, an enormous complex filled with many shops. One of these is a small toy store run by a cantankerous old man (Kingsley). The old man is eventually revealed to be the once-celebrated pioneer filmmaker Georges Méliès, who remains bitter about the destruction of so much of his life's work and since has lived as a near-recluse. But aided by Méliès's charming niece (Chloë Grace Moretz) and the efforts of a film scholar, Hugo eventually manages to bring Méliès back into the world. (The subject of regaining film's lost heritage was important to Scorsese, who in 1990 had founded the Film Foundation, dedicated to preserving American films, and in 2007 the World Cinema Foundation, dedicated to preserving films from around the world.) *Hugo* was nominated for 11 Oscars, the most of any 2011 film, including nods for best picture and best director.

Scorsese won an Emmy Award for another of his musical documentaries, *George Harrison: Living in the Material World* (2011), which examined the life of the former Beatle. Scorsese branched out further into television as the executive producer of *Boardwalk Empire* (2010–), an HBO drama series about gangsters in Atlantic City during Prohibition. He also directed the show's first episode, for which he received an Emmy in 2011.

He returned to his familiar New York City haunts with *The Wolf of Wall Street* (2013), a cautionary tale based on the memoir by Jordan Belfort (DiCaprio), a stock trader who fell afoul of the law but not before showering himself and his associates in tremendous wealth. The film divided critics, who saw it as either condemning or celebrating Belfort and his excesses. Scorsese received his eighth Oscar nomination for best director, and the film itself was nominated for best picture.

In the 2010s Scorsese also directed *The 50 Year Argument* (2014), about the influence of the *New York Review of Books*, and HBO television series *Vinyl* (2015), on the work and life of Richie Finestra, a record label producer in 1970s New York City. In late 2015, Scorsese also wrapped up filming of *Silence*, a historic-drama film based on *Chimmoku* (1966; *Silence*) by Japanese novelist Endō Shūsaku. The plot is built around a fictionalized account of Portuguese priests who traveled to Japan and the subsequent slaughter of their Japanese converts.

ASSESSMENT

Despite the diversity in his chosen subject matter, Scorsese's work contains common elements. His simultaneous fondness for and rebellion against old Hollywood is demonstrated by his exploring anew clichéd plot devices that often culminate in bleak irony and moral ambiguity. He has been praised for his use of the subjective camera to portray the protagonist's point of view, an approach characterized by such subtle touches as right-to-left camera pans that move contrary to normal eye movement and thereby create a slightly disconcerting effect and suggest a subjectively distorted world. Scorsese's films tend to be concerned with people rather than plots, and he is fond of placing his characters in volatile situations and allowing events to unfold naturally, as determined by the characters' instincts, lusts, and obsessions. One of the most important filmmakers of the late 20th and early 21st centuries, Scorsese reflects in his work both a cynicism toward modern culture and an obvious love of the cinema.

ROBERT DE NIRO

(b. Aug. 17, 1943, New York, N.Y., U.S.)

R obert De Niro is an American actor famous for his uncompromising portrayals of violent and abrasive characters.

The son of two Greenwich Village artists, De Niro dropped out of school at age 16 to study at the Stella Adler Conservatory of Acting. After working in a few Off-Off-Broadway plays, he appeared in his first film, Brian De Palma's *The Wedding Party* (filmed 1963, released 1969). Thereafter he appeared in several minor films, the most notable being *The Gang That Couldn't Shoot Straight* (1971). It was not until his performance in *Bang the Drum Slowly* (1973) that he was widely recognized as an excellent actor. *Mean Streets* (1973) marked De Niro's first association with director Martin Scorsese, with whom he would do some of his most celebrated work. Director Francis Ford Coppola, whose massively popular *The Godfather* (1972) had won the Academy Award for best picture, was so impressed by De Niro in *Mean Streets* that he offered the actor the part of young Vito Corleone in *The Godfather: Part II* (1974), forgoing even a screen test. De Niro's brilliant take on the part that was created by Marlon Brando in the first *Godfather* film earned him a best supporting actor Oscar and made him an international star.

Following *The Godfather: Part II*, De Niro worked with some of cinema's most noted directors in such films as Bernardo Bertolucci's *1900* (1976), Elia Kazan's *The Last Tycoon* (1976), and Michael Cimino's *The Deer Hunter* (1978), the last one receiving the Oscar for best picture. But it was his films with Scorsese for which De Niro acquired a reputation for masterfully portraying extremely dark and unappealing figures. He received an Oscar nomination for his role as the isolated and violent Travis Bickle in *Taxi Driver* (1976) and won the best actor Oscar for his portrayal of boxer Jake La Motta in *Raging Bull* (1980). Known for his intense role preparation, De Niro spent weeks driving a taxi in New York City before filming *Taxi Driver*, and he gained more than 50 pounds (about 23 kg) to portray La Motta. By the end of the 1970s, he was widely considered one of the best actors of his generation.

In the 1980s he appeared in a series of box office failures that have nevertheless become cult favourites. Scorsese's *The King of Comedy* (1983), which offered a desolate look at the hazards of celebrity, won critical praise but little public interest, whereas Sergio Leone's epic *Once upon a Time in America* (1984) suffered from postproduction studio interference, as did Terry Gilliam's futuristic satire *Brazil* (1985). De Niro also performed in more conventional films during that era, including *True Confessions* (1981), *Falling in Love* (1984), *The Mission* (1986), and De Palma's *The Untouchables* (1987). He revealed a talent for comedy in *Midnight Run* (1988) and won some of the best notices of his career for his depiction of a catatonic patient in *Awakenings* (1990). *GoodFellas* (1990) reunited De Niro with Scorsese for a brutal look at organized crime. Most critics agreed that Scorsese and De Niro had returned to form, but two further collaborations, *Cape Fear* (1991) and *Casino* (1995), were met with mixed reviews.

De Niro later appeared in Michael Mann's crime thriller *Heat* (1995), which pitted him against actor Al Pacino. He continued to explore his comedic side in such films as the satirical *Wag the Dog* (1997); *Analyze This* (1999) and its sequel, *Analyze That* (2002); and *Meet the Parents* (2000) and its sequels, *Meet the Fockers* (2004) and *Little Fockers* (2010). In 2008 De Niro reteamed with Pacino in the police drama *Righteous Kill*, and the following year he starred in *Everybody's Fine*, portraying a widower who discovers various truths about his adult children. He later took supporting roles in the thrillers *Machete* (2010) and *Limitless* (2011), the action drama *Killer Elite* (2011), and the ensemble romantic comedy *New Year's Eve* (2011).

In 2012 De Niro starred as a destitute writer reconnecting with his estranged son in the drama *Being Flynn* and played another paternal role in the seriocomic *Silver Linings Playbook*. The latter film earned him his first Oscar nomination in more than two decades. In *The Family* (2013) De Niro starred as a mobster turned informant whose family moves to France in the witness protection program. He then teamed with Morgan Freeman, Michael Douglas, and Kevin Kline in the buddy comedy *Last Vegas* (2013). De Niro's later credits include *Grudge Match* (2013), in which he and Sylvester Stallone played superannuated boxers who reunite for one last fight, the crime dramas *The Bag Man* (2014) and *Heist* (2015), and the comedy-drama *Joy* (2015).

In addition to acting, De Niro also directed several films. In 1993 he made his directorial debut with *A Bronx Tale*, a movie about the Mafia set in the 1960s. He later directed the highly acclaimed *The Good Shepherd* (2006), which centres on the origins of the CIA and the compromises made by an agent over the span of his career. In 2009 De Niro was named a Kennedy Center honoree, and two years later he received the Cecil B. DeMille Award (a Golden Globe for lifetime achievement).

GEORGE LUCAS

(b. May 14, 1944, Modesto, Calif., U.S.)

George Walton Lucas, Jr., or simply George Lucas, is an American motion-picture director, producer, and screenwriter who created several of the most popular films in history.

EARLY WORK

The son of a small-town stationer and a mother who was often hospitalized for long periods for ill health, Lucas was an early reader of classic adventure stories such as Daniel Defoe's *Robinson Crusoe* and Robert Louis Stevenson's *Treasure Island*, an avid collector of comic books, and a keen student of history. He became interested in filmmaking while in high school. He was also a car-racing fanatic as a teenager until a near-fatal crash at age 18 convinced him to give up the sport.

Lucas's interest in moviemaking was encouraged by cinematographer Haskell Wexler. In 1966 Lucas received a bachelor's degree from the film department of the University of Southern California in Los Angeles. While there, future director John Milius, a classmate, introduced Lucas to the work of Japanese director Kurosawa Akira, who would be an important influence on Lucas's work. Lucas made several highly acclaimed student films, including the futuristic parable *Electronic Labyrinth THX 1138 4EB*, which took first prize at the National Student Film Festival in 1965. He served a six-month internship in 1967 at Warner Brothers, where he assisted Francis Ford Coppola on *Finian's Rainbow* (1968). He followed that experience by shooting a "making-of" documentary about Coppola's *The Rain People* (1969). Lucas also shot a portion of the documentary *Gimme Shelter* (1970), about the violent Rolling Stones concert at the 1969 Altamont Festival, for Albert and David Maysles and Charlotte Zwerin.

Warner Brothers–Seven Arts signed Lucas to direct a feature-length version of his prizewinning student film, with Coppola executive-producing and Robert Duvall and Maggie McOmie starring as the illicit lovers. A grim fantasy about a robotized, dehumanized society in the distant future, *THX 1138* (1971) was released to respectful reviews, although its obvious debt to George Orwell's novel *Nineteen Eighty-four* and overly deliberate pace kept it from being embraced too enthusiastically by either critics or audiences. The film also was one of the first made through Coppola's American Zoetrope studio, which would go on to create some of the most-memorable films of the 1970s and '80s.

In 1971 Lucas formed the production company Lucasfilm Ltd., which eventually contained a number of divisions, including Industrial Light & Magic (ILM, established 1975), which was regarded as the most prestigious special-effects workshop in American film. His second film, *American Graffiti* (1973), a sympathetic recollection of adolescent American life in the early 1960s, was a surprise success at the box office and was redolent of his youth as a Modesto hot-rodding enthusiast. Shot in less than a month for well under a million dollars, *American Graffiti* became one of the top grossing films of the decade — and with its modest cast of newcomers (including Richard Dreyfuss, erstwhile child star Ron Howard, and Harrison Ford in a small role) may have been among the most profitable as well.

STAR WARS

The success of *American Graffiti* enabled Lucas to finance a project that had been dear to his heart for some time. Science fiction had traditionally been a poor box-office performer, with such rare exceptions as *Planet of the Apes* (1968) and *2001: A Space Odyssey* (1968) only proving the rule. However, with *Star Wars* (1977), which he also wrote, Lucas eschewed the high-tech dystopian allegory then current in science-fiction films in favour of space opera synthesized with vintage Hollywood swashbucklers and frontier adventures. A space fantasy set "a long time ago in a galaxy far, far away," the film centres on Luke Skywalker (played by Mark Hamill), a young man who finds himself embroiled in an interplanetary war between an authoritarian empire and rebel forces. Skywalker, his mentor the wise Jedi Knight Obi-Wan Kenobi (Sir Alec Guinness), and the opportunistic smuggler Han Solo (Ford) are tasked with saving Princess Leia (Carrie Fisher) from captivity on the Death Star, a massive space station commanded by the menacing Darth Vader, whose deep, mechanically augmented voice (contributed by James Earl Jones) became instantly iconic. At the core of the film and the series it initiated are the Jedi Knights—a group of either benevolent or malevolent warriors who harness and manipulate the Force, an all-pervasive spiritual essence that holds in balance the forces of good and evil—and Skywalker's quest to join their ranks.

Star Wars, which borrowed heavily from the ideas of mythographer Joseph Campbell and from the story of

George Lucas (right) and Alec Guinness during the filming of Star Wars *(1977).*

Kurosawa's *Kakushi-toride no san-akunin* (1958; *The Hidden Fortress*), was immediately popular and went on to become the top-grossing motion picture in history. It was the first of Lucas's films to be made with a generous budget, which he extended by shooting on soundstages in England, then far less expensive than Hollywood. The film's success spawned a host of other science-fiction films using the same special-effects technologies developed at ILM that *Star Wars* had used so effectively.

THE GROWTH OF LUCASFILM LTD.

With *Star Wars* in the theatres, Lucas quietly announced his intention to retire from directing and make Lucasfilm an incubator for films to be directed by others under his tutelage. He added, however, that he could envision returning to directing "about 20 years from now," toward the end of the filming schedule for an ambitious series to be born from *Star Wars*. Lucas served as executive producer of the other two episodes in the *Star Wars* saga, *The Empire Strikes Back* (1980) and *Return of the Jedi* (1983). He also created the popular character of the adventurous archeologist Indiana Jones, who was played by Ford in a series of films, beginning with *Raiders of the Lost Ark* (1981), directed by Steven Spielberg and with Lucas as executive producer. Working exclusively as a producer throughout the 1980s and most of the '90s, Lucas had a few minor successes (*Willow*, 1988) and spectacular failures (*Howard the Duck*, 1986). He fulfilled a long-standing ambition by serving as executive producer on Kurosawa's *Kagemusha* (1980).

Lucas created the television series *The Young Indiana Jones Chronicles* (1992–93), about the adventures of Jones as a child and teenager in the early 20th century. The series was not a ratings success, but it allowed Lucas and ILM to experiment with new techniques in special effects. In 1997 he added new computerized effects to the *Star Wars* films and reissued them to great box-office success, though critics were less enthusiastic. Those films generated interest for one of the most highly anticipated releases of the decade, *Star Wars: Episode I—The Phantom Menace* (1999), the first installment in a prequel trilogy about the young Jedi knight Anakin Skywalker. For that film, which received mixed reviews but reaped enormous profits, Lucas returned to the director's chair for the first time in more than 20 years, just as he had foreseen doing in 1977.

Lucas followed with *Star Wars: Episode II—Attack of the Clones* (2002) and *Star Wars: Episode III—Revenge of the Sith* (2005), both of which he also directed, before returning to an executive production role on the fourth Indiana Jones film, *Indiana Jones and the Kingdom of the Crystal Skull* (2008), which Spielberg directed. Lucas created two animated television series, *Star Wars: Clone Wars* (2003–05) and *Star Wars: The Clone Wars* (2008–13). He was then executive producer of *Red Tails* (2012), an action-packed account of the Tuskegee Airmen and his first film in nearly two decades that was not affiliated with either the *Star Wars* or *Indiana Jones* franchises.

Apart from the films he directed and produced, among them some of the most-profitable productions in Hollywood history, Lucas enjoyed as part of his legacy Lucasfilm's network of properties, studios, and subsidiary companies. In 2012 the Walt Disney Company purchased Lucasfilm for $4 billion and announced that it would make a third *Star Wars* trilogy. In 2015 Lucas provided the story behind *Strange Magic*, a 3D computer-animated musical produced by Lucasfilm.

Lucas was named a Kennedy Center honoree in 2015.

STEVE MARTIN

(b. Aug. 14, 1945, Waco, Tex., U.S.)

Steve Martin is an American comedian, writer, and producer who began his career as a stand-up comic and eventually achieved success in motion pictures, television, Broadway, and literature.

Martin attended State College in Long Beach, California. His interest in performing was honed during this period as he worked as a musician and magician at Disneyland and debuted his comedy-and-banjo-playing act in local nightclubs. He soon transferred to the University of California at Los Angeles, where he majored in theatre. In 1967, while still a student, he accepted a contract to write for the hit television show *The Smothers Brothers Comedy Hour*, for which he won an Emmy Award in 1969. Within a few years, he was writing for *The Sonny and Cher Comedy Hour* and other top variety shows of the era.

Martin acquired a modest but loyal following during the early 1970s as he performed his stand-up routine on numerous television shows, particularly *The Tonight Show Starring Johnny Carson*. His breakthrough came in 1976 when he hosted an episode of NBC's *Saturday Night Live*, the first of more than 25 appearances on the show throughout the years. Within months, Martin was the top comic in the United States and was drawing standing-room-only crowds to some of the country's largest performing venues. His exclamations "Well, excuuuuse me!" and "I am a wild and crazy guy!" became national catchphrases. It was also during this period that Martin had success as a recording artist: his *Let's Get Small* (1977) and *A Wild and Crazy Guy* (1978) comedy albums earned Grammy Awards, and his hit single "King Tut" (1978) sold more than a million copies.

Martin wrote and starred in his debut film, the Academy Award-nominated short subject *The Absent-Minded Waiter*, in 1977. This led to an extended collaboration with writer-director-actor Carl Reiner on the hit comedies *The Jerk* (1979), *Dead Men Don't Wear Plaid* (1982), *The Man with Two Brains* (1983), and *All of Me* (1984). These films established Martin as a movie star of the first rank, and he subsequently retired from stand-up comedy. He demonstrated his willingness to take chances with critically praised limited-audience fare such as *Pennies from Heaven* (1981), *The Lonely Guy* (1984), *L.A. Story* (1991), and *Leap of Faith* (1992), and he maintained his popular appeal in such films as *Little Shop of Horrors* (1986), *Roxanne* (1987), *Planes, Trains and Automobiles* (1987), *Parenthood* (1989), *Father of the Bride* (1991), and *Father of the Bride, Part II* (1995). At the beginning of the 21st century, his box-office success continued with *Bringing Down the House* (2003) and *Cheaper by the Dozen* (2003) and its sequel (2005). He later portrayed Inspector Jacques Clouseau, a character made famous by Peter Sellers, in *The Pink Panther* (2006) and *The Pink Panther 2* (2009). Martin's other films include *It's Complicated* (2009), *The Big Year* (2011), and *Home* (2015).

Martin's noteworthy writing endeavours include a play, *Picasso at the Lapin Agile*, which premiered at Chicago's Steppenwolf Theatre in 1993 and went on to win best play and best playwright honours from the New York Outer Critics Circle in 1996. He also wrote a series of well-received satiric articles for *The New Yorker* magazine, later published in the best-selling collection *Pure Drivel* (1998). His novella *Shopgirl* (2000) was produced as a film in 2005 with Martin in a starring role, and his follow-up, *The Pleasure of My Company* (2003), topped best-seller lists. His autobiography, *Born Standing Up: A Comic's Life*, was published in 2007, and he received a Kennedy Center Honor later that year. In private life, Martin was an art connoisseur, and he explored the New York art world in the novel *An Object of Beauty* (2010).

In 2009 Martin released *The Crow*, a collection of original banjo compositions that featured guest performances by banjo virtuoso Béla Fleck and country legends Earl Scruggs and Dolly Parton. A radical departure from the novelty and kitsch of "King Tut," *The Crow* was critically lauded and ultimately won the Grammy Award for bluegrass album of the year. Martin continued in that stylistic vein with *Rare Bird Alert* (2011), on which he performed with the bluegrass band the Steep Canyon Rangers, and *Love Has Come for You* (2013), a collaboration with singer-songwriter Edie Brickell.

In addition, Martin hosted the Academy Awards ceremony in 2001 and 2003 and cohosted the event with Alec Baldwin in 2010. Martin received an honorary Oscar in 2013.

DAVID LYNCH

(b. Jan. 20, 1946, Missoula, Mont., U.S.)

David Lynch is an American director and screenwriter noted for his disturbing and dark films.

Trained as an artist, Lynch studied in Europe and began experimenting with film in the late 1960s. In 1977 he made his first feature, *Eraserhead*, a grotesque and nightmarish film that became a cult favourite. He next directed the critically acclaimed *The Elephant Man* (1980), for which he received Academy Award nominations for best director and for adapted screenplay. After directing the science-fiction film *Dune* (1984), Lynch directed *Blue Velvet* (1986), a bizarre mystery that earned him another Oscar nomination for best director. His later films include *Wild at Heart* (1990), which won the Golden Palm at the Cannes film festival; *Lost Highway* (1997); and *The Straight Story* (1999), an unexpectedly simple film about an elderly man who rides a lawn mower several hundred miles to visit his brother. In 2001 Lynch directed *Mulholland Drive*, a surrealist thriller set in Hollywood; he was named best director at Cannes and later was nominated for an Oscar. Lynch's other works include *Inland Empire* (2006) as well as numerous short films. He also created the offbeat television series *Twin Peaks* (1990–91).

Twin Peaks was publicized and greeted as an extraordinary piece of television "art" that would redefine the boundaries of small-screen drama. It reaped critical acclaim and attracted considerable public attention even before airing. Its two-hour pilot was a massive success in the ratings, and the show managed to hook viewers with its unique Lynchian sensibility, combining a strange, dreamy mise-en-scène with an artistic tone and moments of black humour. In 2014, 14 years after the show initially aired, Lynch announced plans to revive *Twin Peaks* with a new season to be aired on Showtime in early 2016.

STEVEN SPIELBERG
(b. Dec. 18, 1946, Cincinnati, Ohio, U.S.)

Steven Allan Spielberg is an American motion-picture director and producer whose diverse films—which ranged from science-fiction fare, including such classics as *Close Encounters of the Third Kind* (1977) and *E.T.: The Extra-Terrestrial* (1982), to historical dramas, notably *Schindler's List* (1993) and *Saving Private Ryan* (1998)—enjoyed both unprecedented popularity and critical success.

EARLY LIFE AND WORK

Spielberg developed an interest in filmmaking as a child, and during his teens his *Escape to Nowhere* (1962), a

40-minute war movie, won first prize at a film festival. He next directed *Firelight* (1964), a feature-length science-fiction yarn, which was followed by an accomplished short about hitchhikers called *Amblin'* (1968). An executive at Universal Studios saw the latter film and tendered a contract to Spielberg, who began working in the studio's television division after attending California State College, Long Beach (now California State University, from which he would eventually receive a B.A. in 2002). He directed episodes of various TV series, notably *Columbo*, *Marcus Welby, M.D.*, and *Owen Marshall: Counselor at Law*. In 1971 he made his first television movie, *Duel*, a taut, almost claustrophobic exercise in psychosis that was more intense than typical TV fare (it was released theatrically in Europe). Although Spielberg permitted star Dennis Weaver—who played a motorist chased by a homicidal truck driver—to register a one-note impression of sweaty terror throughout the movie, his handling of the action sequences was staged and executed with bravado. The success of *Duel* enabled Spielberg to make theatrically released motion pictures, beginning with *The Sugarland Express* (1974), a chase picture with deft accents of comedy but an inexorable movement toward tragedy; it was anchored by Goldie Hawn's performance.

COMMERCIAL SUCCESS

Spielberg's next movie, *Jaws* (1975), established him as a leading director, and it was one of the highest-grossing films ever. It featured Roy Scheider as the police chief of a resort town who battles a man-eating white shark. Joining him are Richard Dreyfuss as a marine biologist and Robert Shaw as a shark hunter. The highly praised thriller received an Academy Award nomination for best picture, and its ominous soundtrack by John Williams won an Oscar. The film all but created the genre of summer blockbuster—big action-packed movie released to an audience grateful to be in an air-conditioned theatre—and it established many of the touchstones of Spielberg's work: an ordinary but sympathetic main character is enlightened through a confrontation with some extraordinary being or force that gradually reveals itself as the narrative unfolds.

Spielberg then directed the mystical science-fiction tale *Close Encounters of the Third Kind* (1977), which he also wrote. Dreyfuss was cast as the lead, and he submitted one of the best performances of his career, as a telephone lineman who encounters an unidentified flying object and subsequently becomes obsessed with UFOs. For the film, Spielberg received his first Academy Award nomination for best director. Vilmos Zsigmond's cinematography earned the film's only Oscar, though the special effects were also praised. Spielberg became just the second director in history to score back-to-back $100 million grosses.

After the disappointing *1941* (1979)—which was received as an unfunny comedy, despite the presence of John Belushi and Dan Aykroyd—Spielberg directed *Raiders of the Lost Ark* (1981), a loving, expert (if slightly redundant) tribute to old adventure serials. The film and its sequels, which starred Harrison Ford as handsome archaeologist Indiana Jones, used rich colour cinematography, brisk editing, memorable musical soundtracks, and inventive special effects to create a cinematic experience that was typically light yet highly suspenseful. Spielberg received his second Academy Award nomination for best director; the film was also a best picture nominee.

Spielberg's next film was even more successful. *E.T.: The Extra-Terrestrial* (1982) was a moving exploration of an alien encounter that cleverly eschewed the epic scale of *Close Encounters* for the microcosm of its effect on a single California family. Henry Thomas gave a strong performance as the boy who discovers and befriends the stranded alien, and Dee Wallace portrayed his sympathetic mom. The film also featured Drew Barrymore in one of her first roles. As with most Spielberg films to that point, the special effects were a large part of the movie's appeal—in this case, the wonderfully articulated E.T.—but it was Spielberg's mastery of human (and alien) emotion that made the movie a blockbuster. Both Spielberg and the film were nominated for Academy Awards, as were Melissa Mathison's screenplay, Allen Daviau's cinematography, and Williams's score; only the latter won.

After directing *Indiana Jones and the Temple of Doom* (1984), Spielberg adapted Alice Walker's Pulitzer Prize-winning novel *The Color Purple* (1985). The film explores an African American woman's almost unbearably harsh, yet ultimately fulfilling, life. Color was roundly criticized for downplaying the novel's lesbian element, for perpetuating stereotypes about black men, and for sentimentalizing life in the Deep South. Nevertheless, it found an audience that appreciated the cast—which included Whoopi Goldberg, Margaret Avery, and Oprah Winfrey, all of whom were nominated for Academy Awards—as well as the script (by Menno Meyjes) and the score (by coproducer Quincy Jones), both of which were also Academy Award-nominated. The film received a nomination for best picture, but Spielberg failed to earn an Oscar nod, a slight that created a small scandal at the time. More important, however, Spielberg had made one of the few commercially successful films about the experience of African Americans, paving the way for similar projects to be green-lighted.

George Lucas (centre), Steven Spielberg (seated left), and Harrison Ford during the filming of Indiana Jones and the Last Crusade *(1989).*

Spielberg chose another critically acclaimed book as the basis of his next film. *Empire of the Sun* (1987), scripted by Tom Stoppard, was a carefully detailed re-creation of the World War II prison-camp milieu of J.G. Ballard's autobiographical novel of the same name. But where *The Color Purple* was able to convey emotional truth, *Empire of the Sun* almost let the story about its young protagonist (Christian Bale) drown under a wave of pyrotechnics. It was a box-office failure. Spielberg closed out the 1980s with *Indiana Jones and the Last Crusade* (1989) and *Always* (1989), an adaptation of the 1943 film *A Guy Named Joe.* Although *Indiana Jones* was a hit, *Always* failed to find an audience.

Spielberg's tendency toward broad storytelling may have hampered his attempts at more complex filmmaking, and *The Color Purple* and *Empire of the Sun*, in the view of many critics, lacked emotional depth or insight. Yet the aggressive commercialism and optimism of Spielberg's films became the prevailing style in Hollywood in the late 20th century. His pervasive influence was recognized in 1986 by the Academy of Motion Picture Arts and Sciences when it honoured him with the Irving G. Thalberg Award, given for excellence in producing.

THE 1990S

Spielberg's opening film of the 1990s was *Hook* (1991), a retelling of J.M. Barrie's *Peter Pan*. Despite a cast that included major stars Robin Williams and Julia Roberts, the movie was a critical and commercial failure. Spielberg, however, returned to form in dramatic fashion with not one but two enormously popular 1993 releases. The first, *Jurassic Park*, was an adaptation of Michael Crichton's best-selling novel (1990) about dinosaurs re-created and running amok on a remote isle. Its scenes of peril are less deftly blended with character-focused downtime activity than in *Jaws*, but technology is employed to great effect, and there are enough potent shocks to indicate that Spielberg was still a master of Alfred Hitchcock-worthy suspense.

Spielberg's second film from 1993, *Schindler's List*, tells the true story of a group of Polish Jews who avoided Nazi extermination camps with the aid of German industrialist Oskar Schindler during World War II. The drama—which featured notable performances by Liam Neeson, Ben Kingsley, and Ralph Fiennes—quieted many of Spielberg's critics. It was shot with unflinching detail in black and white, and it won Spielberg his first Academy Award for best director. In addition, the film garnered six other Oscars, including best picture.

In 1994 Spielberg joined with multimedia moguls Jeffrey Katzenberg and David Geffen to found a new studio, DreamWorks, which was particularly successful as a creator of such popular animated films as *Antz* (1998), the *Shrek* series (2001, 2004, 2007, 2010), and *Puss in Boots* (2011). In 2006 the partners sold the company to Viacom for $1.6 billion.

On the directorial front, Spielberg's *The Lost World: Jurassic Park* (1997) failed to attain the majesty of *Jurassic Park*, but it had many compelling moments. Based on a 1995 best seller by Crichton, who reportedly wrote the book at the behest of Spielberg himself, the film repeats the *Jurassic Park* formula with a largely new cast—Julianne Moore, Vince Vaughn, Pete Postlethwaite, and Arliss Howard—and returnee Jeff Goldblum, who again plays a scientist who knows this manipulation of nature for profit is both crass and morally indefensible. There are numerous thrills, and the dinosaur special effects equal those of the earlier film.

Amistad (1997) found Spielberg in social historian mode. The film centres on the slave revolt that took place aboard the Spanish slave ship *Amistad* in 1839 and the subsequent trial in the United States for which the slaves were tried for insurrection on the high seas only to be ruled by the court to have been kidnap victims. Matthew McConaughey was effective as a defense lawyer, and Anthony Hopkins earned an Academy Award nomination for his showy role as former U.S. president John Quincy Adams, who is importuned to defend the slaves before the Supreme Court. As Cinque, the leader of the Africans, Djimon Hounsou gave a memorable performance. The film was well received critically, but it did only modest business at the box-office.

In 1998 Spielberg returned to World War II with *Saving Private Ryan*. The drama stands as one of the high points of his career, both praised and criticized for presenting some of the most realistic battle scenes staged in a Hollywood war movie. Of particular note is the 27-minute-long opening that depicts the invasion by U.S. troops at Omaha Beach on D-Day. After that harrowing sequence, the film settles into a more conventional narrative as a group of soldiers search for a paratrooper named Ryan in order to extract him from combat before he is killed, just as his three brothers recently were. Tom Hanks portrayed Captain John Miller, who leads the mission, and the strong cast also includes Matt Damon in the title role, along with Tom Sizemore, Edward Burns, Barry Pepper, Adam Goldberg, Giovanni Ribisi, Ted Danson, and Vin Diesel. *Saving Private Ryan* was nominated for 11 Academy Awards, including best picture, and Spielberg won his second Academy Award as best director. The film was the biggest commercial success of any release in the United States that year.

2000 AND BEYOND

A.I. Artificial Intelligence (2001), based on a short story by British author Brian Aldiss, was a project conceived in the 1970s by Stanley Kubrick, who some 20 years later, with the movie still in its planning stages, began to think Spielberg was a more likely director. After Kubrick died in 1999, Spielberg was approached by the Kubrick estate, and he agreed to helm the project. He cast Haley Joel Osment as David, a young humanoid robot who has been programmed to express love, and Jude Law appeared as a robotic male prostitute named Gigolo Joe. Their fates soon become intertwined and remain so even thousands of years into the future. Spielberg's facility for science fiction helped make the film provocative and often moving, but its inconsistent tone might be traced to Spielberg's and Kubrick's dueling sensibilities.

For the futuristic *Minority Report* (2002), Spielberg turned to another science-fiction short story, this time by Philip K. Dick. But what he aspired to went far beyond the scope of Dick's yarn. Tom Cruise played John Anderton, the head of the Pre-Crime division of the Washington, D.C., police department, which relies on three mutated beings, known as Pre-Cogs, who can predict which citizens are about to commit violent crimes. Anderton is haunted by the absence of his young son, who disappeared years ago and is likely dead. Consumed by guilt, and now divorced, he numbs himself by taking an illegal drug to which he has become addicted. Anderton faces further difficulties with the arrival of a cynical inspector (Colin Farrell) who has concerns about the integrity of the Pre-Crime department. Their strained relationship takes a deadly turn when Cruise is "seen" by the Pre-Cogs in the act of committing a murder, grounds for immediate arrest. To save himself, Cruise kidnaps the head Pre-Cog (Samantha Morton) and goes on the run, hoping to solve the mystery of why he was envisioned as a killer. *Minority Report* functions as both a hard-boiled police procedural and a paranoid vision of the future, and it stands as one of the best of the adaptations from Dick's oeuvre, though only a fraction of it derives from the original short story. The film was both a box-office and a critical success, though complaints about the somewhat pat ending were not uncommon.

The radically different *Catch Me If You Can* was also released in 2002, and it was even more widely admired. The biopic was based on the memoir of con man extraordinaire Frank Abagnale, Jr., who as a teenager in the 1960s bilked both people and organizations out of millions of dollars, posing variously as a doctor, a lawyer, and even a Pan Am airline pilot. He also was a genius at the craft of forgery, a skill that eventually brought the FBI onto his trail. Hanks was highly entertaining as the indefatigable federal agent Carl Hanratty, who pursues Abagnale for years and eventually bonds with his target. But the film belongs to Leonardo DiCaprio, who, as the precocious Abagnale, a charismatic and likable criminal, gave one of his most appealing performances. Christopher Walken played Frank's disgraced father, and Amy Adams played a doctor's aide whom Frank romances. A critical and commercial hit, the film was adapted into a well-received Broadway musical in 2011.

In 2004 Spielberg directed the lighthearted comedy *The Terminal*. Hanks again starred, this time as Viktor Navorski, a visitor from a fictional country in central Europe who lands at a New York airport only to find that civil war in his home country has invalidated his passport, keeping him from entering the United States. Since he now cannot return to his war-torn homeland, he is trapped at the airport. Stanley Tucci portrayed a pitiless customs supervisor who does everything he can to force Navorski to leave, while a more sympathetic eye was cast by Catherine Zeta-Jones as a flight attendant. The film plays like a fable, right up to the happy ending, although it was based on a real-life incident that found a man stranded in the Charles de Gaulle Airport in France for 17 years. Financially, *The Terminal* was probably Spielberg's least-successful film of the decade, and it received mixed reviews.

War of the Worlds (2005) marked Spielberg's return to blockbuster territory in the realm of science fiction. Cruise lent his star power to this version of the H.G. Wells classic, which had already been adapted into a highly regarded film in 1953. Despite a number of effective set pieces, including the opening scene—in which giant alien tripods emerge from underneath the streets of modern-day Newark, N.J., to wreak havoc on the populace after having been interred underground for thousands of years (a touch unique to Spielberg's version)—the film's approach to the story rarely generated excitement in its audiences, who may have been primed for more action than watching Cruise hiding in a farmhouse with a nutty survivor (Tim Robbins). The film was a box-office success, though some critical dissent was registered.

Munich (2005) was a far more serious and controversial piece of work. Eric Bana starred as Avner, an agent of Israel's Mossad who is asked by Prime Minister Golda Meir to head a team of assassins whose mission is to hunt down and execute the Palestinian terrorists responsible for killing 11 Israelis at the 1972 Olympics in Munich. Avner resigns from the Mossad (to ensure total deniability) and assembles a team of experts in explosives, document forgery, and other skills who set about searching for their targets. Daniel Craig, Ciarán Hinds, Hanns Zischler, and Geoffrey Rush (as Avner's handler) are just a few members of the international cast. The film's strength is also its weakness: its meticulous attention to detail and verisimilitude, which demand respect but can exhaust viewers. *Munich* was named one of the year's best films by a number of critics, despite the heated debates—too pro-Israel for some, too anti-Israel for others—that surrounded its release. The film was nominated for an Academy Award as best picture, and Spielberg received another best director nomination.

Made 19 years after *Indiana Jones and the Last Crusade*, Spielberg's next film, *Indiana Jones and the Kingdom of the Crystal Skull* (2008), was set in 1957, with Harrison Ford (now a rugged 64) repeating his signature role as professor and adventurer extraordinaire Indiana Jones. This time he falls afoul of the Soviet Union, agents of which want him to locate an ancient crystal skull that legend claims possesses psychic powers. Shia LaBeouf played Mutt, a motorcycle-riding tough who turns out to be Indy's son by way of Karen Allen's character Marion from the first Indy movie. Allen returns after her 37-year hiatus from the series to good effect, joined by Cate Blanchett as a deadly Russian agent and Ray Winstone as a British agent who secretly is in the pay of the Soviets and double-crosses Indy. Deliberately made with a retro style, the film found favour with audiences, becoming the third biggest movie at the box-office that year.

The Adventures of Tintin (2011) was an adaptation of the long-running comic strip created by the French artist Hergé. The character Tintin had long fascinated Spielberg, who had acquired film rights from Hergé's widow in the early 1980s only to have them lapse when the project failed to develop. But with filmmaker Peter Jackson, who functioned as producer, Spielberg was able to get the project off the ground some 20 years later. He and Jackson decided on utilizing a motion-capture technique (such as Jackson had used for the character of Gollum in his Lord of the Rings trilogy) rather than live-action or pure animation. The film's reception by both the box office and the critics was little more than mediocre in the United States, though in Europe, where Tintin was much more familiar, it fared better.

In 2011 Spielberg helmed another adaptation, War Horse. The drama was based on a popular Broadway play, which itself was developed from a 1982 children's novel by Michael Morpurgo. The story opens shortly before the start of World War I, when a horse named Joey is sold to a cavalry officer by the father of the horse's young owner, Albert, to buy food. The officer promises Albert that he will return Joey at war's end, but he soon is slain, and Joey falls into the hands of a succession of new owners. Albert, who was too young to enlist at the beginning of the war, finally makes it onto the battlefields, and after enormous effort he locates the now-injured Joey and saves him from being put down. The film carried high expectations, given its Broadway pedigree and Spielberg's reputation, and it was nominated for a best picture Academy Award. However, it received a tepid response from moviegoers.

In 2012 Spielberg released *Lincoln*, with a screenplay by Tony Kushner. Based in part on Doris Kearns Goodwin's study *Team of Rivals: The Political Genius of Abraham Lincoln* (2006), the film chronicles the fraught politicking that preceded the passage of the Thirteenth Amendment, which formally abolished slavery, in the closing months of the Civil War. With Daniel Day-Lewis as Abraham Lincoln, Spielberg's film captures the president's complex psychology, a blend of good humour and cynical despair. Although some critics complained that it took a few historical shortcuts and underplayed the role of abolitionists outside Congress, the film enjoyed box-office success. It also received 12 Oscar nominations, including best picture and director.

In 2015 Spielberg directed *Bridge of Spies*, a historical drama starring Tim Hanks based on the 1960 U-2 incident, which occurred during the Cold War. The film was commercially successful and received positive reviews from critics.

DAVID LETTERMAN
(b. April 12, 1947, Indianapolis, Ind., U.S.)

David Letterman is an American late-night talk-show personality, producer, and comedian, best known as the host of the long-running *Late Show with David Letterman*.

After graduating from Ball State University (1969) with a degree in telecommunications, Letterman tried his hand at television as a wisecracking weatherman in Indianapolis. In 1975 he moved to Los Angeles, where he began performing regularly at the Comedy Store, a club for fledgling stand-up comedians. In 1978 he made the first of 22 appearances on *The Tonight Show Starring Johnny Carson*. The following year, Letterman, who had revered Carson since childhood, served as the show's guest host, the first of many such appearances. In 1979 the visibility Letterman gained as a guest host won him an NBC midmorning show, *The David Letterman Show*. However, his unconventional humour—exemplified by the time he sent an audience member out to fetch him coffee—failed to engage daytime viewers. Although it received two Emmy Awards, the show was canceled after three months.

Letterman did not gain a following until he moved to late-night television with the critically acclaimed *Late Night with David Letterman*, which premiered in 1982 on NBC. The show ran immediately after Carson's *The Tonight Show*, and its ironic and offbeat humour was a hit with viewers. *Late Night* featured top-10 lists; sarcastic interplay between Letterman and his comic foil, bandleader Paul Shaffer; nonsensical skits, notably "Stupid Pet Tricks"; and roving cameras that captured ordinary people and placed them in the limelight. Letterman also became known for antagonizing some notable guests; Cher, for example, was moved to curse him on camera. If his behaviour turned off some guests, it excited the critics, who saw in his work an attempt to parody talk shows. Letterman insisted, however, that doing a funny talk show, not a parody, was his main intent. *Late Night with David Letterman* earned five Emmy Awards and 35 nominations.

When Carson announced his retirement in 1992, a very public search ensued for his replacement. Although it was believed that Carson favoured Letterman as host—Carson later regularly sent Letterman jokes for his monologues—NBC executives eventually chose Jay Leno, leaving Letterman in the time slot immediately after in an attempt to retain his high ratings. The following year, however, Letterman announced that he was leaving NBC to join competing network CBS. His new show, the *Late Show with David Letterman*, was placed opposite *The Tonight Show*. Critics immediately questioned whether Letterman and his ironic, abrasive, flippant humour would appeal to the mainstream audience of the earlier hour. Following its August 1993 debut, however, the *Late Show with David Letterman* put that concern to rest by drawing considerably more viewers than Jay Leno's *The Tonight Show*, which, under Carson, had reigned for nearly three decades as the leading American late-night offering.

In 1995 Letterman was selected to host that year's Academy Awards ceremony, but his performance—which included a running gag involving the first names of Oprah Winfrey and Uma Thurman—earned mixed reviews. That year also saw his *Late Show* lose its ratings edge over *The Tonight Show*, which began to consistently attract more viewers. In January 2000 Letterman underwent emergency quintuple heart bypass surgery. His emotional return in February was among the show's highest-rated episodes. On February 1, 2012, Letterman celebrated 30 years as a late-night talk-show host, which was the longest tenure in American television history. By then the *Late Show* had received numerous Emmys. Later that year he was named a Kennedy Center honoree. In 2014 Letterman announced that he was retiring from the *Late Show* the following year, and Stephen Colbert was later announced as his successor. Letterman hosted his last show on May 20, 2015.

Behind the camera, Letterman ran his own film and television production company, Worldwide Pants. Its shows included the hit sitcom *Everybody Loves Raymond* (1996–2005). He also co-owned a race-car team.

LARRY DAVID
(b. July 2, 1947, Brooklyn, New York, N.Y., U.S.)

Lawrence Gene David, known simply as Larry David, is an American comedian and actor who was best known as the cocreator of the television series *Seinfeld* (1989–98) and as the star of *Curb Your Enthusiasm* (2000–).

David attended the University of Maryland and graduated (1970) with a degree in history. He then returned to Brooklyn and found work with a bra wholesaler, one of the many David biographical details—including quitting a job and then returning to work as if the resignation never happened, stealing an answering machine tape so that a girlfriend would not hear the message he had left, and starting a soon-to-be infamous self-denial contest with his friends—that would later turn up in the life of Seinfeld's "lovable loser" George Costanza.

David met comedian Jerry Seinfeld in 1976, and the two soon began collaborating on stand-up material. As Seinfeld's stand-up career took off, David worked as a writer and performer (1980–82) on the ABC television sketch comedy series *Fridays* and as a writer (1984–85) for *Saturday Night Live*, but he never gained much public notice. David was known as "a comic's comic" whose antagonistic, bitingly sarcastic act often alienated the audience but delighted his fellow comedians. In 1988 Seinfeld was offered a sitcom pilot by NBC, and he and David created *Seinfeld*. The series premiered in 1989 and became a huge critical and commercial success. Described as the "show about nothing," it centred on a comedian (played by Seinfeld) and his self-involved best friends: George Costanza, Elaine Benes, and Kramer. David served as the head writer and continuity supervisor for the first seven seasons and occasionally appeared on-screen in memorable cameos. He left the series in 1996 to write and direct the film *Sour Grapes* (1998).

After returning to *Seinfeld* to cowrite the series finale in 1998, David was offered a comedy special on the cable channel HBO. He took an unorthodox approach to the project and produced a "mockumentary" about the making of an HBO special, *Larry David: Curb Your Enthusiasm* (1999). The mostly improvised program received enthusiastic reviews, and HBO turned it into an ongoing series simply called *Curb Your Enthusiasm*. David's new show took the ethos of *Seinfeld*—described by David as "no hugging, no learning"—and amplified it to include even more socially awkward plot points and even-less-redeemable (but still strangely likable) characters. In 2009 he starred in the Woody Allen film *Whatever Works*. After a small role in *The Three Stooges* (2012), David cowrote and appeared in the HBO film *Clear History* (2013), a comedy about a marketing executive who sells his stake in a start-up that later becomes a multibillion-dollar company. In 2015 David wrote and starred in the Broadway play *Fish in the Dark*, which focuses on fifteen different characters' reactions to the death of their family patriarch.

ANDREW LLOYD WEBBER

(b. March 22, 1948, London, Eng.)

Andrew Lloyd Webber, Baron Lloyd-Webber of Sydmonton, (also called Sir Andrew Lloyd Webber, is an English composer and theatrical producer, whose eclectic rock-based works helped revitalize British and American musical theatre beginning in the late 20th century.

Lloyd Webber studied at Magdalen College, Oxford, and at the Royal College of Music. While a student, he began collaborating with Timothy Rice on dramatic productions, with Rice writing the lyrics to Lloyd Webber's music. Their first notable venture was *Joseph and the Amazing Technicolor Dreamcoat* (1968), a pop oratorio for children that earned worldwide popularity in a later full-length version. It was followed by the rock opera *Jesus Christ Superstar* (1971; filmed 1973), an extremely popular though controversial work that blended classical forms with rock music to tell the story of Jesus' life. That show became the longest-running musical in British theatrical history. Lloyd Webber's last major collaboration with Rice was on *Evita* (1978; filmed 1996), a musical about Eva Perón, wife of the Argentine dictator Juan Perón. The Broadway production won seven Tony Awards, including best musical and best score.

In his next major musical, *Cats* (1981), Lloyd Webber set to music verses from a children's book by T.S. Eliot. In 1989 the London production of *Cats* surpassed *Jesus Christ Superstar* as the longest-running British production of a musical; it held that distinction until 2006, when it was overtaken by *Les Misérables*, another blockbuster show originating in the 1980s. In 1997 the Broadway version of *Cats* (which had won the Tony Award for best musical and best score) eclipsed the record set by the American musical *A Chorus Line* to become the longest-running show ever on Broadway. The Broadway and London productions of *Cats* closed in 2000 and 2002, respectively, after more than 7,000 performances each. Lloyd Webber experienced nearly the same level of commercial success with *Starlight Express* (1984; lyrics by Richard Stilgoe), in which performers notoriously donned roller skates to portray anthropomorphic toy trains; the show ran in London for more than 17 years.

With lyricists Charles Hart and Richard Stilgoe, he then composed *The Phantom of the Opera* (1986; filmed 2004), a hugely popular musical version of Gaston Leroux's melodramatic novel. After opening on Broadway in 1988, it won best musical at the Tony Awards, and in 2006 it surpassed *Cats* to become the longest-running Broadway show. A sequel, *Love Never Dies* (lyrics by Glenn Slater and Charles Hart), debuted in London in 2010.

Lloyd Webber maintained his focus on romantic melodrama with *Aspects of Love* (1989; lyrics by Don Black and Charles Hart), which was based on a David Garnett novel. He followed it with *Sunset Boulevard* (1993; lyrics by Don Black and Christopher Hampton), a musical adaptation of the classic Hollywood film. Commercially, both shows fared better in London than on Broadway, where they were plagued with financial difficulties. However, *Sunset Boulevard* became the third Lloyd Webber musical to win Tony Awards for both best musical and best score. His other musicals include *Jeeves* (1975; reworked in 1996 as *By Jeeves*), a collaboration with Alan Ayckbourn that was based on the novels of P.G. Wodehouse; *Song and Dance* (1982), which incorporated ballet; *Whistle Down the Wind* (1998), set in 1950s Louisiana; *The Beautiful Game* (2000), about an association football (soccer) team in strife-torn Belfast, N.Ire.; and *The Woman in White* (2004), an adaptation of Wilkie Collins's mystery novel of the same name. In 2015, the musical *School of Rock* had its world premiere on Broadway to critical and popular acclaim, with music by Lloyd Webber, lyrics by Glenn Slater, and a book by Julian Fellowes.

Lloyd Webber's best musicals were flashy spectacles that featured vivid melodies and forceful and dramatic staging. He was able to blend such disparate genres as rock and roll, English music-hall song, and operatic forms into music that had a wide popular appeal. In addition, Lloyd

Webber was an astute businessman, founding in 1977 the Really Useful Company (later the Really Useful Group), which managed all his productions thereafter. Under its aegis Lloyd Webber personally produced a number of other shows, including the Bollywood-themed *Bombay Dreams* (2002; with music by A.R. Rahman) and a 2006 revival of Richard Rodgers and Oscar Hammerstein II's *The Sound of Music*. Lloyd Webber was knighted in 1992, and in 1997 he was created a life peer.

MERYL STREEP
(b. June 22, 1949, Summit, N.J., U.S.)

Meryl Streep (original name Mary Louise Streep) is an American film actress known for her masterly technique, expertise with dialects, and subtly expressive face.

Streep started voice training at age 12 and took up acting in high school. In 1971 she graduated from Vassar College in Poughkeepsie, New York, with a degree in drama and costume design. After working in summer stock theatre, Streep studied drama at Yale University, where she earned a master of fine arts degree in 1975. She then moved to New York City to begin a professional career as an actress.

Streep made her Broadway debut in 1975 with *Trelawny of the "Wells."* Two years later she appeared in her first feature film, *Julia* (1977), but it was her performance in *The Deer Hunter* (1978) that earned Streep widespread recognition. Though her role was relatively small, she displayed a quiet softness that contrasted sharply with the bravado of the male characters and deepened the film's testament to the devastating effects of the Vietnam War on young Americans. That same year she also starred in the television miniseries *Holocaust*, for which she won an Emmy Award.

Over the next 10 years, Streep confirmed her reputation as one of Hollywood's finest dramatic actresses. Her performances in *Kramer vs. Kramer* (1979)—as a mother who leaves her young son and then fights to regain his custody—and *Sophie's Choice* (1982)—as a Polish survivor of a Nazi concentration camp—earned her Academy Awards for supporting actress and leading actress, respectively. She further demonstrated her range and her gifts for rendering complex emotional states and seamless characterization in such roles as a modern-day actress portraying a Victorian woman of mystery in *The French Lieutenant's Woman* (1981), a factory-worker-turned-activist in *Silkwood* (1983), and the aristocratic Danish author Isak Dinesen in *Out of Africa* (1985). She won the Cannes film festival and New York Film Critics' Circle awards for best actress for her moving performance in *A Cry in the Dark* (1988) as Lindy Chamberlain, the real-life Australian mother accused of having murdered her baby daughter although she claimed that the child was carried off by a dingo.

By the late 1980s Streep's reputation as a brilliant technical actress came to be a burden. Her name was typically associated with a serious, often depressing sort of film, and some critics complained that her performances lacked compassion. As a result, Streep tried to change her popular image by appearing in a handful of comedies, including *Postcards from the Edge* (1990) and *Death Becomes Her* (1992), and in the action-adventure film *The River Wild* (1994). For the most part, these films were not well received, and Streep returned to dramatic films that required more technical skill and less personal charisma. She gave memorable performances in *The Bridges of Madison County* (1995), *Marvin's Room* (1996), *One True Thing* (1998), and *The Hours* (2002).

In 2003 Streep received an unprecedented 13th Academy Award nomination—for best supporting actress

Meryl Streep in The Devil Wears Prada *(2006)*.

in *Adaptation* (2002); Katharine Hepburn originally held the record with 12 nominations. Streep earned another Oscar nomination (for best actress) for her portrayal of an overbearing fashion magazine editor in *The Devil Wears Prada* (2006). In 2008 she played a middle-aged woman reunited with three of her former lovers in the musical *Mamma Mia!* and later that year starred with Philip Seymour Hoffman in *Doubt*, about a nun who suspects a priest of having inappropriate relationships with children at a Catholic school; her performance in the latter film earned Streep another Academy Award nomination. She also garnered critical acclaim for her portrayal of famed American chef Julia Child in *Julie & Julia* (2009), a role for which she received a Golden Globe Award and her 16th Oscar nomination.

Streep later provided the voice of Mrs. Fox in the animated *Fantastic Mr. Fox* (2009), a film adaptation of Roald Dahl's children's book, and costarred with Alec Baldwin and Steve Martin in *It's Complicated* (2009), a comedy about a divorced woman having an affair with her remarried ex-husband. She then stepped into the role of Margaret Thatcher in *The Iron Lady* (2011), a portrait of the former British prime minister. For her performance, Streep earned her eighth Golden Globe Award and third Oscar. In the lighthearted *Hope Springs* (2012), she and Tommy Lee Jones starred as a couple trying to save their stagnant marriage. She evinced a razor-tongued matriarch whose husband has committed suicide in *August: Osage County* (2013), adapted from Tracy Letts's play; for her performance, Streep earned her 18th Oscar nomination. Streep next appeared as the dispassionate leader of an ostensibly utopian community in *The Giver* (2014), based on the novel for young readers by Lois Lowry; as a minister's wife who cares for mentally ill women in the western *The Homesman* (2014); and as a vengeful witch in the film of

Stephen Sondheim's musical *Into the Woods* (2014). She was nominated for an Academy Award for best supporting actress for the latter role. Streep then slipped into the role of a feckless (and unsuccessful) rock-and-roll singer who attempts to reconcile with her family in *Ricki and the Flash* (2015). She then depicted woman-suffrage pioneer Emmeline Pankhurst in *Suffragette* (2015).

In addition to her numerous acting awards, Streep was made Commander in the Order of Arts and Letters (the highest cultural award presented by the French government) in 2002. In 2010 she was elected an honorary member of the American Academy of Arts and Letters. The following year Streep received a Kennedy Center Honor.

PEDRO ALMODÓVAR

(b. Sept. 25, 1949, Calzada de Calatrava, Spain)

Pedro Mercedes Almodóvar Caballero, or simply Pedro Almodóvar, is a Spanish filmmaker known for colourful melodramatic films that often feature sexual themes.

As a young man, Almodóvar moved to Madrid with the hopes of attending the Spanish national film school, but it had recently been closed under dictator Francisco Franco's rule. With this avenue blocked, he purchased a Super-8 camera and began making his own short films.

Almodóvar's first feature-length film, *Pepi, Luci, Bom y otras chicas del montón* (1980; *Pepi, Luci, Bom, and Other Girls like Mom*), which he also wrote, explores the punk rock scene in Madrid in the years after Franco's death. Ostensibly a comedy, the film also traffics in themes of rape, corruption, and revenge. After several other early efforts, Almodóvar wrote and directed a series of films starring Antonio Banderas. The first two films, *Matador* (1986) and *La ley del deseo* (1987; *Law of Desire*), deal with the intersection between violence and sexual desire. A dizzying farce called *Mujeres al borde de un ataque de nervios* (1988; *Women on the Verge of a Nervous Breakdown*) won international acclaim, including an Academy Award nomination for best foreign-language film. Almodóvar followed it with ¡Átame! (1990; *Tie Me Up! Tie Me Down!*), which attracted criticism from women's advocacy groups for a plot in which a mentally ill man (played by Banderas) successfully persuades a woman he has kidnapped to fall in love with him. *Carne trémula* (1997; *Live Flesh*), based on a Ruth Rendell novel and starring Javier Bardem, examines the tangled consequences of an accidental gunshot.

Almodóvar's reputation soared with *Todo sobre mi madre* (1999; *All About My Mother*), which he also wrote. The film—the bittersweet story of a woman's search for her recently deceased son's father—won an Academy Award for best foreign-language film, and Almodóvar was

Daniel Giménez Cacho (centre) and Pedro Almódovar (right) on the set of La mala educación *(2004), which Almódovar directed.*

honoured as best director at the Cannes film festival. He received similar praise for the emotionally charged *Hable con ella* (2002; *Talk to Her*), for which he garnered an Oscar for best original screenplay, in addition to a nomination for best director. Almodóvar subsequently directed *La mala educación* (2004; *Bad Education*), which takes on sexual abuse within the Roman Catholic Church; the family drama *Volver* (2006; "To Return"); and *Los abrazos rotos* (2009; *Broken Embraces*), a stylish exercise in film noir. The latter two films starred Penélope Cruz.

After more than 20 years, Almodóvar reteamed with Banderas for *La piel que habito* (2011; *The Skin I Live In*), a psychological thriller about a plastic surgeon who performs experiments on a woman he holds captive. The campy, socially pointed comedy *Los amantes pasajeros* (*I'm So Excited!*), set aboard an airplane preparing for an emergency landing, followed in 2013. In 2016, Almódovar released his twentieth feature film, *Silencio* ("Silence"), which followed the protagonist Julieta's life over a twenty-year span from 1985 to 2015.

BILL MURRAY

(b. Sept. 21, 1950, Wilmette, Ill., U.S.)

William James Murray, or simply Bill Murray, is an American comedian and actor best known for his trademark deadpan humour on television's *Saturday Night Live* and for his film roles.

Murray, one of eight children, began his acting career on the *National Lampoon Radio Hour* (1975) alongside fellow comedians John Belushi and Dan Aykroyd. From 1977 to 1980 Murray performed on NBC's *Saturday Night Live* comedy sketch show, on which he popularized a seedy, shifty comedic persona. He launched his film career with a string of commercial hits, including *Meatballs* (1979),

Caddyshack (1980), and *Stripes* (1981). In 1984 Murray starred with Aykroyd and Harold Ramis in *Ghostbusters*, which became one of the highest-grossing films of the decade.

A run of unsuccessful films led Murray into a self-imposed hiatus until he directed and starred in *Quick Change* (1990). After playing a burned-out weatherman in the existential comedy *Groundhog Day* (1993), Murray began tackling more thoughtful and challenging parts, including supporting roles in Tim Burton's *Ed Wood* (1994) and Wes Anderson's *Rushmore* (1998).

In addition to earning an Academy Award nomination, Murray won a Golden Globe Award and a British Academy of Film and Television Arts (BAFTA) Award for his role as a

Bill Murray and Anjelica Huston in The Life Aquatic with Steve Zissou *(2004).*

washed-up American actor visiting Japan in the acclaimed film *Lost in Translation* (2003). The depth and sensitivity of his performance surprised critics and solidified his place as an accomplished dramatic actor. Murray also earned critical acclaim for his performance as a longtime bachelor who reexamines his romantic choices in Jim Jarmusch's *Broken Flowers* (2005).

After *Rushmore*, Murray appeared in several other films by Anderson, including *The Royal Tenenbaums* (2001); *The Life Aquatic with Steve Zissou* (2004), in which he starred as a world-weary oceanographer; *The Darjeeling Limited* (2007); *Moonrise Kingdom* (2012); and *The Grand Budapest Hotel* (2014). He provided the voice of the sardonic cat Garfield in two commercially successful films (2004 and 2006) based on the eponymous comic strip, as well as the voice of a badger in Anderson's *Fantastic Mr. Fox* (2009), an animated film adaptation of Roald Dahl's children's book.

Murray also took supporting roles as a funeral director in the whimsical Depression-era comedy *Get Low* (2009) and as a mobster in the thriller *Passion Play* (2010). In 2012 he starred as U.S. Pres. Franklin D. Roosevelt in *Hyde Park on Hudson*, which focused on the president's private life during a weekend in 1939 when he entertained British royalty. Murray later played a member of the Monuments, Fine Arts, and Archives (MFAA) unit, which recovered works of art stolen by the Nazis during World War II, in *The Monuments Men* (2014). His turn as a bibulous profanity-spewing ne'er-do-well in the ensemble comedy *St. Vincent* (2014) was singled out by critics as particularly praiseworthy, as was his evocation of a depressed widower opposite star Frances McDormand in the HBO television miniseries *Olive Kitteridge* (2014).

ROBIN WILLIAMS

(b. July 21, 1951, Chicago, Ill., U.S.–d. Aug. 11, 2014, Tiburon, Calif., U.S.)

Robin McLaurin Williams was an American comedian and actor known for his manic stand-up routines and his diverse film performances. He won an Academy Award for his role in *Good Will Hunting* (1997).

Williams's father, Robert, was an executive for the Ford Motor Company, and his mother was a former fashion model. He early learned to use humour to entertain classmates and was a fan of comedian Jonathan Winters. When he was 16, his father retired, and the family moved to the San Francisco area. Williams studied political science at Claremont Men's College (now Claremont McKenna College), where he began taking courses in improvisation. He then attended the College of Marin to study acting but later received a scholarship to study at the Juilliard School in New York City. Williams eventually moved back to California, where he began appearing in comedy clubs in the early 1970s.

By the mid-1970s Williams was guest starring on several television shows, including *The Richard Pryor Show* and *Laugh-In*. After guest appearances as the alien Mork on *Happy Days*, Williams was given his own show, *Mork & Mindy* (1978–82). The series offered Williams the opportunity to transfer the enthusiasm of his stand-up performances to the small screen and provided an outlet for his prolific improvisational talents. *Mork & Mindy* proved an immense success and was instrumental in launching Williams's film career.

Williams's early movie appearances included leads in *Popeye* (1980) and *The World According to Garp* (1982), but his first major role came with *Good Morning, Vietnam* (1987), in which he portrayed the irreverent military disc jockey

Adrian Cronauer. The role earned Williams his first Academy Award nomination. His second came soon after for his performance as an inspirational English teacher at a preparatory school in *Dead Poets Society* (1989). In the early 1990s he lent his talents to a number of successful family-oriented films, including *Mrs. Doubtfire* (1993), in which he played a divorced man who impersonates a female nanny in order to be close to his children, and the animated feature *Aladdin* (1992), in which he voiced a frenetic genie.

While undoubtedly a successful comedic actor, Williams was equally adept at more-sober roles. He played a distressed former professor in *The Fisher King* (1991) and a psychiatrist who mentors a troubled but mathematically gifted young man (played by Matt Damon) in *Good Will Hunting* (1997). Both films earned Williams Academy Award nominations, and for *Good Will Hunting* he finally received an Oscar.

As his career progressed, Williams continued to take both comedic and serious roles. He starred as a doctor who attempts to heal his patients with laughter in *Patch Adams* (1998) and portrayed a psychotic photo-lab technician who stalks a suburban family in *One Hour Photo* (2002). A 2002 stand-up performance led to the hugely successful *Robin Williams: Live on Broadway* (2002), which was released as both an album and a video. He later portrayed Teddy Roosevelt in the comedy *Night at the Museum* (2006) and two sequels (2009, 2014). He provided voices for the animated films *Happy Feet* (2006) and *Happy Feet Two* (2011). Williams was sidelined with heart problems in early 2009, but he returned to work shortly thereafter, promoting his films and resuming his Weapons of Self-Destruction comedy tour. Later that year he starred in the family comedy *Old Dogs*.

In 2011 Williams—who had appeared in a 1988 Off-Broadway production of Samuel Beckett's *Waiting for*

Godot—made his Broadway acting debut in *Bengal Tiger at the Baghdad Zoo*, a surreal comic drama set during the Iraq War. In 2013 he returned to movies, portraying a priest in the star-studded farce *The Big Wedding* and U.S. President Dwight D. Eisenhower in Lee Daniels' *The Butler*. The TV series *The Crazy Ones*, in which he played the head of an ad agency, premiered later that year; it was canceled in 2014. Williams then portrayed a man who attempts to reconcile with friends and family following a terminal diagnosis in the comedy *The Angriest Man in Brooklyn* (2014). *Boulevard* (2014), in which he played a closeted gay man who befriends a male prostitute, was released after his death.

Williams was active with a number of charities, including Comic Relief and the Christopher and Dana Reeve Foundation, an organization founded by the late *Superman* star that is dedicated to curing spinal cord injury. Through his work with the United Service Organizations, Inc. (USO), he was also a frequent performer for American troops stationed abroad. In 2014 Williams committed suicide.

KATHRYN BIGELOW
(b. Nov. 27, 1951, San Carlos, Calif., U.S.)

Kathryn Ann Bigelow is an American film director and screenwriter, noted for action films that often featured protagonists struggling with inner conflict. She was the first woman to win an Academy Award for best director, for *The Hurt Locker* (2008).

Bigelow studied painting at the San Francisco Art Institute, and in the early 1970s she moved to New York City to participate in the Whitney Museum's independent study program. She soon became interested in filmmaking and eventually earned a scholarship to the graduate film school at Columbia University. There she made the short film *The Set-Up* (1978). After graduating from Columbia in 1979, Bigelow began working on her first feature-length movie, *The Loveless*, which she cowrote and codirected (with Monty Montgomery). The 1982 drama, starring a then unknown Willem Dafoe, focused on a motorcycle gang's visit to a small Southern town and the ensuing violence. Bigelow was subsequently sent a number of scripts, most of which were high-school comedies. Uninterested in the offers, she instead began teaching at the California Institute of the Arts in 1983.

In 1987 Bigelow returned to the big screen with *Near Dark*, a vampire film that became a cult classic. Two years later she married director James Cameron (divorced 1991). She described *Blue Steel* (1989), which she cowrote and directed, as a "woman's action film." The crime drama starred Jamie Lee Curtis as a policewoman who is stalked by a serial killer. Bigelow's next film, *Point Break* (1991), centres on a FBI agent (played by Keanu Reeves) whose loyalty is tested when he infiltrates a charismatic gang of bank-robbing surfers. In addition to being a box-office success, it solidified Bigelow's place in the traditionally male-dominated world of action films. With the science-fiction movie *Strange Days* (1995), she created a stylish drama involving futuristic technology that enables the transmission of thoughts and memories from one person to another. After *The Weight of Water* (2000), Bigelow helmed *K-19: The Widowmaker* (2002). Based on a true event, it focuses on a Soviet nuclear submarine that suffers a radiation leak. The action film, which starred Harrison Ford and Liam Neeson, received mixed reviews and failed to find an audience.

Bigelow's next directorial project was the Iraq War drama *The Hurt Locker* (2008). The low-budget film follows an elite squad of bomb detonators working in Iraq. Avoiding the politics of the war, she explored the dangers of armed conflict and the attraction it holds for some soldiers. In addition to Bigelow's Oscar win for director, the movie earned five other Academy Awards, including best picture. Bigelow subsequently reteamed with *The Hurt Locker* screenwriter Mark Boal to make *Zero Dark Thirty* (2012), an unflinching account of the U.S. military and intelligence operation to capture Osama bin Laden.

ROSEANNE BARR
(b. Nov. 3, 1952, Salt Lake City, Utah, U.S.)

Roseanne Cherrie Barr, also called Roseanne Arnold, is an American comedian and actress who achieved stardom with the popular and innovative television situation comedy *Roseanne* (1988–97).

After dropping out of high school in her native Salt Lake City, Utah, Barr lived for a time in an artists' colony in Colorado before marrying and raising a family in Denver. Encouraged by friends, she began doing stand-up comedy, developing her salty comic persona, initially self-labeled the "Domestic Goddess." A particularly winning appearance on *The Tonight Show* in 1985 set the stage for major stardom and for her lead role as the wisecracking mother of a working-class family in the successful *Roseanne*, for which she won an Emmy Award. Barr made further forays into television with *The Roseanne Show* (1998–2000), a syndicated talk show, and *Roseanne's Nuts* (2011), a reality series about her life as a macadamia farmer in Hawaii. Additionally, she acted in a number of films, including *She Devil* (1989), *Even Cowgirls Get the Blues* (1994), and *Blue in the Face* (1995).

Throughout her career, a significant element of Barr's public persona was her bluntly voiced advocacy for women and the working class. While her political outspokenness contributed to her appeal, it also made her something of a controversial figure, and, at the height of her popularity, her personal life—she was married and divorced several times, most notably to actor Tom Arnold—was the subject of much tabloid journalism. In 2012 Barr, after failing to win the Green Party's nomination for president of the United States, ran as the candidate of the Peace and Freedom Party. On the ballot in three states, she received a total of about 60,000 votes.

Among the books Barr has written are *Roseanne: My Life as a Woman* (1989), *My Lives* (1994), and *Roseannearchy: Dispatches from the Nut Farm* (2011).

JERRY SEINFELD

(b. April 29, 1954, Brooklyn, New York, N.Y., U.S.)

Jerry Seinfeld, the byname of Jerome Seinfeld, is an American comedian whose television show *Seinfeld* (1989–98) was a landmark of American popular culture in the late 20th century.

Seinfeld's interest in comedy was sparked at an early age through the influence of his father, a sign maker who was also a closet comedian. By age eight Seinfeld was putting himself through a rigorous comic training, watching television day and night to study the techniques of comedians. Over the years, he developed a unique style of comedy that centred on his wry observations on life's mundanities. He made his stand-up debut in 1976 and worked his way to an appearance on *The Tonight Show* in 1981, which gave Seinfeld his first national exposure. By the late 1980s he was one of the highest-profile stand-up comedians in the United States.

Principal cast members of the Seinfeld *television series were, left to right in foreground, Jason Alexander, Julia Louis-Dreyfus, Michael Richards, and Jerry Seinfeld.*

In 1988 Seinfeld was asked to develop a sitcom with NBC. He teamed with friend and fellow comedian Larry David to create *Seinfeld*, which was first broadcast the following year. Produced and sometimes cowritten by Seinfeld, the quirky widely watched show emphasized loosely structured stories, seemingly insignificant subject matter, and a buddy system of comedy in which the Jerry character often played a straight man to his three tightly wound screwball friends. The show reached unprecedented levels of popular and critical acclaim, and many of its catchphrases and plot elements became part of the cultural lexicon. *Seinfeld* ran for nine seasons and was still the highest-rated show in the United States when its final episode aired in 1998. His later television credits include appearances as himself on David's comedy series *Curb Your Enthusiasm*; the *Seinfeld* cast reunited for several episodes of that program in 2009. The following year *The Marriage Ref*, which Seinfeld created and produced, premiered. The reality series featured celebrity guests who mediated arguments between married couples.

Seinfeld returned to stand-up comedy in the late 1990s, embarking on multiple national tours of comedy clubs and theatres, one of which was documented in the 2002 film *Comedian*. He also wrote *Seinlanguage* (1993), a best-selling book of humorous observations, and the children's book *Halloween* (2003). In 2007 he provided the voice of the lead character in the animated *Bee Movie*, which he also cowrote.

JAMES CAMERON
(b. Aug. 16, 1954, Kapuskasing, Ont., Can.)

James Cameron is a Canadian filmmaker known for his expansive vision and innovative special-effects films, most notably *Titanic* (1997), for which he won an Academy Award for best director, and *Avatar* (2009).

Cameron studied art as a child; he later provided the drawings that figured prominently in *Titanic*. In 1971 his family moved to California. After studying physics at California State University at Fullerton, Cameron worked at a series of jobs, including machinist and truck driver, before a viewing of *Star Wars* (1977) inspired him to try his hand at moviemaking.

In 1980 Cameron was hired as a production designer, and the following year he made his directorial debut with *Piranha II: The Spawning*. A flop at the box office, the movie encouraged Cameron to write his own material. The result was *Terminator* (1984), an action thriller about a robot hit man that made actor Arnold Schwarzenegger a star and established Cameron as a bankable filmmaker. A series of high-tech and big-budget pictures followed, including *Aliens* (1986) and *The Abyss* (1989), each of which received an Oscar for best visual effects, *Terminator 2: Judgment Day* (1991), and *True Lies* (1994). In 1992 Cameron formed his own production company, Lightstorm Entertainment, and the following year he cofounded Digital Domain, a state-of-the-art effects company.

Although his films met with success at the box office, many viewers complained that the films lacked substance and relied too heavily on visual effects. In 1998 Cameron defied critics with *Titanic*, his screen adaptation of the doomed ocean liner's 1912 maiden voyage. Written, directed, and coproduced by Cameron, *Titanic* was one of the most expensive movies ever made, but it broke box-office records and tied *Ben-Hur* (1959) for most Academy Awards won (11). Skillfully blending special effects with a fictional love story between a penniless artist (played by Leonardo DiCaprio) and an unhappily engaged first-class passenger (Kate Winslet), *Titanic* stood atop the American charts for an unprecedented 15 weeks and earned more than $1.8 billion to become the highest-grossing movie in the world.

Following *Titanic*'s unparalleled success, Cameron took a break from feature films. He created and coproduced *Dark Angel* (2000–01), a science-fiction television series about a genetically altered female warrior, and he made several documentaries. *Expedition: Bismarck* (2002) took the director and his crew deep into the Atlantic Ocean, where they captured footage of the sunken Nazi battleship *Bismarck*. The documentary won an Emmy Award. Other underwater excursions were chronicled in *Ghosts of the Abyss* (2003), which explored the *Titanic*, and *Aliens of the Deep* (2005).

In 2009 Cameron returned to feature films with *Avatar*, a science-fiction thriller that was noted for its special effects. A major box-office success, it surpassed *Titanic* to become the highest-grossing movie in the world, earning more than $2.5 billion. The movie also received critical acclaim. At the Golden Globes ceremony in 2010, Cameron received the award for best director, and the film was named best picture.

Cameron remained involved in underwater exploration. In 2012 he debuted the *Deepsea Challenger*, a submersible that he codesigned. Described as a "vertical torpedo," the one-person vehicle performed quick ascents and descents and was able to withstand extreme pressure. In March Cameron completed a test dive in which he traveled to a depth of approximately 5 miles (8 km), a record for a solo mission. Later that month he journeyed nearly 7 miles (11 km) below the Pacific Ocean to explore the Challenger Deep, the world's deepest known recess, in the Mariana Trench. In 2014 he released a documentary, *Deepsea Challenge 3D*, which chronicled the construction of the submersible and debuted striking footage captured during its voyages beneath the waves.

DENZEL WASHINGTON
(b. Dec. 28, 1954, Mount Vernon, N.Y., U.S.)

Denzel Washington is an American actor celebrated for his engaging and powerful performances. Throughout his career he has been regularly praised by critics, and his consistent success at the box office helped to dispel the perception that African American actors could not draw mainstream white audiences.

After graduating from Fordham University (B.A., 1977), Washington began to pursue acting as a career and joined the American Conservatory Theater in San Francisco. After several successful stage performances in California and New York, he made his screen debut in the comedy *Carbon Copy* (1981). He first began to receive national attention for his work on the television drama *St. Elsewhere* (1982–88). For the film *Cry Freedom* (1987), he portrayed South African activist Stephen Biko, and he received an Academy Award nomination for best supporting actor. Two years later he won the Oscar for best supporting actor for his performance as a freed slave fighting in the Union army in the American Civil War film *Glory* (1989).

Washington's skill as an actor and his popular appeal as a leading man were firmly established in the 1990s. He gave memorable performances in the romantic comedy Mississippi Masala (1991), the Shakespearean comedy *Much Ado About Nothing* (1993), the courtroom drama *Philadelphia* (1993), the hard-boiled mystery *Devil in a Blue Dress* (1995), and the military thriller *Crimson Tide* (1995). The latter was the first of several popular movies he made with director Tony Scott. During this time he also frequently worked with director Spike Lee, starring in *Mo' Better Blues* (1990), *He Got Game* (1998), and most significantly *Malcolm X* (1992). Portraying the civil rights activist Malcolm X, Washington gave a complex and powerful performance and earned an Academy Award nomination for best actor. He received a second best-actor nomination for his portrayal of boxer Rubin Carter in the film *The Hurricane* (1999).

In *Training Day* (2001), Washington played a corrupt and violent police detective, the performance for which he became only the second African American actor (the first was Sidney Poitier) to win an Oscar for best actor. After starring in director Jonathan Demme's 2004 update of the 1962 thriller *The Manchurian Candidate*, Washington reteamed with Lee for the crime drama *Inside Man* (2006). He later appeared as a drug kingpin opposite Russell Crowe's determined narcotics officer in *American Gangster* (2007) and as a dispatcher caught in the middle of a

Denzel Washington in Flight *(2012).*

subway train hijacking in Scott's *The Taking of Pelham 1 2 3* (2009). In 2010 Washington starred in the postapocalyptic action drama *The Book of Eli* and collaborated again with Scott on the action thriller *Unstoppable*. He subsequently portrayed a rogue CIA agent in South Africa in the spy thriller *Safe House* (2012) before giving an Oscar-nominated performance in *Flight* (2012) as a heroic airplane pilot hiding a substance-abuse problem. The action comedy *2 Guns*, in which Washington played a covert drug-enforcement operative, followed in 2013. The following year Washington played a mysterious vigilante in the action thriller *The Equalizer*.

Additionally, Washington directed and appeared in the biographical films *Antwone Fisher* (2002), about a U.S. serviceman with a troubled past, and *The Great Debaters* (2007), about an inspirational debate coach at an African American college in the 1930s.

In addition to his film work, Washington occasionally acted onstage. In 2005 he starred as Brutus in *Julius Caesar*. Five years later he appeared in the Broadway revival of August Wilson's *Fences*, a family drama set in the 1950s that explores issues of identity and racism. For his performance, Washington won a Tony Award in 2010.

NATHAN LANE
(b. Feb. 3, 1956, Jersey City, N.J., U.S.)

Nathan Lane (original name Joseph Lane) is an American stage and film actor, best known for his work in musical comedies, notably the Broadway production of *The Producers*.

Lane discovered his flair for musical comedy when he appeared in a high-school production of *No, No, Nanette*, and after graduation he embarked on a career in theatre. Among his early productions was a dinner-theatre staging of *Guys and Dolls*, in which he played Nathan Detroit. When he was about to join Actors' Equity and learned that there was already a Joe Lane in the membership, he took that character's first name. He moved to New York City in the late 1970s, appeared in some Off-Broadway productions, and—in addition to taking odd jobs to help support himself—put together a comedy act with another actor, Patrick Stark. The team, known as Stark and Lane, spent more than two years performing in nightclubs and as the opening act at concerts in Los Angeles, before Lane returned to New York.

Lane had a part in a short-lived 1982 television sitcom, *One of the Boys*, and shortly thereafter he was cast in a Broadway production of the Noël Coward play *Present Laughter*. Such plays as *Love* and *She Stoops to Conquer* (both in 1984) followed, and in 1987 Lane made his motion picture debut in *Ironweed*. An Off-Broadway role in Terrence McNally's *The Lisbon Traviata* (1989) attracted critical praise, as did his performances in McNally's *Lips Together, Teeth Apart* (1991) and the film *Frankie and Johnny* (1991). In 1992 he reprised his role in *Guys and Dolls*, this time on

Broadway. The following year Lane's stage performance in the Neil Simon comedy *Laughter on the 23rd Floor* received rave reviews. He further charmed audiences with his voicing of the meerkat Timon in the animated film *The Lion King* (1994), his performance in McNally's play *Love! Valour! Compassion!* (1994), and his role as the drag queen Albert in the movie *The Birdcage* (1996). Lane then went on to play the lead character Pseudolus in a Broadway revival of *A Funny Thing Happened on the Way to the Forum* (1996), a performance that garnered him his first Tony Award. In 1999–2000 he provided a voice for the animated television series *George and Martha*, and in 2000 he appeared onstage in *The Man Who Came to Dinner* as well as in television productions of that play and of *Laughter on the 23rd Floor*.

Lane received new praise in 2001 for his masterfully hilarious turn as con man Max Bialystock in Mel Brooks's blockbuster Broadway musical comedy *The Producers*. The production, which also starred Matthew Broderick, broke sales records, and Lane received a Tony for his performance; he also starred in the 2005 film adaptation. After a year, Lane left the Broadway production but later returned (with Broderick) in 2003–04. His subsequent theatre work included *Trumbo* (2003), *Butley* (2003, 2006–07), and *Dedication or the Stuff of Dreams* (2005). From 2005 to 2006 he appeared in a remake of Simon's *The Odd Couple*, and in 2008 he starred in David Mamet's *November*, portraying a president on the eve of an election. The following year Lane played Estragon in a well-received Broadway revival of Samuel Beckett's *Waiting for Godot*, and in 2010–11 he starred in the musical *The Addams Family*. He returned to Broadway in *The Nance* (2013) as a closeted gay man in the 1930s who performs a caricature of homosexuality as a burlesque routine. In 2014, Lane and Broderick appeared in an updated production of Terrence McNally's *It's Only a*

Play, which explored the dynamics of Broadway theatre production.

Lane's additional film credits in the 21st century include *The Nutcracker in 3D* (2010), based on Pyotr Ilyich Tchaikovsky's popular ballet, and *Mirror Mirror* (2012), a comedic version of the Snow White tale. Although a pair of sitcoms in which he starred (1998–99, 2003) were short-lived, he enjoyed recurring roles on the television series *The Good Wife* and *Modern Family* in the early 2010s.

TOM HANKS

(b. July 9, 1956, Concord, Calif., U.S.)

Thomas J. Hanks is an American film actor whose cheerful everyman persona made him a natural for starring roles in many popular films. In the 1990s he expanded his comedic repertoire and began portraying lead characters in dramas.

After a nomadic childhood, Hanks majored in drama at California State University and performed in summer stock in Cleveland, Ohio, playing a variety of classical roles. In the late 1970s he moved to New York City, where he had a small part in a horror film in 1980.

Hanks gained notice for his comic abilities as a costar of the television series *Bosom Buddies* (1980–82). His work in the hit film *Splash* (1984) earned him leads in other comedies, including *Bachelor Party* (1984), *Volunteers* (1985), and *The Money Pit* (1986). He successfully mixed comedy with drama in *Nothing in Common* (1986) and *Punchline* (1988), and his portrayal of a boy in an adult body in *Big* (1988) earned him an Academy Award nomination and launched him on the path to becoming one of the era's most popular stars.

After starring opposite actress Meg Ryan in the romantic comedy *Joe Versus the Volcano* (1990), Hanks reteamed

with her in *Sleepless in Seattle* (1993) and *You've Got Mail* (1998), both directed by Nora Ephron. He portrayed the drunken manager of a women's baseball team in the comedy *A League of Their Own* (1992) and delivered an Oscar-winning performance as a gay lawyer with AIDS in *Philadelphia* (1993). Another Academy Award, for the phenomenally popular *Forrest Gump* (1994), made him the first actor to win back-to-back best actor Oscars since Spencer Tracy.

Hanks earned further Oscar nominations for outstanding dramatic performances in *Saving Private Ryan* (1998), which was directed by Steven Spielberg, and *Cast Away* (2000). Additional dramatic roles came in *Apollo 13* (1995), *The Green Mile* (1999), and *Road to Perdition* (2002). In the blockbuster *Toy Story* series (1995, 1999, 2010), Hanks provided the voice of the animated cowboy Woody.

In 2002 Hanks starred with Leonardo DiCaprio in Spielberg's *Catch Me If You Can*, and he portrayed Robert Langdon, a professor of symbology, in the 2006 film adaptation of Dan Brown's hugely popular *The Da Vinci Code*. In *Charlie Wilson's War* (2007), he appeared as real-life senator Charlie Wilson, who assisted the Afghan resistance to the Soviets in the 1980s. Hanks reprised his role as Langdon in *Angels & Demons* (2009), and he portrayed a father killed in the September 11 attacks in the drama *Extremely Loud & Incredibly Close* (2011). For the mystical epic *Cloud Atlas* (2012), which wove together multiple narratives, he took on six roles, ranging from a 19th-century surgeon to a postapocalyptic tribesman. In 2013 Hanks made his Broadway debut in *Lucky Guy*, a play by Ephron based on the life of journalist Mike McAlary, and he captured a Tony Award nomination for his starring performance as the colourful hard-nosed newsman. Later that year he returned to the big screen with *Captain Phillips*, a drama based on the true story of an American cargo ship hijacked by Somali pirates in 2009, and *Saving Mr. Banks*, a comedy based on the efforts of Walt Disney to obtain the film rights to P.L. Travers's novel *Mary Poppins* (1934).

In addition to his acting, Hanks wrote and directed the comedy *That Thing You Do!* (1996), about a fictional 1960s rock band. He later cowrote, directed, and starred opposite Julia Roberts in the romance *Larry Crowne* (2011), playing an unemployed man who enrolls in community college. Hanks also produced a number of films and such television miniseries as *From the Earth to the Moon* (1998), which documents the Apollo space program, and the World War II dramas *Band of Brothers* (2001) and *The Pacific* (2010). In 2009 he narrated *Beyond All Boundaries*, a documentary about World War II that used animation, archival footage, and sensory effects, including shaking seats; the 35-minute film was produced for the National World War II Museum in New Orleans.

Hanks was the recipient of numerous acting awards. In addition, he received a Kennedy Center Honor in 2014.

SPIKE LEE

(b. March 20, 1957, Atlanta, Ga., U.S.)

S helton Jackson Lee, better known by his byname of Spike Lee, is an American filmmaker known for his uncompromising, provocative approach to controversial subject matter.

The son of the jazz composer Bill Lee, he was reared in a middle-class Brooklyn neighbourhood. He majored in communications at Atlanta's Morehouse College, where he directed his first Super-8 films and met his future coproducer, Monty Ross. In 1978 Lee entered New York University's Graduate Film School, where he met another future collaborator, cinematographer Ernest Dickerson. He gained national attention with his master's thesis, the short subject *Joe's Bed-Stuy Barbershop: We Cut Heads* (as he explained at the time, the barbershop "is second only in importance to the church in the black community"), which earned him the Academy of Motion Picture Arts and Science's Student Award.

Lee's feature film debut was *She's Gotta Have It* (1986), a prismatic character study about the love life of a contemporary black woman. Establishing a career-long pattern, Lee not only wrote, produced, directed, and edited the film but also played a key supporting role. The film, which was made on a $175,000 budget, was hailed as "Godardesque" at the Cannes film festival. His next film, based on his experiences at Morehouse, was *School Daze* (1988), a scatological satire of colour prejudice, snobbery, and betrayal within the black academic community.

The infamous Beach incident (1986), in which a black man in Queens, N.Y., was chased and killed by rampaging white youths, was the inspiration for Lee's third feature, *Do the Right Thing* (1989), an impassioned but evenhanded work that neither blamed any specific group for racial violence nor absolved any from it. Most of his subsequent films dealt head-on with issues of race and racism in the United States—for instance, with interracial relationships in *Jungle Fever* (1991) and with the diversity of opinions within the black community in *Get on the Bus* (1996).

With the notable exception of his monumental biographical film *Malcolm X* (1992), many of Lee's later works received mixed reviews. Some observers complained about the excessive length of his films; others criticized his perpetuation of ethnic stereotypes, notably the Jewish characters in *Mo' Better Blues* (1990) and the Italian Americans in *Summer of Sam* (1999); while still others condemned his treatment of his female characters. The outspoken Lee cited what he perceived as Hollywood's antiblack bias, noting that, while *Do the Right Thing*, *Malcolm X*, and his poignant documentary *4 Little Girls* (1997)—about the 16th Street Baptist Church bombing—all received Academy Award nominations, he was repeatedly denied an Oscar win.

Lee's subsequent films include *He Got Game* (1998), a family drama that is both an exposé of college basketball recruiting practices and a paean to the sport, and *25th Hour* (2002), which focuses on the last day of freedom for a convicted drug dealer (played by Edward Norton). *Inside Man* (2006), starring Denzel Washington and Jodie Foster, centres on the negotiations between the police and the bank robbers engaged in a hostage situation, while the mystery *Miracle at St. Anna* (2008) focuses on the experiences of African American soldiers in World War II. Lee returned to Brooklyn, the setting for several earlier films, for the drama *Red Hook Summer* (2012). *Oldboy* (2013) was a violent revenge drama based on a Japanese manga (which had previously been adapted as a South Korean film). *Da Sweet Blood of Jesus* (2014) told the tale of a wealthy, black American anthropologist who, once stabbed by an ancient dagger from the Ashanti empire, becomes a vampire. *Chiraq* (2016) satirized the gang violence prevalent in Chicago.

Lee also continued to direct nonfiction films, including *The Original Kings of Comedy* (2000), which showcased African American stand-up comedians, and *When the Levees Broke* (2006), a four-part HBO series outlining the U.S. government's inadequate response to Hurricane Katrina. A follow-up series, *If God Is Willing and da Creek Don't Rise*, aired in 2010. Lee's other directorial credits include several music videos as well as the Broadway production of *Mike Tyson: Undisputed Truth* (2012), a one-man show performed by the former heavyweight boxing champion.

Many of Lee's films can be classified as family affairs: his father, Bill, contributed music to *She's Gotta Have It* and *Mo' Better Blues*, among others; his sister, Joie, played major roles in several productions; and his brother David Charles Lee was the still photographer.

DANIEL DAY-LEWIS

(b. April 29, 1957, London, Eng.)

D aniel Day-Lewis (full name Sir Daniel Michael Blake Day-Lewis) is a British actor known for his on- and offscreen intensity and exhaustive preparation for roles.

Day-Lewis was the second child of Cecil Day-Lewis, one of the leading British poets of the 1930s, and actress Jill Balcon and was the grandson of motion-picture producer Sir Michael Balcon. He began acting at Bedales, a liberal school in Petersfield, England, and at age 13 he landed a small role in the film *Sunday Bloody Sunday* (1971). He then went on to perform with the Bristol Old Vic and Royal Shakespeare theatrical companies before appearing in his first adult roles in the films *Gandhi* (1982) and *The Bounty* (1984). In 1985 Day-Lewis displayed his versatility by playing a homosexual hooligan in *My Beautiful Laundrette* and a staid Edwardian-era Englishman in an adaptation of E.M. Forster's *A Room with a View*; the films brought him international acclaim, as did his performance as an adulterous surgeon in *The Unbearable Lightness of Being* (1988). His portrayal of Christy Brown, an artist almost completely disabled by cerebral palsy, in the film *My Left Foot* (1989) won him numerous awards, including an Academy Award for best actor. In the course of making the film, Day-Lewis spent the entire time in a wheelchair and learned to paint with his left foot.

Day-Lewis subsequently starred in a number of successful films, including *The Last of the Mohicans* (1992), as the frontiersman Natty Bumppo; *The Age of Innocence* (1993), Martin Scorsese's film adaptation of Edith Wharton's novel; *In the Name of the Father* (1993), which earned him an Academy Award nomination; and *The Crucible* (1996), based on Arthur Miller's play. After appearing in *The Boxer* (1997), Day-Lewis took a break from acting and worked for a time as a cobbler's apprentice in Italy.

In 2002 he returned to the screen as a murderous anti-immigrant gang leader in Scorsese's *Gangs of New York*, a drama set in the mid-19th century. He subsequently starred in the intimate *The Ballad of Jack and Rose* (2005), which was written and directed by Miller's daughter Rebecca, whom he had married in 1996. In 2008 Day-Lewis won a second Academy Award, for his transformative performance as self-made oil tycoon Daniel Plainview in *There Will Be Blood* (2007). His later film roles include an Italian film director in the star-studded musical *Nine* (2009) and U.S. Pres. Abraham Lincoln in Steven Spielberg's biographical *Lincoln* (2012). For his nuanced performance in the latter film, he won an unprecedented third best-actor Oscar. Day-Lewis was named a knight bachelor in 2014.

ELLEN DEGENERES
(b. Jan. 26, 1958, Metairie, La., U.S.)

Ellen Lee DeGeneres is an American comedian and television host known for her quirky observational humour.

DeGeneres briefly attended the University of New Orleans, where she majored in communications. Dissatisfied with university life, she left to work in a law firm and later held a string of jobs, including waitress, bartender, house painter, and oyster shucker. After putting together a comedy routine for a group of friends, DeGeneres was asked to perform in local coffeehouses in the late 1970s. She was soon traveling through the United States on the comedy club circuit, earning applause with her quirky, naive stories that were punctuated with her loose-limbed gestures. Her style was compared to those of Mary Tyler Moore and Lucille Ball. DeGeneres's act also caught the attention of Showtime, and the cable network named her Funniest Person of the Year in 1982. Her career hit a high note in 1986 after she was invited to perform on *The Tonight Show Starring Johnny Carson*. Following her humorous rendition of "Phone Call to God," Carson motioned DeGeneres to sit and chat—the first time a female comedian had been given that honour.

Besides appearing on television in stand-up comedy routines, DeGeneres had parts in such television shows as *One Night Stand* (1989), *Open House* (1989–90), and *Laurie Hill* (1992). In 1994 she starred in *These Friends of Mine*; its name changed to *Ellen* the following season. The show was a success, earning nominations for Golden Globe, American Comedy, and Emmy awards. In 1997 DeGeneres revealed that she was gay, and *Ellen* became the first prime-time show to feature an openly gay lead character. After the show ended in 1998, DeGeneres eventually moved to the daytime arena, launching her own syndicated talk show, *The Ellen DeGeneres Show*, in 2003. The show earned more than 20 Daytime Emmy Awards in its first five seasons. In September 2009 it was announced that DeGeneres would be a judge on the reality series *American Idol*, but she left the program after just one season, saying that she felt uncomfortable criticizing the talent show's contestants.

In addition to her television work, DeGeneres appeared in such films as *Coneheads* (1993), *Mr. Wrong* (1996), and the animated feature film *Finding Nemo* (2003), in which she provided the voice of the forgetful but lovable Dory. DeGeneres later reprised the role for the sequel *Finding Dory* (2016). She also hosted a number of awards shows, notably the Academy Awards in 2007. Her comedic essays were collected in the best-selling books *My Point... and I Do Have One* (1995), *The Funny Thing Is...* (2003), and *Seriously...I'm Kidding* (2011). In 2012 DeGeneres received the Kennedy Center's Mark Twain Prize for American Humor.

MADONNA

(b. Aug. 16, 1958, Bay City, Mich., U.S.)

Madonna Louise Ciccone, better known as simply Madonna, is an American singer, songwriter, actress, and entrepreneur whose immense popularity in the 1980s and '90s allowed her to achieve levels of power and control unprecedented for a woman in the entertainment industry.

Born into a large Italian-American family, Madonna studied dance at the University of Michigan and with the Alvin Ailey American Dance Theater in New York City in the late 1970s before relocating briefly to Paris as a member of Patrick Hernandez's disco revue. Returning to New York City, she performed with a number of rock groups before signing with Sire Records. Her first hit, "Holiday," in 1983, provided the blueprint for her later material—an upbeat dance-club sound with sharp production and an immediate appeal. Madonna's melodic pop incorporated catchy choruses and her lyrics concerned love, sex, and relationships—ranging from the breezy innocence of "True Blue" (1986) to the erotic fantasies of "Justify My Love" (1990) to the spirituality of later songs such as "Ray of Light" (1998). Criticized by some as being limited in range, her sweet, girlish voice nonetheless was well suited to pop music.

Madonna was the first female artist to exploit fully the potential of the music video. She collaborated with top designers (Jean-Paul Gaultier), photographers (Steven Meisel and Herb Ritts), and directors (Mary Lambert and David Fincher), drawing inspiration from underground club culture or the avant-garde to create distinctive sexual and satirical images—from the knowing ingenue of "Like a Virgin" (1984) to the controversial red-dressed "sinner" who kisses a black saint in "Like a Prayer" (1989). By 1991 she had scored 21 Top Ten hits in the United States and sold some 70 million albums internationally, generating $1.2 billion in sales. Committed to controlling her image and career herself, Madonna became the head of Maverick, a subsidiary of Time-Warner created by the entertainment giant as part of a $60 million deal with the performer. Her success signaled a clear message of financial control to other women in the industry, but in terms of image she was a more ambivalent role model.

In 1992 Madonna took her role as a sexual siren to its full extent when she published *Sex*, a soft-core pornographic coffee-table book featuring her in a variety of "erotic" poses. She was criticized for being exploitative and overcalculating, and writer Norman Mailer said she had become "secretary to herself." Soon afterward Madonna temporarily withdrew from pop music to concentrate on a film career that had begun with a strong performance in *Desperately Seeking Susan* (1985), faltered

Madonna performs live at the 57th Grammy Awards on February 8, 2015.

with the flimsy *Shanghai Surprise* (1986) and *Dick Tracy* (1990), and recovered with *Truth or Dare* (1991, also known as *In Bed with Madonna*), a documentary of one of her tours. She scored massive success in 1996 with the starring role in the film musical *Evita*. That year she also gave birth to a daughter.

In 1998 Madonna released her first album of new material in four years, *Ray of Light*. A fusion of techno music and self-conscious lyrics, it was a commercial and critical success, earning the singer her first musical Grammy Awards (her previous win had been for a video). Her experimentation in electronica continued with *Music* (2000). In 2005 she returned to her roots with *Confessions on a Dance Floor*. Despite a marriage in the 1980s to actor Sean Penn and another to English director Guy Ritchie (married 2000; divorced 2008), with whom she had a son, Madonna remained resolutely independent. (She also adopted a boy and a girl from Malawi.) That independent streak, however, did not prevent her from enlisting the biggest names in music to assist on specific projects. This fact was clear on *Hard Candy* (2008), a hip-hop infused effort with writing and vocal and production work by Justin Timberlake, Timbaland, and Pharrell Williams of the hit-making duo the Neptunes. With *MDNA* (2012), which featured cameos from women rappers M.I.A. and Nicki Minaj, she continued to prove herself a shrewd assimilator of cutting-edge musical styles. Madonna's follow-up effort, *Rebel Heart* (2015), was critically acclaimed, although its release was plagued by a series of unexpected leaks of digital recordings ahead of schedule. Nonetheless, the album, which blended elements of electronic music, hip-hop, and acoustic rock, fared well commercially, topping the charts in many countries. It was promoted by the Rebel Heart Tour, which also received mostly positive reviews from critics. Madonna was inducted into the Rock and Roll Hall of Fame in 2008.

In addition to acting in movies—she also starred in the romantic comedy *The Next Best Thing* (2000) and in Ritchie's *Swept Away* (2002)—Madonna pursued work behind the camera. She cowrote and directed *Filth and Wisdom* (2008), a comedy about a trio of mismatched flatmates in London, as well as the drama *W.E.* (2011), which juxtaposed the historical romance between Wallis Simpson and King Edward VIII with the fictional story of a woman in the 1990s researching Simpson's life.

TIM BURTON

(b. Aug. 25, 1958, Burbank, Calif., U.S.)

Timothy William Burton is an American director known for his original, quirky style that frequently drew on elements of the fantastic and the macabre.

Burton, who became interested in drawing and filmmaking while quite young, attended the California Institute of the Arts and later worked as an animator at Disney Productions. After making a series of short films, including the horror-movie homage *Frankenweenie* (1984), Burton directed his first feature film, *Pee-Wee's Big Adventure*, in 1985. A box-office success, the family movie centred on a man-child (played by Paul Reubens) looking for his stolen bicycle. With the dark comedy *Beetlejuice* (1988), Burton established himself as an unconventional filmmaker. He turned to more mainstream fare with the big-budget *Batman* (1989) and its sequel *Batman Returns* (1992). Both films were major hits. Burton was also responsible for the concept and general design of the stop-motion animation film *The Nightmare Before Christmas* (1993), which was directed by Henry Selick.

Edward Scissorhands (1990) marked Burton's first collaboration with actor Johnny Depp. The two subsequently worked on such movies as *Ed Wood* (1994), a biopic about a

Michael Keaton plays the role of Batman in the 1989 film of the same name, directed by Tim Burton.

cross-dressing filmmaker who was called the worst director ever; *Sleepy Hollow* (1999), which was based on Washington Irving's story *The Legend of Sleepy Hollow*; and *Charlie and the Chocolate Factory* (2005), an adaptation of Roald Dahl's children's book of the same name.

In 2001 Burton's remake of the science-fiction classic *The Planet of the Apes* (1968) was released. During its filming, he had begun a romantic relationship with one of its stars, Helena Bonham Carter, and the two became long-time partners. After directing *Big Fish* (2003), he made *Corpse Bride* (2005), which was nominated for an Academy Award for best animated feature. The film featured voice work by Depp and Bonham Carter, both of whom subsequently reteamed with Burton on *Sweeney Todd: The Demon Barber of Fleet Street* (2007), based on Stephen Sondheim's musical; *Alice in Wonderland* (2010), a special-effects-enhanced adaptation of the Lewis Carroll story; and *Dark Shadows* (2012), a comedic interpretation of a cult-favourite soap opera from the 1960s. A feature-length stop-motion remake of *Frankenweenie*, directed by Burton, was released in 2012. *Big Eyes* (2014) told the true story of painter Margaret Keane, whose husband took credit for her work during the early part of her career.

MICHAEL JACKSON

(b. Aug. 29, 1958, Gary, Ind., U.S.–d. June 25, 2009, Los Angeles, Calif., U.S.)

Michael Joseph Jackson was an American singer, songwriter, and dancer who was the most popular entertainer in the world in the early and mid-1980s. Reared in Gary, Ind., in one of the most acclaimed musical families of the rock era, Michael Jackson was the youngest and most talented of five brothers whom his father, Joseph, shaped into a dazzling group of child stars known as the Jackson 5. In addition to Michael, the members of the Jackson 5 were Jackie Jackson (byname of Sigmund Jackson; b. May 4, 1951, Gary), Tito Jackson (byname of Toriano Jackson; b. Oct. 15, 1953, Gary), Jermaine Jackson (b. Dec. 11, 1954, Gary), and Marlon Jackson (b. March 12, 1957, Gary).

Motown Records president Berry Gordy, Jr., was impressed with the group and signed them in 1969. Sporting the loudest fashions, the largest Afros, the snappiest choreography, and a youthful, soulful exuberance, the Jackson 5 became an immediate success. They scored four consecutive number one pop hits with "I Want You Back," "ABC," "The Love You Save," and "I'll Be There" in

1970. With Michael topping the pop charts as a solo performer with "Ben" and reaching number two with "Rockin' Robin," and with the Jackson 5 producing trendsetting dance tracks such as "Dancing Machine," the family's string of hits for Motown lasted through 1975. As Michael matured, his voice changed, family tensions arose, and a contract standoff ensued. The group finally broke with Motown, moving to Epic Records as the Jacksons. Jermaine remained at Motown as a solo performer and was replaced by his youngest brother, Randy Jackson (in full Steven Randall Jackson; b. Oct. 29, 1961). As a recording act, the Jacksons enjoyed consistent success through 1984, and their sister Janet Jackson embarked on her own singing career in the early 1980s; however, Michael's solo albums took on an entirely different status.

Jackson's first solo effort for Epic, *Off the Wall* (1979), exceeded all expectations and was the best-selling album of the year (it eventually sold more than 20 million copies). Produced by industry veteran Quincy Jones, *Off the Wall* yielded the massive international hit singles "Don't Stop 'til You Get Enough" and "Rock with You," both of which showcased Michael's energetic style and capitalized on the contemporary disco dance fad. Three years later he returned with another collaboration with Jones, *Thriller*, a tour de force that featured an array of guest stars and elevated him to worldwide superstardom. *Thriller* captured a slew of awards, including a record-setting eight Grammys; remained on the charts for more than two years; and sold more than 40 million copies, long holding the distinction of being the best-selling album in history. The first single on the album, "The Girl Is Mine," an easygoing duet with Paul McCartney, went to number one on the rhythm-and-blues charts and number two on the pop charts in the fall of 1982. The follow-up single, "Billie Jean," an electrifying

Michael Jackson performs live on Aug. 1, 1984, in New York City, N.Y.

dance track and the vehicle for Jackson's trademark "moonwalk" dance, topped the pop charts, as did "Beat It," which featured a raucous solo from famed guitarist Eddie Van Halen. Moreover, "Beat It" helped break down the artificial barriers between black and white artists on the radio and in the emerging format of music videos on television.

By 1984 Jackson was renowned worldwide as the "King of Pop." His much anticipated Victory reunion tour with his brothers was one of the most popular concert events of 1984. In 1985 Jackson and Lionel Richie cowrote "We Are the World," the signature single for USA for Africa, an all-star project aimed at famine relief. Further solo albums—*Bad* (1987), which produced five chart-topping hits, and *Dangerous* (1991), much of which was produced by New Jack Swing sensation Teddy Riley—solidified Jackson's dominance of pop music. In 2001 he was inducted into the Rock and Roll Hall of Fame; the Jackson 5 were inducted in 1997.

Jackson's eccentric, secluded lifestyle grew increasingly controversial in the early 1990s. His reputation was seriously damaged in 1993 when he was accused of child molestation by a 13-year-old boy he had befriended; a civil suit was settled out of court. In 1994 Jackson secretly married Lisa Marie Presley, daughter of Elvis Presley, but their marriage lasted less than two years. Shortly thereafter Jackson married again, this marriage producing children, though it too ended in divorce. While he remained an international celebrity, his image in the United States was slow to recover, and it suffered even more in November 2003 when he was arrested and charged with child molestation. After a 14-week trial that became something of a media circus, Jackson was acquitted in 2005.

In the wake of these events, Jackson suffered a financial collapse that resulted in the sale of many of his considerable assets, including, ultimately, his lavish Neverland ranch. He was preparing for a series of high-profile concerts he hoped would spark a comeback when he died suddenly of cardiac arrest on June 25, 2009 — prompting a widespread outpouring of grief from his fans that culminated in a memorial celebration of his life and legacy on July 7 at the Staples Center in Los Angeles, featuring tributes by friends and luminaries such as Stevie Wonder, Berry Gordy, Jr., Brooke Shields, and Al Sharpton. In August 2009 the coroner ruled Jackson's death a homicide; the cause was a lethal combination of sedatives and propofol, an anesthetic. In November 2011 Jackson's personal physician was found guilty of involuntary manslaughter.

The documentary film *This Is It*, which drew from more than 100 hours of footage compiled during rehearsals for Jackson's scheduled 50-concert comeback engagement in London, premiered in October 2009. Also in 2009 Jackson's 14-minute music video "Thriller" (1983), directed by John Landis, was inducted into the National Film Registry of the Library of Congress — the first music video to be so honoured.

EDDIE MURPHY

(b. April 3, 1961, Brooklyn, New York, N.Y., U.S.)

Edward Regan Murphy is an American comedian and actor who was a dominant comedic voice in the United States during the 1980s. His comedy was largely personal and observational and at times raunchy and cruel. He was also a skillful impersonator.

Murphy began doing stand-up comedy in New York City as a teenager and was only 19 years old when he joined the cast of *Saturday Night Live* in 1980. He quickly emerged as the show's top performer, creating memorable characters such as Mister Robinson (a spoof on the children's show host Mister Rogers), convict-poet Tyrone Green, and a very grumpy take on the animated clay character Gumby. Murphy scored a major hit in his first film, *48 Hrs.* (1982). He followed with three more box-office successes—*Trading Places* (1983), *Beverly Hills Cop* (1984), and *The Golden Child* (1986). He left *Saturday Night Live* in 1984 to focus on his film and stand-up career. In addition to sequels to *48 Hrs.* and *Beverly Hills Cop*, Murphy showed his versatility in *Eddie Murphy Raw* (1987), which documented two of his live performances, and the comedy *Coming to America* (1988), in which he played four different roles. He recorded several comedy albums during the 1980s and also scored a minor pop music hit with the single "Party All the Time" in 1985. He wrote, directed, and starred in *Harlem Nights* (1989), which was a critical and commercial disappointment.

After a series of flops in the early 1990s, Murphy triumphed again with *The Nutty Professor* (1996) and *Dr. Dolittle* (1998), both updated versions of previous films. He also found success with animated family films, providing the voice of Mushu in *Mulan* (1998) and that of Donkey in the *Shrek* series (2001, 2004, 2007, and 2010). In 2007 Murphy earned his first Academy Award nomination—for best supporting actor—for his performance in *Dreamgirls* (2006). His later films include *Imagine That* (2009), *Tower Heist* (2011), *A Thousand Words* (2012), and *Henry Joseph Church* (2016). In 2015 it was announced that he would receive the Kennedy Center's Mark Twain Prize for American Humor.

GEORGE CLOONEY
(b. May 6, 1961, Lexington, Kent., U.S.)

George Clooney (full name George Timothy Clooney) is an American actor and filmmaker who emerged in the 1990s as a popular leading man, known for his good looks and versatility, and who later became a respected director and screenwriter.

Although his family had a show-business background—his father, Nick Clooney, was a broadcast journalist, and Rosemary Clooney, his aunt, was a famous singer and actress—Clooney initially wanted to be a baseball player. After an unsuccessful tryout with the Cincinnati Reds, he moved to Los Angeles at age 21 to pursue an acting career. Two years later he began appearing in television sitcoms. Although Clooney soon had recurring roles on the popular series *The Facts of Life* and *Roseanne*, most of his early television work was forgettable. In 1994, however, he earned his big break when he was cast as Dr. Doug Ross on the drama *ER*.

After starring in a series of films—including *Batman & Robin* (1997), *The Peacemaker* (1997), and *Out of Sight* (1998)—Clooney left *ER* in 1999 to concentrate on his movie career. Later that year he appeared in the critically acclaimed *Three Kings*. The comedy-drama centred on U.S. soldiers at the end of the Persian Gulf War. Clooney then starred in the quirky Coen brothers film *O Brother, Where Art Thou?* (2000) and earned a Golden Globe Award for his performance as an escaped convict.

Clooney's next film, *Ocean's Eleven* (2001), followed a group of con artists as they robbed a casino. His portrayal of Danny Ocean, the group's ringleader, continued throughout the movie's sequels, *Ocean's Twelve* (2004) and *Ocean's Thirteen* (2007). Clooney made his film directorial debut during one of the breaks between shooting for the Ocean's trilogy with *Confessions of a Dangerous Mind* (2002), which was based on the life of Chuck Barris, a television host who claimed to have been a hit man for the Central Intelligence Agency (CIA).

In 2006 Clooney won his first Academy Award, as best supporting actor for his portrayal of a cynical CIA agent in *Syriana* (2005). The complex thriller took a critical look at the oil industry and its impact on international affairs. Clooney was also nominated for best director and best screenwriter for *Good Night, and Good Luck* (2005). The film—shot in black-and-white and featuring actual news-reel footage—documented journalist Edward R. Murrow's confrontation with Sen. Joseph McCarthy. Both films reflected Clooney's growing liberal political activism. He was involved in causes to end world poverty and to stop the humanitarian crisis in the Darfur region of Sudan.

In 2007 Clooney starred in the critically acclaimed *Michael Clayton*, portraying a corporate attorney who pushes ethical boundaries. The following year he directed and starred in the 1920s football film *Leatherheads* and then reteamed with the Coen brothers for *Burn After Reading*, a CIA comedy in which he played an adulterous federal marshal. Clooney later starred as a U.S. soldier trained to use mind control in the comedy *The Men Who Stare at Goats* (2009), and he provided the voice of the title character in *Fantastic Mr. Fox*, an animated film adaptation of Roald Dahl's children's book. In *Up in the Air* (2009), Clooney appeared as a consultant who specializes in firing people, and he portrayed an assassin on assignment in Italy in the thriller *The American* (2010). He moved behind the camera again for the tense political drama *The Ides of March* (2011), casting himself as a presidential candidate in a cutthroat primary campaign.

In the seriocomic *The Descendants* (2011), Clooney starred as an indifferent father forced to reassess his life after his wife suffers a coma-inducing accident. He earned a Golden Globe for the role. In 2013 he and Sandra Bullock portrayed astronauts in *Gravity*, a sci-fi drama about a space mission that goes awry. Clooney then cowrote, directed, and starred in the film *The Monuments Men* (2014), which fictionalized the efforts of the international

Monuments, Fine Arts, and Archives (MFAA) unit to recover art stolen by the Nazis during World War II. He next starred in the fantastical *Tomorrowland* (2015), about a quest to access a utopian civilization.

Clooney also worked as a producer of various television programs and films, including the Oscar-winning *Argo* (2012). In recognition of his multifaceted career, he received the Cecil B. DeMille Award (a Golden Globe for lifetime achievement) in 2015.

After his marriage (1989–93) to actress Talia Balsam, Clooney vowed never to remarry, and his various relationships became fodder for the tabloids. In 2014, however, he wed Lebanese English lawyer Amal Alamuddin.

JIM CARREY
(b. Jan. 17, 1962, New Market, Ont., Can.)

James Eugene Carrey, better known as Jim Carrey, is a Canadian comedian who established himself as a leading comedic actor with a series of over-the-top performances and who won plaudits for his more-serious portrayals as his career progressed.

Carrey grew up in and around Toronto. At age eight he began making faces before a mirror and discovered a talent for doing impressions. After leaving school in 1978 to help support his family, Carrey worked for two years as a janitor in a factory. He made his professional debut as a stand-up comedian in a Toronto club at age 15 and by 1979 he was able to make a living as a comedian. He wrote most of his own material as an opening act for such comics as Buddy Hackett and Rodney Dangerfield. Known for his racing energy level and frenetic improvisation, he had a comic appeal that was mainly visual. He was a technically brilliant mimic and boasted more than 100 characterizations, with a repertoire ranging from Humphrey Bogart to Kermit the Frog.

At age 19 Carrey moved to Hollywood, where he acted in films and on television. In 1983 he played a role in the Canadian television film *Introducing...Janet*. The following year he made his feature film debut in Finders Keepers, which was followed by a leading role in the film *Once Bitten* (1985). Carrey then played an intergalactic alien named Wiploc in the comedy *Earth Girls Are Easy* (1988). His first TV special, *Jim Carrey: Unnatural Act* (1991), received rave reviews and led to a regular role on the television sketch comedy series *In Living Color*. The show ended in 1994, and Carrey concentrated on his film career. He scored an immediate hit with *Ace Ventura: Pet Detective* and had continued box-office success with *Dumb and Dumber* (1994) and *The Mask* (1994). In the latter film Carrey played a timid bank clerk who becomes a hip wisecracking green-faced dandy when he dons a magical mask. His performance earned Carrey the first of several Golden Globe Award nominations. He subsequently starred in *Ace Ventura: When Nature Calls* (1995) and played the Riddler in *Batman Forever* (1995).

After the black comedy *The Cable Guy* (1996)—which fared poorly at the box office—Carrey scored a hit with *Liar Liar* (1997). In that film he played a fast-talking lawyer forced—by a magic spell invoked by his young son's birthday wish—to tell the truth for one day. Carrey received Golden Globes for his work in *The Truman Show* (1998), a tale of a man who discovers that his apparently ordinary life is really a popular television show, and *Man on the Moon* (1999), in which he portrayed the comedian Andy Kaufman. In 2000 he appeared in the film adaptation of *Dr. Seuss's How the Grinch Stole Christmas*. After receiving mixed reviews for *The Majestic* (2001) and *Bruce Almighty* (2003), Carrey earned critical acclaim for his performance as a man who decides to have his memories of a former girlfriend erased in *Eternal Sunshine of the Spotless Mind*

(2004). He subsequently starred in such films as *Lemony Snicket's A Series of Unfortunate Events* (2004), the mystery-thriller *The Number 23* (2007), and *Yes Man* (2008).

In 2009 Carrey provided the voice of Ebenezer Scrooge in *A Christmas Carol*, an animated adaptation of Charles Dickens's novel. That year he also starred as a homosexual con man who, while in prison, falls in love with a fellow inmate in the dark comedy *I Love You Phillip Morris*. In the family comedy *Mr. Popper's Penguins* (2011), based on the children's book of the same name, Carrey portrayed a businessman who inherits several gentoo penguins. His later credits include *The Incredible Burt Wonderstone* (2013), *Kick-Ass 2* (2013), and *Dumb and Dumber To* (2014).

JON STEWART
(b. Nov. 28, 1962, New York, N.Y., U.S.)

Jonathan Stuart Leibowitz, known by his byname of Jon Stewart, is an American comedian best known for hosting the satiric television news program *The Daily Show*.

Stewart graduated from the College of William and Mary in Williamsburg, Va., in 1984 and then held a series of odd jobs before pursuing a career in comedy. In the late 1980s he began performing stand-up comedy under the name Jon Stewart and quickly became popular on the club circuit. By the early 1990s he was appearing regularly on television, and, after hosting the MTV series *You Wrote It, You Watch It* (1992), he was given his own program, *The Jon Stewart Show*. Featuring celebrity interviews and comedy sketches, it debuted in 1993 but lasted only two years, despite receiving positive reviews. Stewart, who made his big-screen debut in the 1994 film *Mixed Nuts*, also appeared in a number of films, including *Half Baked* (1998), *The Faculty* (1998), and *Big Daddy* (1999).

He returned to hosting in January 1999 when he replaced Craig Kilborn on *The Daily Show*, a fake news program on the Comedy Central cable network that satirized media, politics, and pop culture. With Stewart as anchor, the show increased its viewership dramatically. During the 2000 U.S. presidential campaign, its satiric and comprehensive "Indecision 2000" coverage—featuring *The Daily Show* correspondents reporting from the caucuses and national conventions—became so popular that on election night its viewership rivaled that of some traditional news programs. Indeed, many prominent politicians, journalists, and pundits began to appear on the show to discuss current affairs (and exchange jokes) with Stewart. The program also launched the careers of many of its correspondents, including Stephen Colbert, Steve Carell, and Lewis Black. *The Daily Show* earned Peabody Awards in 2000 and 2004 and garnered a number of Emmy Awards. Stewart left the show in August 2015 and was replaced by South African comedian Trevor Noah.

Stewart's influence on the public extended past the reach of his broadcasts. On October 30, 2010, Stewart and Colbert hosted the Rally to Restore Sanity and/or Fear at the Mall in Washington, D.C. The rally, which drew more than 200,000 attendees and was broadcast live on Comedy Central, was a satiric response to conservative media personality Glenn Beck's Restoring Honor rally the previous summer. While Stewart and Colbert's event was chiefly an ironic send-up of the vituperative rallies on both ends of the political spectrum, it also aimed to promote civility in political discourse.

Stewart hosted several awards shows, most notably the Academy Awards in 2006 and 2008. His books include *Naked Pictures of Famous People* (1998) and (with the writing staff of *The Daily Show*) the popular *America (the Book): A Citizen's Guide to Democracy Inaction* (2004) and *Earth (the*

Book): A Visitor's Guide to the Human Race (2010). The audio-book versions of the latter two titles earned Grammy Awards for Stewart and *The Daily Show* staff.

Stewart made his directorial debut with *Rosewater* (2014), adapted from a memoir by journalist Maziar Bahari (played by Gael García Bernal in the film), who was detained in Iran in 2009 on suspicion of espionage while covering election protests there; Bahari had appeared in a Daily Show segment that satirized Iranian paranoia about spying, a fact that Iranian authorities in part used to justify his imprisonment.

QUENTIN TARANTINO
(b. March 27, 1963, Knoxville, Tenn., U.S.)

Quentin Jerome Tarantino is an American director and screenwriter whose films are noted for their stylized violence, razor-sharp dialogue, and fascination with film and pop culture.

Tarantino worked in a video store in California before selling two screenplays that became *True Romance* (1993) and Oliver Stone's *Natural Born Killers* (1994). In 1992 he made his directing debut with *Reservoir Dogs*, a violent film about a failed jewelry store robbery. Two years later he established himself as a leading director with *Pulp Fiction*. The provocative film, which featured intersecting crime stories, won the Palme d'Or at the Cannes film festival, and Tarantino later received (with Roger Avary) an Academy Award for best original screenplay. For *Jackie Brown* (1997), he adapted an Elmore Leonard novel about a flight attendant entangled in criminal activities.

Tarantino subsequently wrote and directed *Kill Bill: Vol. 1* (2003) and *Kill Bill: Vol. 2* (2004), which centre on a trained assassin (played by Uma Thurman) and her quest for revenge. *Grindhouse* (2007), an homage to B-movie double features, paired Tarantino's *Death Proof*, a thriller about a homicidal stuntman, with Robert Rodriguez's horror film *Planet Terror*. Tarantino's next two films took an irreverent approach to history. *Inglourious Basterds* (2009), set during World War II, follows a group of Jewish American soldiers trained to kill Nazis in German-occupied France. *Django Unchained* (2012), set in the antebellum American South, tells the lively tale of a freed slave attempting to rescue his wife from a cruel plantation owner. For writing the screenplay of that film, Tarantino won another Academy Award. He also wrote and directed *The Hateful Eight* (2015). In addition to writing and directing, Tarantino also worked as an actor and producer.

BRAD PITT
(b. Dec. 18, 1963, Shawnee, Okla, U.S.)

Brad Pitt (full name William Bradley Pitt) is an American actor known for his good looks and portrayal of unconventional characters.

EARLY LIFE AND WORK

Pitt grew up in Springfield, Missouri, and attended (1983–87) the University of Missouri before dropping out just short of graduation to move to California and pursue an acting career. After playing minor television and movie roles, Pitt captured the public's attention as a charming scoundrel in the film *Thelma & Louise* (1991). He followed up with such movies as *A River Runs Through It* (1992), *Interview with the Vampire* (1994), and *Legends of the Fall* (1994). Pitt then starred as a police detective in the gritty thriller *Se7en* (1995) and as a demented malcontent in the fantasy *Twelve Monkeys* (1995), for which he won a Golden Globe Award and was nominated for an Academy Award.

Films from the Late 1990s and Beyond

Pitt deliberately played against type as Austrian mountain climber Heinrich Harrer in *Seven Years in Tibet* (1997), an Irish Republican Army terrorist in *The Devil's Own* (1997), a modern-day personification of death in *Meet Joe Black* (1998), and an underground boxer in *Fight Club* (1999). In 2000 Pitt married actress Jennifer Aniston. The following year he starred in *Ocean's Eleven*, a comedy caper about con artists. The film was a major success and led to the sequels *Ocean's Twelve* (2004) and *Ocean's Thirteen* (2007). In 2004 Pitt portrayed the Greek warrior Achilles in *Troy*.

The action comedy *Mr. & Mrs. Smith* (2005) paired Pitt with actress Angelina Jolie, with whom he became romantically involved. Pitt continued to lend his talents to films covering a wide range of subject matter, including *Babel* (2006), a film that traces the intersecting lives of characters from divergent backgrounds, and the period western *The Assassination of Jesse James by the Coward Robert Ford* (2007). Pitt further demonstrated his versatility in 2008, portraying a dim-witted would-be blackmailer in the Coen brothers' *Burn After Reading* and a man who ages backward in the poignant fantasy *The Curious Case of Benjamin Button*. His chameleonic turn in the latter film earned him an Academy Award nomination for best actor.

In 2009 Pitt starred in Quentin Tarantino's *Inglourious Basterds*, a World War II drama about a group of Jewish American soldiers trained to kill Nazis in German-occupied France. The following year Pitt provided the voice of the superhero rival of the titular villain in the animated film *Megamind*. In Terrence Malick's impressionistic drama *The Tree of Life* (2011), he played a domineering father in 1950s Texas. Pitt later scored another best actor Oscar nomination, for his performance as real-life general manager Billy Beane in the baseball drama *Moneyball*

(2011). The film chronicles how Beane assembled successful teams with the Oakland Athletics by using statistics to acquire cheaper, less-well-known players. Pitt subsequently starred as a mob enforcer in the crime drama *Killing Them Softly* (2012) and as a former United Nations investigator fighting to contain a zombie pandemic in the thriller *World War Z* (2013).

Pitt had supporting roles in *12 Years a Slave* (2013)—which was based on the true story of Solomon Northup, a free person of colour who was kidnapped and sold into slavery in the mid-19th century—and in the crime drama *The Counselor* (2013). In *Fury* (2014) he played an American army sergeant commanding the remnants of a decimated battalion during the last days of World War II. Pitt reteamed with Jolie on *By the Sea* (2015), a marital drama she also wrote and directed. He then portrayed a morally grounded former investment banker in the black comedy *The Big Short* (2015), about the 2008 financial crisis.

In addition to acting, Pitt headed his own film-production company, Plan B Entertainment. The company partnered with several others to produce *12 Years a Slave*, and Pitt won an Academy Award for his producing role when that film was named best picture.

PERSONAL LIFE AND HUMANITARIAN CAUSES

Pitt's involvement with Jolie and his 2005 divorce from Aniston were intensely scrutinized by the tabloid press. In 2006 Pitt adopted Jolie's two children, Maddox and Zahara, whom she had adopted from Cambodia and Ethiopia, respectively. The couple had their first biological child, Shiloh, in May 2006. The next year they adopted a boy, Pax, from Vietnam, and in 2008 they added biological twins, Knox and Vivienne, to their family. Pitt and Jolie married in 2014.

The couple often used their celebrity status as a platform for speaking out on behalf of a number of humanitarian causes. Pitt cofounded and was actively involved in Not on Our Watch, a campaign that directed resources to developing countries in crisis, notably the Sudanese province of Darfur. In 2006 he established Make It Right, a multimillion-dollar project to construct environmentally friendly homes in New Orleans for people displaced by Hurricane Katrina.

STEPHEN COLBERT
(b. May 13, 1964, Washington, D.C., U.S.)

Stephen Tyrone Colbert is an American actor and comedian, perhaps best known as the host of *The Colbert Report* (2005–14), an ironic send-up of television news programs.

After graduating with a theatre degree (1986) from Northwestern University in Evanston, Ill., Colbert joined the Second City comedy improv troupe in Chicago. There he met Amy Sedaris and Paul Dinello, with whom he created the award-winning sketch show *Exit 57* (1995–96) and the bizarre sitcom *Strangers with Candy* (1999–2000), both on the Comedy Central cable network. Colbert worked on several other television projects before joining in 1997 Comedy Central's *The Daily Show*, which was hosted by Jon Stewart. For eight years he was a correspondent and writer on the news parody, where he became a fan favourite for such segments as "This Week in God," a look at religious issues in the news, and "Even Stevphen," a mock debate between Colbert and fellow correspondent Steve Carell.

In 2005 Colbert became the host of his own spin-off show, *The Colbert Report*, and took on the guise of a self-important conservative commentator, a persona meant to parody certain cable-news personalities, most notably Bill O'Reilly. During his first show Colbert coined the word "truthiness" to express a kind of unchanging "truth" derived from a gut feeling rather than from any known facts. ("Truthiness" was named the Word of the Year in 2005 by the American Dialect Society.) The neologism became the organizing principle for the show, where Colbert's rants about political and cultural issues and his expressions of personal idiosyncrasies (such as an unyielding hatred of bears) were treated with the same amount of seriousness. *The Colbert Report* earned various honours, including Emmy Awards for outstanding writing (2008, 2010, 2013–14) and outstanding variety series (2013–14) and a Peabody Award (2008).

In April 2006 Colbert blurred the line between entertainment and political critique in a very public forum when he was the featured speaker at the White House Correspondents' Association dinner—an annual event that traditionally featured good-natured ribbing between the president and the press. He performed in character, lampooning George W. Bush's administration and the mainstream media with a degree of harshness (or candour, depending on one's political leanings) not common to the event. The resulting publicity raised Colbert's national profile and helped turn him into something of a political tastemaker for many young liberals.

Colbert was also notable for other moments when his character entered into "real world" events. The egotistical host would often call upon his dedicated fans—whom he dubbed the "Colbert Nation"—to vote for him as a write-in candidate in various online public polls, which resulted in Colbert's winning the naming competitions for, among others, a bridge in Budapest and a node on the International Space Station (amid public outcry, his name was disqualified in both instances). In 2009 he organized a fund-raising effort by the Colbert Nation to sponsor the U.S. speed-skating team during the 2010 Olympic Winter Games in Vancouver.

On October 30, 2010, Colbert and Stewart hosted the Rally to Restore Sanity and/or Fear at the Mall in Washington, D.C. More than 200,000 people attended the nationally televised rally, which was a satirical response to the Restoring Honor rally held by conservative media personality Glenn Beck the previous August. Although it was primarily sardonic in nature, Colbert and Stewart's rally was also a genuine appeal to civility in political discourse.

In 2011 Colbert made another audacious foray into the political realm when he founded the political action com-mittee (PAC) "Americans for a Better Tomorrow, Tomorrow." The PAC was what is commonly known as a "Super PAC," an organization that—in the wake of the U.S. Supreme Court's 2010 *Citizens United v. Federal Election Commission* decision—can accept unlimited contributions from individuals, corporations, or labour unions, which can then be spent on political causes, though the money cannot be given directly to political candidates or parties. Colbert used the donations received by his Super PAC to purchase mock television advertisements during the 2012 presidential campaign. In January 2012 he briefly handed over control of his Super PAC to Stewart in order to pave the way for a short-lived potential presidential run, as a candidate's business partner may legally run a Super PAC. Many media observers and political activists hailed Colbert for highlighting the murky details of campaign-finance rules through his continued promotion of the Super PAC on *The Colbert Report*.

In addition to his acting credits, Colbert provided vocal talent for various projects, including *Saturday Night Live*'s "TV Funhouse" cartoon and the animated films

Monsters vs. Aliens (2009) and *Mr. Peabody & Sherman* (2014). He coauthored *Wigfield* (2003) with Sedaris and Dinello and starred with them in a feature film adaptation of *Strangers with Candy* (2005). In 2007 Colbert published *I Am America (And So Can You!)*, in which he used his television-pundit persona to comment on—and frequently deride—various aspects of American society, including religion, the media, higher education, and dating. In 2012 he published the picture book *I Am a Pole (And So Can You!)*—which, although described as a children's book, was for adults—and *America Again: Re-becoming the Greatness We Never Weren't.*

In 2014 Colbert was named to succeed David Letterman as host of the CBS late-night talk show the *Late Show*; Letterman had announced that he intended to retire from the program in 2015. In anticipation of the move, *The Colbert Report* ended in December 2014. Colbert's debut on the *Late Show* came on September 8, 2015, with high ratings.

CHRIS ROCK

(b. Feb. 7, 1966, Georgetown, S.C., U.S.)

Chris Rock is an American comedian whose popular stand-up routine—which often addressed racial matters—led to a successful film career.

Rock grew up in the impoverished Bedford-Stuyvesant section of Brooklyn, N.Y.. After dropping out of high school at 17 (he later received a high-school-equivalency diploma), Rock played small clubs in the New York area, where he was discovered by comedian-actor Eddie Murphy. After landing parts in Murphy's film *Beverly Hills Cop II* (1987) and director Keenen Ivory Wayans's *I'm Gonna Git You Sucka* (1988), Rock got his big break by earning a spot in 1990 as a cast member of *Saturday Night Live*.

He left the show in 1993 to join the Fox network's *In Living Color*, which was taken off the air shortly thereafter. After starring in and writing the script for the film *CB4* (1993), he covered the 1996 presidential campaign for ABC's *Politically Incorrect*. Rock then appeared in the first of his HBO comedy specials, *Big Ass Jokes* (1994), which won a CableACE Award. Soon after, however, Rock found his popularity as an actor and comedian beginning to fade.

In an effort to reignite his career, Rock went on the road in 1996, playing small clubs. There he honed his comedic repertoire, touching on subjects that were often considered taboo, such as race relations, drug addiction, and black poverty, all the while revealing the humorous aspects of some of the more serious, painful truths of the black experience. Bolstered by the positive reaction he received while touring, Rock once again appeared in an HBO special, *Bring the Pain* (1997), which won two Emmy Awards and brought Rock widespread fame and critical acclaim. Riding the crest of his newfound popularity, Rock went on to star in the television series *The Chris Rock Show* (1997–2000), write the best-selling book *Rock This!* (1997), costar in the film *Lethal Weapon 4* (1998), and provide the voice for Rodney the guinea pig in another Murphy movie, *Dr. Dolittle* (1998).

In 1999 Rock starred in his third HBO comedy special, *Bigger and Blacker*, and then appeared in a series of films, including *Nurse Betty* (2000) and *Down to Earth* (2001). In 2001 he provided the voice of the title character in the animated movie *Osmosis Jones*. He later starred opposite Anthony Hopkins in the thriller *Bad Company* (2002). In 2003 Rock made his directorial debut with *Head of State*, which centred on a presidential election. After the popular HBO comedy special *Never Scared* (2004), he cocreated a television series based on his childhood, *Everybody Hates Chris*. The show premiered in 2005 and was a critical and commercial success. Rock also hosted the Academy Awards ceremony that year. He hosted again in 2016.

Rock's subsequent films include *The Longest Yard* (2005), in which he costarred with Adam Sandler, and the animated *Madagascar* series (2005, 2008, 2012), for which he provided the voice of a zebra. In 2007 he starred in *I Think I Love My Wife*, a remake of Eric Rohmer's *L'Amour l'après-midi* (1972; *Chloe in the Afternoon*) that he also cowrote and directed. Two years later Rock investigated the hairstyles of African American women in the documentary *Good Hair*. He next appeared in *Death at a Funeral* (2010), a comedy about a chaotic funeral, and *Grown Ups* (2010), in which he, Sandler, and several other comedians played high-school friends reuniting as adults; a sequel followed in 2013. In 2011 Rock made his Broadway debut in *The Motherfucker with the Hat*, portraying an AA sponsor. The following year he had a role in the film *What to Expect When You're Expecting*, an ensemble comedy about parenting, and starred opposite actress and filmmaker Julie Delpy in her culture-clash comedy *2 Days in New York*. Rock then wrote, directed, and starred in *Top Five* (2014), about a comedian struggling to transition to more serious fare. The film was lauded for successfully situating Rock's cutting humour in a moving and believable narrative.

WILL FERRELL

(b. July 16, 1967, Irvine, Calif., U.S.)

John William Ferrell, better known as simply Will Ferrell, is an American comedy actor, writer, and producer known for his impersonations and for his portrayal of dim-witted but endearing characters.

Ferrell grew up in suburban Irvine, Calif., where he played varsity football and drew laughs for reading the high school's morning announcements in a variety of voices. He later studied sports journalism at the University of Southern California in Los Angeles. After graduating in 1990, he worked as a sports broadcaster on local cable before studying acting and comedy. After a year of training with the Los Angeles improv comedy group the Groundlings, he became a member of the company, and in 1995 he was invited to join the television sketch show *Saturday Night Live* (*SNL*).

With his manic energy, outlandish gags, and energetic commitment even to a failing joke, Ferrell became a fixture on *SNL*. He was well known for his impersonations, notably of game show host Alex Trebek, sportscaster Harry Caray, and U.S. Pres. George W. Bush. While on *SNL*, Ferrell also appeared in such feature films as the James Bond parody *Austin Powers: International Man of Mystery* (1997); *Dick* (1999), a satire of the Watergate scandal; and *Zoolander* (2001).

In 2002 Ferrell left *SNL* to focus on a film career, often collaborating with Adam McKay, a writer and director he had met on *SNL*. The following year Ferrell was one of the stars in *Old School*, and he took the lead role in *Elf* (2003), playing a charmingly naive human raised in Santa's village who ventures to New York City. Both films were box office successes. He then starred in a string of hit comedies, notably *Anchorman: The Legend of Ron Burgundy* (2004) and the NASCAR spoof *Talladega Nights: The Ballad of Ricky Bobby* (2006), both of which he cowrote with McKay. In 2005 Ferrell portrayed a Nazi playwright in the musical comedy *The Producers*, and he played equally outlandish characters in the sports comedies *Blades of Glory* (2007) and *Semi-Pro* (2008).

His subsequent film roles include a bumbling scientist in the adventure comedy *Land of the Lost* (2009) and an alien supervillain in the animated *Megamind* (2010). Although most of Ferrell's film work was broadly comic in

(From left to right) Matthew Broderick, Will Ferrell, and Nathan Lane star in the movie The Producers *(2005).*

tone, he occasionally took on more serious roles, including a methodical Internal Revenue Service agent in *Stranger than Fiction* (2006) and an alcoholic selling his possessions in *Everything Must Go* (2010), an adaptation of a Raymond Carver short story.

In 2006 Ferrell and McKay launched Gary Sanchez Productions. Through that company they produced several other movies in which Ferrell starred, including the farcical *Step Brothers* (2008), which they cowrote; the buddy-movie parody *The Other Guys* (2010); *Casa de mi padre* (2012; "My Father's House"), a Spanish-language send-up of Mexican telenovelas; the political satire *The Campaign* (2012); and *Anchorman 2: The Legend Continues*

(2013). The production company was also behind Funny or Die (funnyordie.com), a website that first garnered notice with a short video of Ferrell being intimidated by his landlady, a beer-swigging potty-mouthed toddler. Ferrell voiced a tyrannical businessman in *The LEGO Movie* (2014), a computer-animated film that used renderings of plastic LEGO toys as the characters and set pieces. In the racially charged satire *Get Hard* (2015) he played a hedge-fund manager who, after being framed for insider trading, looks to a black employee (Kevin Hart) for assistance on learning how to survive in prison. In 2015 Ferrell also starred in the made-for-television movie *A Deadly Adoption* and the comedy *Daddy's Home*.

In 2009 Ferrell made his Broadway debut in the one-man play *You're Welcome America. A Final Night with George W. Bush*, which he wrote. The play featured Ferrell's Bush giving some imaginative reminiscences and defenses of his administration. It earned a Tony Award nomination for special theatrical event and was broadcast on the cable channel HBO at the end of the stage production's run in March 2009. Ferrell periodically returned to the small screen for guest appearances, notably on several episodes of the sitcoms *30 Rock* (in 2010 and 2012) and *The Office* (in 2011). He was also featured in the comic miniseries *The Spoils of Babylon* (2014) and *The Spoils Before Dying* (2015) as a bloviating author and director. In 2011 he received the Mark Twain Prize for American Humor.

LOUIS C.K.

(b. Sept. 12, 1967, Washington, D.C., U.S.)

L ouis Szekely, better known by his byname Louis C.K., is an American comedian, writer, director, and producer known for his ribald confessional stand-up comedy and for his television show *Louie* (2010–).

Szekely was raised in Mexico City until age seven, when his family moved to Massachusetts. In elementary school he began styling his name "Louis C.K.," using a phonetic rendering of his surname. After graduating from high school, he worked as an auto mechanic while trying out stand-up comedy routines at Boston-area open-mike nights. In 1989 C.K. moved to New York City, where he continued to hone his stand-up and began making short films.

He joined the writing staff of *Late Night with Conan O'Brien* in 1993, beginning a career writing for the television shows of respected comedians such as Conan O'Brien, David Letterman, and Chris Rock. C.K. won an Emmy Award in 1999 for his work on *The Chris Rock Show*, and in 2001 he wrote and directed the eccentric feature film *Pootie Tang*, a box-office disappointment that later earned a cult following. He also was a writer on the Rock-starring films *Down to Earth* (2001) and *I Think I Love My Wife* (2007).

While C.K. was making a name for himself as a writer, his candid stand-up routines grew in popularity and gradually earned him a reputation as a "comic's comic." He was known for exploring the darker side of human nature in his stage show—often mining the most intimate details of his personal life for material—and being someone who said the things an audience would not admit to thinking. Aided by his savvy use of the Internet via his blog and oft-proliferated YouTube clips of his performances, C.K. established himself as a prominent U.S.-touring stand-up comedian by the middle of the first decade of the 2000s.

In 2006 C.K. created, cowrote, and starred in *Lucky Louie*, a television series on the HBO cable channel that recalled working-class sitcoms of the past, such as The Honeymooners and All in the Family. *Lucky Louie* met with mixed reviews from critics and lasted just one season before being cancelled.

In 2010 C.K. created for the FX cable channel a second television series, *Louie*, an offbeat, loosely structured show that consisted of short, often-surreal narrative segments—which were not always comedic in nature—interspersed with clips of C.K.'s stand-up performances. He had even more creative control in this second attempt at running a television show: he wrote, directed, edited, and starred in the program. *Louie* was a hit with critics, and C.K. received Emmy Awards for his writing (2012 and 2014) as well as multiple nominations for best lead actor in a comedic series (2011–15).

C.K.'s extremely hands-on approach to his projects extended to his 2011 stand-up special *Louis C.K.: Live at the Beacon Theater*. He produced, directed, and edited the Emmy-winning special, which, before airing on television, was distributed on C.K.'s website for a low price ($5) to make it more accessible to his fans and to discourage illegal downloads. He was widely praised for this novel (for the comedy world, at least) business model. In 2014 C.K. released a feature-length film that he had directed in 1998, *Tomorrow Night*, via a $5 download from his website. C.K. also produced conventionally released audio and video recordings of his stand-up performances, one of which, *Hilarious* (2011), won a Grammy Award for best comedy album.

In addition, C.K. acted in such films as *The Invention of Lying* (2009), Woody Allen's *Blue Jasmine* (2013), David O. Russell's *American Hustle* (2013), and *Trumbo* (2015). He also had a recurring role on the sitcom *Parks and Recreation*.

TINA FEY

(b. May 18, 1970, Upper Darby, Penn., U.S.)

Elizabeth Stamatina Fey, better known as Tina Fey, is an American writer and actress whose work on the television shows *Saturday Night Live* (*SNL*; 1997–2006) and *30 Rock* (2006–13) helped establish her as one of the leading comedians in the early 21st century.

Fey was educated at the University of Virginia, where she studied drama. Following graduation in 1992, she moved to Chicago to take classes at The Second City, a training ground for comedians. After about two years of instruction in improvisational comedy, she joined the Second City cast, first as a touring company understudy and later as a performer on the company's main stage. In 1997 Fey submitted samples of her sketch writing to the *Saturday Night Live* television show staff. The show's executive producer, Lorne Michaels, interviewed her, and within a week he hired her to be one of the show's few female writers. In 1999 Fey became the first woman to be named *SNL*'s head writer, and during the 2000–01 season she debuted onscreen as coanchor of the show's "Weekend Update" feature. She went on to join the cast as a regular. In 2002, with the rest of the show's writing staff, she shared the Emmy Award for outstanding writing for a variety, music, or comedy program.

In 2004 Fey extended her reach into motion pictures with the teenage-angst comedy *Mean Girls*, writing the screenplay and appearing as one of the supporting characters. In 2006 she left *Saturday Night Live* to produce, write, and star in *30 Rock*, a comedy based on her *SNL* experiences. Fey played Liz Lemon, the uptight head writer of a comedy sketch show. During the seven-season run of *30 Rock*, she, with the other producers, won three consecutive Emmy Awards for outstanding comedy series (2007–09), and she earned additional Emmys in 2008 for her portrayal of Lemon and for her writing for the show. Also in 2008 Fey returned multiple times as a guest on *SNL* in order to satirize Republican vice presidential nominee Sarah Palin, to whom she bore a striking resemblance.

While still working on *30 Rock*, Fey continued to star in motion pictures, notably *Baby Mama* (2008), a female buddy movie that also featured Fey's former *SNL* costar Amy Poehler, and *Date Night* (2010), an action comedy about mistaken identities that paired her with Steve Carell. She also appeared in a supporting role in *The Invention of Lying* (2009), and she lent her voice to the animated films *Ponyo*—the English version of Miyazaki Hayao's *Gake no ue no Ponyo* (2008; "Ponyo on the Cliff")—and *Megamind* (2010). Fey later starred in the romantic comedy *Admission* (2013), as a university admissions officer thrown into a midlife crisis. She played a Russian prison guard in *Muppets Most Wanted* (2014) and a woman who has to return home to sit shivah for her dead father in the

Tina Fey (left) is shown co-hosting the 70th Annual Golden Globe Awards with Amy Poehler in 2013.

comedy *This Is Where I Leave You* (2014). Fey narrated the nature documentary *Monkey Kingdom* (2015). In late 2015 she co-starred with Poehler in the comedy *Sisters*.

In 2010 Fey received the Kennedy Center's Mark Twain Prize for American Humor. The following year she released the memoir *Bossypants*, which included humorous essays on work and motherhood. She cohosted (with Poehler) the Golden Globe ceremony in 2013, 2014, and 2015.

CHRISTOPHER NOLAN
(b. July 30, 1970, London, Eng.)

C hristopher Nolan is a British film director acclaimed for his noirish visual aesthetic and unconventional, often highly conceptual narratives.

Nolan was raised by an American mother and a British father, and his family spent time in both Chicago and London. As a child, he attended Haileybury, a boarding school just outside of London. From a young age Nolan was interested in moviemaking and would use his father's Super-8 camera to make shorts. He was influenced by George Lucas's *Star Wars* trilogy and by the dystopic, immersive films of Ridley Scott. After attending University College London, where he studied English literature, Nolan began directing corporate and industrial training videos. At the same time he was working on his first full-length release, *Following* (1998). The film centred on a writer going to dangerous lengths to find inspiration; it took Nolan 14 months to complete. On the strength of its success on the festival circuit, he and his producer wife moved to Hollywood.

Nolan's breakthrough came with the 2000 film *Memento*, a sleeper hit that he adapted from a short story written by his brother Jonathan. It used a destabilizing reverse-order story line to mirror the fractured mental state of its protagonist, a man with short-term amnesia who is trying to track down the person who murdered his wife. The film was a critical and popular success and garnered the Nolan brothers an Academy Award nomination for best original screenplay. Nolan followed up with *Insomnia* (2002), a thriller set in the Alaskan wilds, which starred Al Pacino as a compromised police detective.

In 2003 Warner Brothers enlisted Nolan to direct an installment of the *Batman* franchise, the first since 1997's poorly received *Batman & Robin*. Nolan's highly anticipated *Batman Begins* (2005), starring Christian Bale, focused on the superhero's origins and featured settings and tone that were grimmer and more realistic than those of previous *Batman* films. Hugely well received, it became a forerunner of a new trend in superhero films: a move toward realism and away from the genre's comic-book roots.

Nolan's next project was *The Prestige* (2006), a story of two warring illusionists in early 20th-century London. He then began work on a second *Batman* film, cowritten with his brother Jonathan. *The Dark Knight* leaned even more heavily on the moral and structural decay of its setting, fictional Gotham City, and it revived such classic *Batman* villains as the Joker (played by Heath Ledger). *The Dark Knight* became one of the highest-grossing movies of all time.

The release of *Inception* (2010) marked the realization of a script Nolan had begun a decade prior. It starred Leonardo DiCaprio as a corporate spy who steals secrets via a technology that allows him to enter people's dreams. The film turns on his character's attempt to move past the boundaries of the technology in order to actually plant an idea in a dreamer's head. *Inception* was another commercial and critical hit and earned Nolan a second Academy Award nomination for best original screenplay. His *Batman* series concluded with the grandiose *The Dark Knight Rises* (2012), in which the superhero's exploits were set against a backdrop of civil unrest. Nolan also helped develop the story for the *Superman* reboot *Man of Steel* (2013). He then helmed *Interstellar* (2014), which he had written with Jonathan. The film depicts the efforts of a group of scientists to relocate humanity from an Earth vitiated by war and famine to another planet by way of a wormhole.

In 2015, the Library of Congress appointed Nolan to its National Film Preservation Board.

DAVE CHAPPELLE
(b. Aug. 24, 1973, Washington, D.C., U.S.)

David Khari Webber Chappelle, better known simply as Dave Chappelle, is an American comedian and actor who is best known for cocreating, writing, and starring in the groudbreaking television sketch comedy program *Chappelle's Show* (2003–06).

Chappelle's childhood was split between Silver Spring, Md., where his mother taught at various local colleges and universities, and Yellow Springs, Ohio, where his father taught at Antioch University. He started performing stand-up comedy in the Washington area at age 14, and, after graduating from the distinguished Duke Ellington School of the Arts in Washington in 1991, he moved to New York City to pursue comedy full-time. Chappelle's star quickly rose, and he performed on television and played a major supporting role in Mel Brooks's *Robin Hood: Men in Tights* (1993) before he turned 20 years old.

Chappelle costarred in the short-lived situation comedy *Buddies* (1996) and had small roles in the films *The Nutty Professor* (1996) and *Con Air* (1997). *Half Baked*, the offbeat marijuana-themed comedy that he cowrote (with

Neal Brennan) and in which he starred, was released in 1998. Although the film later developed something of a cult following, it was not a huge box-office success, and Chappelle resumed his career pattern of taking small roles in Hollywood projects while continuing to perform stand-up.

The stand-up stage was where Chappelle first made a significant impact on the cultural landscape. His material often included no-holds-barred takes on race and society, but he was by no means a typical angry comedian in the vein of Lenny Bruce or Bill Hicks, as Chappelle softened his barbs by delivering his jokes in an impish manner and with a wry smile. By the early 21st century he had established himself as one of the most-revered stand-up comedians of his generation, and his first one-hour stand-up special, *Dave Chappelle: Killin' Them Softly*, aired in 2000 on HBO. Chappelle's stand-up fame helped him strike a deal with the cable channel Comedy Central to produce *Chappelle's Show*, which he cocreated with Brennan. The show—which featured Chappelle introducing sketches in front of a live audience and usually ended with a musical performance by a hip-hop or rhythm and blues artist—featured biting political and cultural satire that was leavened by a playful sense of the absurd. *Chappelle's Show* produced a number of sketches that became word-of-mouth and viral Internet hits, notably an episode consisting of a series of anecdotes about outlandish musician Rick James, in which Chappelle reenacted the events as James while the real James provided occasional commentary. The first season of the show was released on DVD in 2004 and quickly became the best-selling television program in that format's history. That year Chappelle also released a second stand-up special, *Dave Chappelle: For What It's Worth*.

The success of *Chappelle's Show* was a mixed blessing for its star. Whereas the popularity of the show made Chappelle the most famous that he had ever been, he felt pressured by the amount of his time and energy that needed to be dedicated to the show and grew troubled by the production's behind-the-scenes racial dynamics. In April 2005, nearly one year after signing a $50 million contract with Comedy Central, as he was filming the third season of *Chappelle's Show*, he abruptly left the show. Three episodes' worth of material were cobbled together and broadcast sans Chappelle in his hosting role, bringing the grand total of *Chappelle's Show* episodes to just 28, a minuscule number for a program of such influence.

After leaving the show, Chappelle mostly kept out of the public eye for nearly a decade, appearing sporadically to perform stand-up in clubs across the United States and in the documentary *Dave Chappelle's Block Party* (2005), which chronicled a free music and comedy concert Chappelle organized in Brooklyn. In 2013 he launched his first national comedy tour since the end of *Chappelle's Show*.

JIMMY FALLON
(b. Sept. 19, 1974, New York, N.Y., U.S.)

James Thomas Fallon, Jr., better known as Jimmy Fallon, is an American comedian and talk-show host known for his exuberant presence on the sketch comedy show *Saturday Night Live* (*SNL*; 1998–2004) and as host of *Late Night with Jimmy Fallon* (2009–14) and *The Tonight Show* (2014–).

Fallon attended the College of St. Rose, Albany, N.Y., but left before completing a degree to pursue a career in comedy in Los Angeles. Within a few years, however, he went to New York City to audition for a spot on *SNL*, and he joined the cast in 1998. The *SNL* format served as a showcase for Fallon's comedic impressions. He often portrayed celebrities and created memorable characters such as Jarret the stoner and Nick Burns, a patronizing computer expert. On his last four seasons, Fallon cohosted *SNL*'s "Weekend Update" segment with fellow comedian Tina Fey. In the skit the two starred as coanchors, mixing humour with contemporary news stories.

In 2004 Fallon left *SNL* to pursue a movie career. He starred in the comedy *Taxi* (2004) and in the romantic comedy *Fever Pitch* (2005) and also had parts in the drama *Factory Girl* (2006) and the comedy-drama *Whip It* (2009).

Jimmy Fallon hosts his first episode of The Tonight Show.

However, he failed to become a big box-office draw, and he returned to television.

In March 2009 Fallon replaced talk-show host Conan O'Brien on *Late Night with Conan O'Brien. Late Night with Jimmy Fallon* featured comedy sketches, impersonations, musical performances (including guitar solos by Fallon), celebrity guests, and one-on-one upbeat interviews. Fallon's enthusiasm and energy were infectious. He persuaded guests to participate in a number of offbeat sketches; notably, U.S. Pres. Barack Obama appeared with him in "Slow Jam the News," a segment in which they recited headlines over a sexy funk groove.

Fallon took over one of the most-coveted chairs in late-night television when in February 2014 he succeeded Jay Leno as host of *The Tonight Show*. Fallon became the sixth host of the iconic program, which premiered in 1954. At Fallon's request *The Tonight Show* was moved from Burbank, Calif. (where former host Johnny Carson had relocated it in 1972), and returned to the same studio that Carson had previously used in Rockefeller Center, New York City. In addition, his longtime executive producer, Lorne Michaels, and his house band, the hip-hop group the Roots, joined *Tonight*.

Besides fulfilling his hosting duties, Fallon established a strong presence on social media. He had millions of followers on Twitter, and some of the videos that he created with celebrities went viral on YouTube. In 2012 and 2014 Fallon earned Emmy Awards for outstanding guest actor for hosting *SNL*.

ANGELINA JOLIE

(b. June 4, 1975, Los Angeles, Calif., U.S.)

Angelina Jolie (original name Angelina Jolie Voight) is an American actress known for her sex appeal and edginess as well as for her humanitarian work. She won an

Academy Award for her supporting role as a mental patient in *Girl, Interrupted* (1999).

EARLY LIFE

Jolie, daughter of actor Jon Voight, spent much of her childhood in New York before relocating to Los Angeles at age 11. She attended the Lee Strasberg Theatre and Film Institute for two years and then enrolled at Beverly Hills High School. She later studied drama at New York University. In addition to acting in theatre productions, she modeled and appeared in music videos.

FILM ROLES

Jolie's first major movie role was in *Hackers* (1995), during the filming of which she met her first husband, British actor Jonny Lee Miller (married 1996; divorced 1999). The film failed to find an audience, as did a series of subsequent movies. In 1997, however, Jolie garnered much attention portraying the wife of Alabama's segregationist governor in the television movie *George Wallace*, and she later won a Golden Globe Award for her portrayal. The following year she played a supermodel struggling with drug addiction in the HBO movie *Gia*, a performance that earned her multiple honours, including a Golden Globe and a Screen Actors Guild Award. In 1999 she appeared in the comedy *Pushing Tin* with John Cusack and Billy Bob Thornton, and the following year she married Thornton (divorced 2003).

After her Oscar-winning turn in *Girl, Interrupted*, Jolie starred in a series of action movies. She played the girlfriend of a carjacker (Nicolas Cage) in *Gone in Sixty Seconds* (2000) and later adopted a British accent and mastered street fighting and kickboxing for the title roles in *Lara Croft: Tomb Raider* (2001) and *Lara Croft Tomb Raider: The*

Cradle of Life (2003). In 2004 she portrayed the mother of Alexander the Great in Oliver Stone's *Alexander* and also starred opposite Gwyneth Paltrow and Jude Law in *Sky Captain and the World of Tomorrow*, a sci-fi thriller set in 1930s New York City. Both films were box-office disappointments, but Jolie scored a hit with *Mr. & Mrs. Smith* (2005), in which she played an assassin pretending to be a normal housewife; while working on the film, she met Brad Pitt, who became her partner.

In Robert De Niro's *The Good Shepherd* (2006), she was the aggrieved wife of an early CIA agent (Matt Damon). Jolie earned critical acclaim for her performance as Mariane Pearl in *A Mighty Heart* (2007). Based on a true story, the film followed efforts to rescue Pearl's husband, Daniel, who was kidnapped and later murdered by Islamic extremists while reporting in Pakistan for *The Wall Street Journal*. Jolie followed it with *Beowulf* (2007) and *Wanted* (2008). Her immersion into the role of a mother whose son is kidnapped and later replaced by a different child in Clint Eastwood's *Changeling* (2008) resulted in another Oscar nomination.

In 2010 Jolie starred as a CIA operative accused of spying for Russia in the action thriller *Salt* and appeared opposite Johnny Depp in the caper *The Tourist*. She later assumed the role of the titular villain in *Maleficent* (2014). The live-action film attempted to cast the evil fairy from the 1959 Disney animated classic *Sleeping Beauty* in a more-sympathetic light. Jolie also provided voices for several animated films, including *Kung Fu Panda* (2008) and its sequels (2011 and 2016).

DIRECTING

In 2011 Jolie made her directorial and screenwriting debut with the Bosnian-language *In the Land of Blood and Honey*, a turbulent love story set during the Bosnian conflict of the 1990s. She then helmed the World War II drama *Unbroken* (2014). The script for the film, based on the true story of an Olympic runner and U.S. Air Force officer who became a Japanese prisoner of war after his plane crashed, was written by the Coen brothers. In 2015 she directed, wrote, and starred in *By the Sea*, which focuses on a troubled couple in 1970s France; the drama also starred Pitt.

PERSONAL LIFE AND PHILANTHROPIC WORK

Jolie's personal life often attracted at least as much attention as her acting. Her relationship with Pitt became fodder for tabloids, and the birth of the couple's biological children, Shiloh (2006) and twins Knox and Vivienne (2008), caused a media frenzy; Jolie and Pitt married in 2014. Her humanitarian work also drew interest. In 2001 she was named a Goodwill Ambassador for the United Nations High Commissioner for Refugees (UNHCR). After that appointment she traveled to numerous poverty-stricken countries and adopted children from Cambodia and Ethiopia—Maddox and Zahara, respectively. Pitt later adopted the children, and in 2007 the couple adopted a boy, Pax, from Vietnam. In 2013 Jolie made news for having a preventive double mastectomy after discovering mutations in her *BRCA1* gene, which increase the odds of developing breast or ovarian cancer. That year she also received the Jean Hersholt Humanitarian Award from the Academy of Motion Picture Arts and Sciences.

JUSTIN TIMBERLAKE
(b. Jan. 31, 1981, Memphis, Tenn., U.S.)

Justin Randall Timberlake is an American singer and actor who achieved fame as a member of the hugely successful "boy band" *NSYNC before establishing a career as a solo performer.

Along with Britney Spears, Christina Aguilera, and future *NSYNC member J.C. Chasez, Timberlake launched his performing career in the late 1980s on the Disney Channel's *The New Mickey Mouse Club*. In 1996 he and Chasez were recruited for the male pop vocal quintet *NSYNC. The group's self-titled debut, released in 1998, did well commercially after a slow start, and their second effort, *No Strings Attached* (2000), became one of the fastest-selling albums in history, selling more than 14 million copies and featuring a string of hits, including the chart-topping "It's Gonna Be Me." Timberlake began his solo recording career in 2001 after the release of *NSYNC's third album.

During his tenure with *NSYNC, Timberlake had cultivated his role as a songwriter, and his breakup with longtime love interest Spears provided the inspiration for a number of songs on his Grammy Award-winning (best pop vocal album) solo debut, *Justified* (2002), most notably "Cry Me a River" (best male pop vocal performance). In 2003 Timberlake was a guest performer on the Black Eyed Peas' hit "Where Is the Love?" During the halftime performance of the 2004 Super Bowl, Timberlake was involved in a notorious "wardrobe malfunction" when by design he pulled off part of costar Janet Jackson's top. His second solo release, the Prince-influenced *FutureSex/LoveSounds* (2006), featured production work by Timbaland and Rick Rubin and earned four Grammy Awards, including best dance recording for "SexyBack." Timberlake was not always treated kindly by critics, but few would argue that his solo work, solidly in the vein of rhythm-and-blues (R&B) and blue-eyed soul, had not transcended his bubblegum dance-pop origins, and he sold millions of recordings in the process.

Having earned a reputation as an affable and versatile entertainer, Timberlake began to act in films. His first substantial roles were in the gritty dramas *Alpha Dog* (2006) and *Black Snake Moan* (2006). In 2010 he earned accolades for his portrayal of Internet entrepreneur Sean Parker, the cofounder of Napster and the founding president of Facebook, in *The Social Network*, a fictionalized account of Facebook's origins. The same year, he provided the voice of Yogi Bear's diminutive sidekick Boo Boo in *Yogi Bear*, a movie adaptation of the classic TV cartoon. Timberlake subsequently starred in the racy romantic comedy *Friends with Benefits* (2011), the sci-fi thriller *In Time* (2011), and the online-gambling drama *Runner Runner* (2013). In addition, he took supporting roles in *Bad Teacher* (2011) and *Trouble with the Curve* (2012). In 2015 Timberlake announced his involvement in two further films projects, both voicing the lead character in the animated musical comedy *Trolls* and composing the soundtrack for the feature film *The Devil and the Deep Blue Sea*, in which Timberlake's wife Jessica Biel (married October 2012) was starring. Throughout the years Timberlake also gained notice for his frequent appearances on the television sketch-comedy show *Saturday Night Live*.

As Timberlake's focus remained on acting, his future in music became, for his fans, a subject of anxious speculation. In 2013, however, he mounted a comeback with *The 20/20 Experience*, a pair of luxuriant song suites that were recorded in collaboration with Timbaland and released six months apart. Boasting both contemporary electronic production and nods toward old-fashioned R&B, *The 20/20 Experience* found Timberlake sounding relaxed and romantic, particularly on singles such as "Mirrors." The first volume sold nearly one million copies in the United States in its initial week of release, and each of the two albums (which were also sold as a single package) topped the *Billboard* album chart.

In addition to performing, Timberlake embarked on several business ventures. Notably, he took a minority stake in the advertising group Specific Media when it acquired the social networking site Myspace in 2011. Serving as a creative consultant for the company, he helped repurpose Myspace, which had conceded the majority of its former market to Facebook, as a community for musicians and their fans.

BEYONCÉ

(b. Sept. 4, 1981, Houston, Tex., U.S.)

Beyoncé Giselle Knowles—most commonly referred to by her first name alone—is an American singer-songwriter and actress who achieved fame in the late 1990s as the lead singer of the R&B group Destiny's Child and then launched a successful solo career.

At age nine Beyoncé formed the singing-rapping girl group Destiny's Child (originally called Girl's Tyme) in 1990 with childhood friends. In 1992 the group lost on the Star Search television talent show, and three years later it was dropped from a recording contract before an album had been released. In 1997 Destiny's Child's fortunes reversed with a Columbia recording contract and then an eponymous debut album that yielded the hit single "No, No, No Part 2." Their follow-up album, *The Writing's on the Wall* (1999), earned the group two Grammy Awards and sold more than eight million copies in the United States. *Survivor* (2001), the group's third album, reached the number one spot on the *Billboard* 200 chart.

Beyoncé was clearly the leader of the group and wrote hit songs for Destiny's Child, such as the saucy "Bootylicious." Eventually, the group parted ways to pursue individual projects. Beyoncé used her songwriting talents to pen her first solo album, *Dangerously in Love* (2003). The album debuted to rave reviews, and, aided by the exuberant single "Crazy in Love," which featured rapper Jay Z, it topped charts around the world. In 2004 Beyoncé won five Grammy Awards, including best contemporary R&B album and best female R&B vocal performance.

Beyoncé performs at the Super Bowl XLVII Halftime Show in New Orleans, La., on Feb. 3, 2013.

Destiny's Child reunited in 2004 to release *Destiny Fulfilled*. While generally not as acclaimed as the group's previous efforts, the album sold more than seven million copies worldwide and spawned several hit singles. The trio embarked on a world tour in 2005, during which they announced that the group would officially disband. That same year they released *#1's*, a collection of well-known songs and number one hits.

In 2006 Beyoncé released her second solo studio album, *B'Day*, which featured several coproducers, including the hit-making duo the Neptunes. Although much of the album carried echoes of 1970s-style funk, the pop ballad "Irreplaceable" became its most successful single. In 2008 she and Jay Z married, and the union made them one of the top-earning couples in the entertainment industry. Later that year Beyoncé released the double album *I Am... Sasha Fierce*. Whereas the first half (*I Am*) found her in an introspective mood, the second (*Sasha Fierce*) contained songs better suited to the dance floor. The album as a whole generated several hits, including the assertive "Single Ladies (Put a Ring on It)," and it contributed to Beyoncé's dominance of the 2010 Grammy Awards. Her six awards, which included those for song of the year, best female pop vocal performance, and best contemporary R&B album, amounted to the most Grammys collected by a female artist in a single night.

Days after a triumphant headlining performance at England's Glastonbury Festival, Beyoncé released *4* (2011), a genre-bending mix of ballads and dance tracks that evoked influences ranging from Motown-era torch songs to the audio collages of rapper M.I.A. In early 2013 Destiny's Child reunited for a halftime appearance at the Super Bowl and released a new song, "Nuclear." Shortly thereafter Beyoncé collected a Grammy for her single "Love on Top." She returned later in the year with the confidently sensuous and expressive *Beyoncé*, which boasted brand-name producers and appearances from, among others, the Nigerian author Chimamanda Ngozi Adichie and the singer's toddler daughter, Blue Ivy. The record, initially offered exclusively on iTunes, was promoted as a "visual album," with music videos made to accompany each track. Its unexpected release—without prior announcement or promotion—caused frenzy among fans and influenced a new trend among artists of releasing new music digitally without prior promotion. The single "Drunk in Love," which featured Jay Z, was awarded several Grammys, including best R&B song. In 2014 Beyoncé promoted the album with her On the Run Tour, coheadlining alongside her husband Jay Z. Later that year, she rereleased *Beyoncé* with additional bonus tracks.

In 2001 Beyoncé made her acting debut in the television movie *Carmen: A Hip Hopera*, which aired on MTV. Her role as Foxxy Cleopatra in *Austin Powers in Goldmember* (2002) made her a film star and led to parts in *The Fighting Temptations* (2003) and *The Pink Panther* (2006). In 2006 she played Deena Jones in *Dreamgirls*, the film adaptation of the 1981 Broadway musical about a 1960s singing group. Beyoncé's performance was nominated for a Golden Globe Award and her song "Listen" for an Academy Award. She later starred in *Cadillac Records* (2008), in which she portrayed singer Etta James, and the thriller *Obsessed* (2009) before providing the voice of a fairylike forest queen in the animated *Epic* (2013).

LENA DUNHAM
(b. May 13, 1986, New York, N.Y., U.S.)

Lena Dunham is an American actress, writer, director, and producer known for advancing a feminist perspective coloured by the experiences of the millennial generation, most visibly on the television series *Girls* (2012–).

Dunham was born to artist parents; her father was a painter and her mother a photographer. She began writing and acting while attending a private primary and secondary school in Brooklyn. After a brief stint at the New School University, she enrolled at Oberlin College in Ohio, where she studied creative writing. Stymied by poetry and frustrated by the ephemeral nature of theatre, Dunham focused her narrative efforts on script writing. She began producing short films and posting them on the Internet.

One such piece, *The Fountain* (2007), in which a bikini-clad Dunham laves her Rubenesque figure in a campus water feature, presaged the emphasis on body image in her subsequent work. Her efforts reached a wider audience when she launched a Web series titled *Tight Shots* (2007) on the sex and culture website Nerve.com. The series documented the farcical, hormonally charged efforts of a group of student filmmakers to depict the sexual awakening of a young Southern woman.

Following her graduation from Oberlin in 2008, Dunham returned to New York City, where she continued to experiment with film while supporting herself by babysitting and writing for such publications as *The Onion A.V. Club*. The semiautobiographical *Creative Nonfiction* (2009)—which she wrote, directed, and starred in—documents the romantic travails of an aspiring college filmmaker attempting to finish a screenplay. Completed while Dunham was still at Oberlin, it was shown at the SXSW film and music conference in Austin, Texas, in 2009. The short-form Web series *Delusional Downtown Divas* (2009) punctured the pretenses of art-world strivers.

Dunham's second feature, *Tiny Furniture* (2010), documents with acerbic precision the familial and social difficulties of a privileged college graduate attempting to integrate into society at large. Also featured at SXSW, it was picked up by the distributor IFC Films and received a wider theatrical release. Director and producer Judd Apatow saw the film and approached Dunham about developing a television show for cable channel HBO. While that project progressed, she wrote the script for the film *Nobody Walks* (2012) and two other shorts.

The HBO series, ultimately titled *Girls*, debuted in 2012 with Dunham serving as producer, writer, and star. She frequently directed episodes as well. The show depicted the lives of four young women living in New York City with a vérité sensibility that was both humorously critical of their privileged notions of reality and empathetic to their efforts to realize their ambitions in the face of adversity. Dunham and other characters were frequently nude in nonsexual contexts, and scenes that depicted sexual encounters were pointedly devoid of glamour, making the show a flash point for discussion of evolving perceptions of beauty, body image, propriety, and sexuality.

Dunham appeared in a supporting role as the friend of a profligate young woman attempting to mature in the comedy *Happy Christmas* (2014). She also published a humorous volume of memoir and advice, *Not That Kind of Girl: A Young Woman Tells You What She's "Learned"* (2014), which was inspired in part by Helen Gurley Brown's *Having It All* (1982).

GLOSSARY

baroque Characterized by grotesqueness, extravagance, complexity, or flamboyance.

burlesque A kind of entertainment that was popular in the U.S. in the late 19th and early 20th centuries and that included comedy, singing, dancing, and sometimes performances in which women take off their clothes.

byname A secondary name or stage name.

dandy A man who cares too much about his clothing and personal appearance.

droll Having a humorous, whimsical, or odd quality.

eponymous Of, relating to, or being the person or thing for whom or which something is named.

foibles Minor flaws or shortcomings in character or behavior.

Freudian Of, relating to, or according with the psychoanalytic theories or practices of Sigmund Freud..

ingenue The stage role of a naive girl or young woman.

itinerant Traveling from place to place.

Kafkaesque Of, relating to, or suggestive of Franz Kafka or his writings; or having a nightmarishly complex, bizarre, or illogical quality.

mellifluous Having a smooth rich flow.

milieu The physical or social setting in which people live or in which something happens or develops.

minstrelsy The singing and playing of a troupe of

performers typically giving a program of black American melodies, jokes, and impersonations and usually wearing blackface.

mise-en-scène The arrangement of actors and scenery on a stage for a theatrical production; stage setting.

mordant Biting and caustic in thought, manner, or style.

pantomime A performance in which a story is told without words by using body movements and facial expressions.

passé Outmoded; behind the times.

pessimism An inclination to emphasize adverse aspects, conditions, and possibilities or to expect the worst possible outcome.

protégé One who is protected or trained or whose career is furthered by a person of experience, prominence, or influence.

reprise To repeat the performance of something (such as a performance of a role or piece of music).

roman à clef A novel in which real persons or actual events figure under disguise.

self-deprecating Belittling or disparaging toward oneself.

subterfuge The use of deception especially to hide, avoid, or get something.

surreal Marked by the intense irrational reality of a dream.

vaudeville A type of entertainment that was popular in the U.S. in the late 19th and early 20th centuries and that had many different individuals performing songs, dances, and comic acts.

zeppelin A large aircraft without wings that floats because it is filled with gas and that has a rigid frame inside its body to help it keep its shape.

FOR FURTHER READING

Abrams, Dennis. *Spike Lee: Film Director and Producer*. New York, NY: Chelsea House, 2014.

Aldridge, Rebecca. *Stephen Colbert*. New York, NY: Rosen Publishing, 2015.

Aretha, David. *Awesome African-American Rock and Soul Musicians*. Berkeley Heights, NJ : Enslow Publishers, Inc., 2013.

Armstrong, Linda. *African-Americans in Radio, Film, and TV Entertainment*. Philadelphia, PA: Mason Crest, 2013.

Boone, Mary. *Backstage Pass: Full Access to Hollywood's Best and Brightest*. Chicago, IL: Triumph Books, 2014.

Fields, Jan. *Asking Questions about How Hollywood Movies Get Made*. Ann Arbor, MI: Cherry Lake Publishing, 2016.

Furstinger, Nancy. *Today's 12 Hottest Movie Superstars*. North Mankato, MN: 12 Story Library, 2015.

Gitlin, Marty. *Chris Rock: A Biography of a Comic Genius*. Berkeley Heights, NJ: Enslow Publishers, 2014.

Goldsworthy, Kaite. *Entertainment* (Great African Americans). New York, NY: AV2 by Weigl, 2012.

Gorlinski, Gini, ed. *The 100 Most Influential Musicians of All Time*. New York, NY: Britannica Educational Publishing, 2009.

Gottfried Hollander, Barbara. *Ellen DeGeneres: Television's Funniest Host*. New York, NY: Rosen Publishing, 2015.

Hubbard-Brown, Janet. *Tina Fey: Writer and Actress*. New York, NY: Chelsea House, 2014.

Lüsted, Marcia Amidon. *Entertainment* (Inside the Industry). Edina, MN: ABDO Publishing, 2011.

Schuman, Michael. *Beyoncé: A Biography of a Legendary Singer*. Berkeley Heights, NJ: Enslow Publishers, 2014.

Tometich, Annabelle. *Today's 12 Hottest Music Superstars*. North Mankato, MN: 12 Story Library, 2015.

York, M. J. *12 Entertainers Who Changed the World*. North Mankato, MN: 12 Story Library, 2015.

Ziegler, Robert. *Great Musicians*. New York, NY: DK, 2008.

INDEX